Wyrd Ecology

O|R|S

OXFORD RITUAL STUDIES

Wyrd Ecology

Heathen Ritual and Gifting Relations

BARBARA JANE DAVY

OXFORD
UNIVERSITY PRESS

Oxford University Press is a department of the University of Oxford.
It furthers the University's objective of excellence in research, scholarship,
and education by publishing worldwide. Oxford is a registered trade mark of
Oxford University Press in the UK and in certain other countries.

Published in the United States of America by Oxford University Press
198 Madison Avenue, New York, NY 10016, United States of America.

© Oxford University Press 2025

Library of Congress Cataloging-in-Publication Data
Names: Davy, Barbara Jane, 1972- author.
Title: Wyrd ecology : heathen ritual and gifting relations / Barbara Jane Davy.
Description: New York, NY : Oxford University Press, [2025] |
Series: Oxford ritual studies |
Includes bibliographical references.
Identifiers: LCCN 2024056448 (print) | LCCN 2024056449 (ebook) |
ISBN 9780197804919 (hardback) | ISBN 9780197804926 (paperback) |
ISBN 9780197804957 | ISBN 9780197804940 | ISBN 9780197804933 (epub)
Subjects: LCSH: Neopaganism—Ontario—Case studies. | Neopaganism—Rituals—Case studies. |
Gifts—Religious aspects—Neopaganism. | Ecology—Religious aspects—Neopaganism.
Classification: LCC BP605.N46 D38 2024 (print) | LCC BP605.N46 (ebook) |
DDC 299/.9409713—dc23/eng/20250125
LC record available at https://lccn.loc.gov/2024056448
LC ebook record available at https://lccn.loc.gov/2024056449

DOI: 10.1093/9780197804957.001.0001

Paperback printed by Marquis Book Printing, Canada
Hardback printed by Bridgeport National Bindery, Inc., United States of America

Cover image: Skaði god pole. Carving by Ewan.
Photo by Barbara Jane Davy

Contents

Detailed Contents

Acknowledgments

This work is the product of conversations and shared experiences between me and the Heathen communities of Vindisir Kindred and Raven's Knoll, a private campground and spiritual retreat center in eastern Ontario. I am especially grateful to Jade Pichette, Austin Lawrence, Erik Lacharity, Brynja Clark, and Nicole Butler for giving me their time and sharing their knowledge and experience in multiple interviews with me to shape into this narrative. Many more people in these communities entrusted me with their stories, some of which have not made it into print yet. I am grateful for all that has been shared with me, and I hope I can do it justice. Your gifts have reshaped my relations with the world while I shape and share our words to offer them to others.

I am thankful to colleagues for feedback when I presented portions of this work at the conferences of the International Society for the Study of Religion, Nature, and Culture; Crafting the Long Tomorrow; and the American Academy of Religion (especially the Pagan studies unit, formerly known as the Nature Religion Scholars Network, which has influenced and nurtured my academic development over a long period of time). Thanks in particular to Chas Clifton, Douglas Ezzy, Graham Harvey, Michael York, Michael Strmiska, Helen Berger, Jennifer Snook, Jone Salomonsen, Bron Taylor, and Adrian Ivakhiv for your encouragement and appreciation. Thanks also to my colleagues in Environment in our time at the University of Waterloo, especially Kaitlin Kish, Katharine Zywert, Evan Andrews, and Norman Kearney for both commiserating and celebrating together and all the great conversations along the way.

Thanks to Stephen Quilley for providing me with the doctoral research opportunity that facilitated this work. Thank you for pointing me in the direction of ritual and re-enchantment, and giving me an economically and sociologically grounded understanding of gifting. Thanks also for giving me the freedom to pursue this in all the weird and wonderful ways the work took me. Thanks to committee members Sarah Wolfe, Daniel McCarthy, Sheldon Solomon, and Douglas Cowan for sharing key sources and providing feedback on this work. I am especially grateful to Sarah Pike, external examiner of the thesis from which this book took shape, whose attentive reading helped steer it info a better final form.

My research was generously supported by the Faculty of Environment at the University of Waterloo through the Dean's Doctoral Initiative, and the Government of Ontario via Ontario Graduate Scholarships.

Thanks to Mark for being such a good sounding board and for always being my greatest supporter. I am still learning from your generosity. Thanks also to our child for enduring the trauma of being torn away from your childhood home and still becoming the awesome person that you are.

Portions of this work discussing ancestor veneration and racism in Heathenry have been previously published in *Nova Religio: The Journal of Alternative and Emergent Religions* (26[3], 2023, 30–51). Thank you to the University of Toronto Press for permission to include portions of my chapter "To Become Ancestors of a Living Future" (pp. 419–431) from *Health in the Anthropocene: Living Well on a Finite Planet*, edited by Katharine Zywert and Steven Quilley (University of Toronto Press 2020) and to include reworked content from that chapter in this work. This material is reprinted with permission of the publisher. Thank you to Equinox Press for permission to include "Reconstructing the procession of Nerthus: A contemporary Heathen ritual offering of sacrifice," previously published in *The Pomegranate: The International Journal of Pagan Studies* (24[1], 2022), which forms the majority of Chapter 3 "A Procession of Reconnecting."

Introduction

You might find wyrd ecology a bit weird. It may be unfamiliar, but perhaps it will resonate and inspire a deeper look. It might evoke a necessary change in orientation. "Wyrd" is an Old English word often translated as "fate," but it refers to the interconnected strands of relations that make up the web of all that exists. In wyrd ecology, we find ourselves entwined in ecological webs of relations. These webs comprise the complex social ecological systems sustained by the things we are given by others (human and other than human) and what we give to others in turn. Wyrd ecology might give an answer to ritual studies scholar Ronald Grimes's question "What action, rightly performed, can save the planet?" We might question that "saving" the "planet" is what we need to be doing or if joining the "deep world's gift economy," as Grimes recommends, requires something more like re-embedding ourselves in sustainable, adaptive relations with the rest of the world than saving something separate from ourselves.[1]

Wyrd ecology is weirdly entwined with gifting and scholarly analysis of it. Marcel Mauss opens his influential text *The Gift* with a quote from the *Hávamál*, part of *The Poetic Edda*, which some Heathens, who are central to this work, regard as significant to their religion. The gist of the passage Mauss quotes is that giving gifts maintains good relations with friends and can also manage relations with strangers. Mauss interprets historical gifting practices as systems of exchange, but a better interpretation may be that ritual practices of giving gifts sustain systems of relations. Gifting is not so much about exchange as it is about how gratitude for gifts received inspires a desire to give in turn.

Ecology also describes systems of relations. Wyrd ecology interprets these biological relations as gifting relations. Contemporary Heathens, practitioners of a new religious movement, participate in gifting relations with the more-than-human world by making offerings. Offerings are gifts that express gratitude for what nonhuman others have given us. Echoing the *Hávamál*, Heathens often say "A gift demands a gift," meaning that what we have received obligates us and creates a desire to give in turn.

Wyrd Ecology. Barbara Jane Davy, Oxford University Press. © Oxford Univesity Press 2025.
DOI: 10.1093/9780197804957.003.0001

My analysis of Heathen gifting rituals illustrates how religion can shape ethics in practice, specifically how ritual can motivate pro-environmental behavior. My understanding of this is based on ethnographic study of the ritual practices and environmental values of a community of Heathens in Canada. Contemporary Heathens are practitioners of reconstructed and reimagined traditions of the pre-Christian peoples of northern Europe (referred to in some scholarly literature as Old Norse society and often known as "Vikings" in popular sources. Contemporary Heathenry often focuses on Scandinavian and/or Germanic traditions, but can also include revivals of early English, Frankish, Baltic, and other traditions).[2] Some practitioners prefer the term "Ásatrú" (meaning those dedicated to a group of gods and goddesses called the Æsir) or, more rarely, "Vanatru" (those dedicated to the Vanir, a partially overlapping group of goddesses and gods) to "Heathen," and some refer to themselves as Norse or Germanic Pagans.[3] None of the Heathens I have spoken with in Canada expressed a preference for a term other than "Heathen." I consider Heathenry to be a form of contemporary Paganism, though some practitioners may object to being classified in this way. Contemporary Paganism is an umbrella term for revivals and reinventions of the pre-Christian traditions of Europe (see Davy 2006, 2009; Harvey 1997).

The Heathens of Raven's Knoll, a private campground and spiritual retreat center in eastern Ontario, and Vindisir Kindred, a smaller group of Heathens based in southwestern Ontario, welcomed me to learn about their ritual practices and environmental values. I engaged in participant observation and interviews with Vindisir Kindred for two years, from 2018 to 2019, and was also able to include the larger community of Heathens who gather and celebrate rituals together at Raven's Knoll at summer festivals there over the same time. Members of Vindisir participate in and sometimes run events at Raven's Knoll, so the communities overlap. The people who regularly participate in Heathen events at Raven's Knoll form a community of practice, which I refer to in this work as "the Heathens of Raven's Knoll." Members of this community do ritual together at Hail and Horn Gathering, the largest Heathen event in Canada, as well as at other Heathen events at Raven's Knoll, such as Stave and Spindle, and Well and Tree Gathering, which is run by Heathens.[4]

The purpose of my study was to better understand ecological conscience formation and the role of ritual in it. What makes people express an ecological ethic and make pro-environmental choices, and how is ritual involved in this? I chose to investigate Heathen ritual to answer these questions because I suspected that lack of pro-environmental behavior is related to disenchantment and that a tradition that re-enchants nature might remedy this. Like many others in the fields of religion and ecology, and Pagan studies, I assumed this would take place through having a sense of divinity as being immanent in the natural world. If God or the divine more generally resides in or is present in nature or if religious practitioners regard nature as sacred, it makes sense to think that they will treat nature with respect. However, ritual gifting and unconscious motivations proved to be much more significant than beliefs about immanence. Like others whose study of religion was initially influenced by a Protestant predisposition to focus on beliefs, I thought that valuing nature and pro-environmental behavior would be rooted in a belief that nature is sacred or a belief that divinity is immanent in nature. However, belief is not determinant of behavior.[5] Ritual does not just express belief or reflect ideas of the world, but is also actively involved in enacting ways of being in the world and, more specifically, ways of relating.

Defining Ritual

For the purposes of this study, I define ritual as specially framed social action that evokes cultural understandings of how people should relate, whether those people are human or not. It is not necessarily religious, but the people may be gods, goddesses, or entities of any kind that participants might regard as persons. I offer this intentionally broad conceptualization as a corrective to definitions that artificially separate religion from other activity. One of my concerns is to define ritual in a way that recognizes its material effects and to draw attention to the social and ecological consequences of whether or not particular rituals take place.

I see ritual as part of the adaptive functioning of social ecological systems. It can both contribute to the resilience of existing human systems of relation and renegotiate the status quo in various contexts. Anthropologist Roy Rappaport's early work (1968, 1979) gives a strong sense of the adaptive potential of ritual to aid in the flexible self-regulation of social ecological systems. However, his final work defines ritual as "the performance of more or less invariant sequences of formal acts and utterances not entirely encoded by the performers" (Rappaport 1999, 24). Such understandings of ritual in terms of invariance, maintaining order, and the functioning of systems in equilibrium may fit the rituals of well-established, culturally dominant traditions but this is not the only form religion takes. Defining ritual as invariant and formal would preclude recognizing ritual innovation, sometimes discussed in terms of "ritualization" (Bell 2009) and "ritualizing" (Grimes 2014, 193), and may misconstrue or misinterpret rituals of new religious movements such as contemporary Paganism and Heathenry. I am interested in how people collectively construct ritual practices as they revive Heathen traditions and build their communities. These collective constructive processes of collaborative negotiation may also continue in more established religious traditions.

My definition of ritual picks up some common themes in discussions of ritual, namely the framing of the activity as special in some way and conveying some sense of ethical orientation or sense of how things should be while also allowing that ritual is not necessarily about relating with the supernatural, is not necessarily formulaic or unchanging, and can have material effects. Lest my definition of ritual seem to lack boundaries, events and activities are not ritual if they are not specially framed, and making sense of them does not require a cultural understanding of proper relations. Eating a sandwich is not a ritual unless it is done in a particular way for a particular purpose that means something to the one eating it. Ritual practice *means* something about the *right way* to do something.

While I hope my definition of ritual may offer insights into how values are operationalized in other rituals and how people learn how to relate in the dynamics of ritual, it is first and foremost a heuristic developed for understanding how Heathen gifting rituals are involved in conscience formation.[6] To say that ritual "operationalizes" values may sound determinant, but what I mean by this is that ritual practices put values in play. Participating in ritual practices makes particular values come to mind and negotiates the expression of those values in the actions of participants. Thus, ritual practice, in my understanding, negotiates and co-constructs a shared sense of moral order, or how people should relate. Each iteration of a ritual establishes a shared sense of moral order, but it is always negotiated in practice.

This negotiation is not necessarily or wholly through consciously articulated agreements. It takes place as much through imitation of those who people want to emulate and an unconscious following of existent social norms of cultural subgroups as it does through consciously recognized rules. It is a negotiation of norms through practice. Some aspects may be consciously taught and imitated in a desire to conduct "proper" Heathen rites, but others are more a matter of developing a feel for it, going with the flow, and tuning into "what makes sense" in the tradition. Ritual can be like an orchestrated performance in which much of the negotiation is in the past or behind the scenes, or it can be like a jam session with variations on emergent themes. Heathen rituals exhibit both of these tendencies, and the negotiation involved ranges from explicit to largely unspoken. As in walking with someone, conducting ritual together does not necessarily require speaking or narrating what is being done. There are conscious and unconscious components. We can discuss a destination, but getting there may be largely a nonverbal process of continuous adjustment. Sometimes we ask for clarification, but sometimes we just follow or react to the actions of one another. Sometimes we bump along awkwardly, sometimes we effortlessly stay together.

What I am particularly interested in is how practitioners' sense of how we should relate is influenced by participation in rituals. How do people develop a sense of what actions are right and wrong, what is required, what is forbidden, and what is unthinkable? How are ethics taught, learned, absorbed, and/or negotiated through participation in group practices? How does ritual practice evoke cultural understandings of how we should relate with others? I use the word "evoke" intentionally here to refer to how cultural meanings are called forth through ritual practices, how they are brought to mind, and how they emerge in the encounters of ritual practice. Ritual practices do not just invoke preexisting cultural understandings, but also can occasion new meanings.

Dominant Western traditions present ethics as a list of rules applied to produce correct actions and suggest that we deliberate to come to agreement about how we should act. However, our actions are not determined by the rules we consciously endorse. Sometimes we cannot get ourselves to do what we think is right, sometimes we don't notice that what we are doing violates what we otherwise think we should do, and sometimes the rules don't cover the situation at hand. A list of rules cannot cover every contingency. The determinate meaning of words can never fully capture the situation or procedure. The "spirit" of the law matters, and applying the "letter" of the law can create injustice.

I'm particularly interested in the unconscious aspects of the formation of ecological conscience. What are we not aware of that nonetheless shapes how we relate with others? How does participation in a ritual "nudge" behavior in a particular direction? Behavioral economists Richard Thaler and

Cass Sunstein (2009) describe nudges with reference to economic behavior, but these unconscious effects are not limited to the realm of economics. The way choices are presented to us, "choice architecture," nudges behavior by requiring more effort to choose something other than the default option, which means most people will go along with the default option unless they feel strongly about it. The norms of a group are like a default pattern of relations to follow, which requires effort to reject or forge a new path.

Nudges can also take the form of using words or introducing symbols that have known effects on behavior, such as smiley faces that give people a sense of social approval or "priming" effects that make it more likely that certain things come to mind in particular social situations (Thaler and Sunstein 2009, 69–71). Unconscious priming affects our behavior, making us more likely to eat more, for example, when we feel badly about ourselves. Exposure to specific stimuli changes our affect, or emotional disposition, and is reciprocal between our reception of the prime and the physical effects such a stimulus provokes. Behavioral economist Daniel Kahneman illustrates this with examples of how changing our facial expression changes our affect: holding a pencil in your mouth gives the physical effect of smiling without knowing you are smiling, which makes comics seem funnier than they do to people told to hold their eyebrows together, which gives the effect of unconscious frowning (Kahneman 2011, 53–54). Bodily movements can thus change how we feel and affect what we do. Cognitive frame shifts can thus be triggered through bodily movement as a priming effect.

In this work, I explore how ritual can affect our behavior through priming effects. The rituals I focus on are Heathen gifting rituals, which include making offerings to various entities and the ritual known as sumbel. Practitioners give offerings to deities during blót, a ritual practice that is central to Heathenry,[7] and they also make other less formal offerings. Historically, blót included animal sacrifice as an offering shared with deities and/or ancestors, but animal sacrifice is rare in contemporary practice. Some blóts, such as those at Raven's Knoll as part of Hail and Horn Gathering, are large-scale community events that are formally structured and dedicated to one specific deity at a time. I discuss only one particular blót in this work, Dísablót as conducted by Vindisir Kindred. Practitioners also make offerings to various entities in less formal circumstances, either privately or in smaller groups at other times that are also ritual activities. It is fairly standard in the study of religion to regard practices of giving offerings in general as part of ritual practice. Sumbel, an event of sharing drinks and offering toasts and sometimes gifts, is less obviously a ritual and can be entirely secular. I interpret it in terms of ritual because practitioners see it as a ritual. In addition, sumbel paradigmatically illustrates my understanding of how ritual practices of giving gifts can inspire ethical sensibility.

The Heathens of this study also conduct what they call "esoteric rites," which are rituals, but not as much discussed here because I saw less relevance to environmental values in these rites than the ones included. "Esoteric" in this context usually means the ritual involves divination and altered states of consciousness for at least some people involved. The most well-known of these in Heathenry is seiðr (see Blain 2002). In seiðr and other esoteric rites, often a gythia, a female or femme-identified religious officiant, goes into a trance and answers questions from other participants. In Vindisir and at Raven's Knoll, esoteric rituals are typically held at night.[8] Not all practitioners participate in esoteric rites, but some partake in these but not sumbel. There are other rituals that Heathens engage in that I did not have the opportunity to participate in as part of this research, such as the rites of passage of handfasting (a marriage rite), first footing (a baby-welcoming rite in which an infant's feet touch the ground for the first time), and funeral rites. (I did attend memory ales, which are a form of sumbel rather than actual funeral rites.)

My research finds that giving offerings to ancestors prompts gratitude for what practitioners have and fosters a sense of obligation to future generations. Heathen offerings to the regenerative powers of the land (*genius loci*, or *landvaettir* in Heathen terms) can similarly inspire a sense of responsibility in practitioners toward nonhuman others. Giving offerings makes practitioners aware of what they have already received and prompts a desire to give in turn. Giving offerings can support a preference for engaging in ethical consumption and prioritizing humane, pro-environmental production. In addition, my findings suggest that Heathenry supports a sense of self as relational, and this sense of relationality is deeply entwined with the meaning of wyrd and gifting.

Relational Ontology, Gifting Relations, and Wyrd Ecology

Heathen understandings of wyrd, the threads of relations that make up the world, parallel certain aspects of Indigenous lifeways that anthropologists describe in terms of relational ontologies. *Ontology* can be thought of as what it means to be a self, a way of being, or a way of relating in describing relations. Our ontologies can be more relational or more individualized. Relational ontology and individualized ontology can be regarded as poles on a continuum. In this study, I construct them in binary opposition as ideal types to describe differences between dominant modern assumptions about self–other relations and Heathen perspectives. It is not that Heathens have a completely different sense of self or that anyone has a completely individualized sense of self but that the differences between a more individualized and a more relational understanding illuminate shortcomings of the dominant modern way of life[9] and suggest how a more relational ontology may be beneficial.

There are significant differences between Heathen and Indigenous ontologies, and Indigenous ontologies are themselves diverse.[10] While contemporary Heathens revive pre-Christian traditions of northern Europe, it does not make sense to describe Heathens as Indigenous because of the legacies of colonization and ongoing power differentials. This becomes obvious in the context in Norway where the Sámi are Indigenous people, and it does not make sense to regard other Norwegians as Indigenous.[11]

In sociology and studies in political economy, there is also a growing awareness that there is no such thing as a fixed or innate "human nature" but instead various ontologies. These ontologies emerge from or arise in conjunction with different social structures and economic relations.[12] The development of individualized ontology is a historical process that coincides with the disembedding of the economy from society, the erosion of gift economies, and the transition from relational ontologies toward the individualized ontology epitomized by the understanding of humans as *Homo economicus*, or rationally self-interested individuals. People developed a more individualized sense of self as they started to trade goods through markets rather than as part of gifting relations; trade became an exchange cut off from past and future obligations and thus disembedded from social relations.

Relational ontologies do not just describe a way of being as a sense of the self, but also a way of relating within the whole social ecological system. Relational ontology is as much a cosmology—or how everything is related—as it is an ontology because of continuity between self and others and its priority on relationality. When the self is relational, and relations extend in multiplicity, ontology and cosmology describe the larger system. To call it "ontology" in a way continues a priority on the self, but only because of the dominant understanding of the self in modern individualized ontology.

This is why, I think, anthropologist Eduardo Viveiros de Castro describes his "perspectivism" in terms of cosmology rather than ontology, while his account shares much in common with other descriptions of relational ontology (see Holbraad and Pedersen 2017, 162).

Anthropological descriptions of relational ontologies overlap with those of what religion scholar Graham Harvey (2006, 2014) calls "the new animism." Harvey discusses the ontology and etiquette of gift economies as the new animism in contrast to anthropologist Edward Tylor's original understanding of animism as the mistaken or superstitious belief in "souls or spirits" underlying all religion. For Harvey and others reinterpreting animism, the new animism is a form of relational ontology that does not attribute animating spirits to inanimate objects or nonhuman animals but simply describes relations between persons, not all of whom are human. It includes the inherently ethically inflected relations of the more-than-human world, which can be understood in Heathen terms as wyrd.[13]

Heathen gifting practices, in the experience of practitioners, generate and sustain the social web of relations understood as wyrd and model ethical relations more generally, which, in the context of this Heathen community, includes the more-than-human world. For contemporary Heathens "wyrd" refers to the interconnected strands of relations that make up the fabric of reality. In my understanding, wyrd is the process of everything coming into existence and passing on. It is the network of relations that comprise our complex social ecological systems, sustained by the things we are given by others (including human and other-than-human persons[14]) and what we give to others in turn. Some Heathens discuss wyrd in terms of Heathen cosmology or metaphysics, as abstracted from myths recorded in historical sources and current practice, but relational ontology is the description I apply to Heathen practice. I see contemporary Heathens as a particular sort of hybrid, living in modern society and emerging out of individualized ontologies, but forming incipient gift economies and expressing what I call a "gift ethic," with an appreciation for that which is received from others and a desire to give in turn, which nudges practitioners toward sustaining social ecological systems as distributed networks.

Here I focus on the ethical relations sustained by gifting practices. There is, of course, a large literature on gift economies.[15] My assessment is that market economies, in which people pay for goods and services, reduce what were previously gifting relations to dyadic exchanges of goods, separating these transactions from the social contexts that previously would have included relations extending into the past and future and beyond the interhuman in interlacing connections of delayed and indirect reciprocity. Market economies impose symmetry on exchange and eliminate factors of time and obligation (debt owed into the future).[16] This transforms exchange into "tit for tat," rather than "*do ut des*," the Roman ritual phrase meaning "I give so that you may give." Heathen understandings of gifting are influenced by some anthropological literature but also draw directly on some of the same sources Mauss used in developing his understanding of it, such as the *Hávamál*.

Heathen gifting rituals illustrate how gifting practices can inspire ethical relations. I discuss the emergence of a gift ethic in the Heathen ritual sumbel in relation to philosopher Emmanuel Levinas's understanding of the origins of ethical sensibility and his criticisms of reciprocity in the next chapter.[17] While Levinas locates the origin of ethics in a transcendence of being without expectation of reciprocity, in Heathen ritual gifting practices, the gratitude felt for gifts received, and the desire to give in turn, motivates ethical relations. The web of wyrd can be seen as the interlacing connections between all our relations that form complex patterns through what we are given and what we give to others. Participation in sumbel and related gifting practices inspires gratitude and supports the development of relational ontology. Relational ontology and gifting are mutually self-reinforcing. Each promotes the other, which can generate a self-sustaining pattern creating a gift ethic feedback loop.

Interpretive Lenses

Levinas's work is foundational for my understanding of how ethics come to pass and it underlies my interpretation of Heathen gifting practices, but I also employ interpretive lenses from social psychology as well as what may be more familiar framings from ritual studies. *Terror management theory* emerged as an increasingly important tool for interpreting ritual over the course of this work. Terror management theory, often referred to as "TMT" in the literature,[18] explains how thoughts of death and challenges to one's worldview create a sense of threat to one's self-esteem by endangering the system in which self-worth is vested. More than 500 studies have now empirically tested the psychological effects of mortality salience or death awareness (Solomon et al. 2015, 211). When reminded of our mortality, people tend to act in defense of the values underlying their worldviews.

Terror management theory is useful for understanding what prompts ethical action in part for its "dual process model" of cognition as both rational and nonrational, or conscious and unconscious. This adds nuance to the typical strategies of environmental politics of rational discourse, education, and economic incentives. Terror management theory provides a compelling explanation for what motivates people to consume more than they need in affluent consumer society. While I do not think the effects of religion should be explained away through psychology or reduced to social psychological mechanisms, I find terror management studies useful in that they are empirically based rather than just an argument based on theoretical assumptions about what is happening. As religion scholar Bron Taylor (2016, 295) argues, too often in studies in religion and ecology there is a presumption that religion can help solve environmental problems without the collection of any actual evidence of religion having that effect.

When I began this research I was not intending to apply terror management theory as an interpretive lens for understanding ritual, but I kept finding evidence of the presence of mortality salience, or death awareness, in Heathen ritual: references to ancestors, ancient practices of human sacrifice symbolically referenced in current practice, the death of animals in blót, Hel (personification of death, or the goddess who presides over Niflheim or Helheim, the realm of the dead), and going to the realm of the dead for seiðr or other esoteric rites. But this is not all there is to Heathen ritual. Community and gifting practices are deeply important to practitioners and have significant effects in conjunction with morality salience, making the values of sharing, generosity, and community come to mind.

Terror management theory is not the only lens that could be usefully applied to Heathen ritual, and, indeed, it is not the only one I apply. Ritual infelicity, or what can go wrong in ritual, is an important theme in my interpretation of the procession of Nerthus and in explaining the negotiation and emergence of ethics through the dynamics of ritual practice. Various ritual theories are important in my understanding of the social ecological effects of Heathen ritual, but terror management theory is an important interpretive lens because it so well explains the problem of overconsumption in unconscious motivations of human behavior and how ritual in the context of relational ontology might contribute to reducing overconsumption. If there is something in particular about Heathen ritual that works against overconsumption, that is significant. And I think there is: Heathen ritual is part of a system that includes relational ontology and a revival of gifting practices that supports the emergence of a gift ethic.

Methodology

While discussing methodology may be unfashionable or uninteresting to the casual reader, a short discussion is necessary for transparency. I conducted this research through participant observation and interviews aimed at understanding Heathen ritual and environmental values in Vindisir Kindred and at Raven's Knoll, treating these Heathens as a case study. This sort of qualitative research cannot prove the existence of causal relationships between ritual practices or enchantment and environmental values, but instead it seeks to understand how ritual is part of the interplay of values, meaning, and behavior in these groups.

In addition to speaking informally with people at events, I audio-recorded thirty semi-formal interviews. The length of interviews ranged from forty-five minutes to two and a half hours. While I had a formal question list for each interview, some interviews became wide-ranging conversations, with fruitful digressions from my line of questioning. Quotes included in this work are from the audio-recorded interviews or personal communications rather than informal conversations. It should be noted that quotes from interviews illustrate individual perspectives that may not be so much representative of as influential within Vindisir and the Raven's Knoll Heathen community.

I chose Heathens for this study because of personal interest in Heathenry and because they welcomed me into their community. I did not select them for their environmentalism, which does not stand out from other Pagan groups, but for the enchanted perspective Heathenry shares with Paganism more broadly. In the early stages of my research, I approached a number of Pagan groups, and I chose this community for its geographic proximity and personal connections, having felt welcomed at Raven's Knoll and by Vindisir closer to home. I prioritized depth rather than breadth in narrowing my focus to the Heathens of Vindisir and Raven's Knoll.

Vindisir Kindred and the Heathens of Raven's Knoll

The original core of Vindisir is six people, with a group of about thirty people with varying extents of integration participating in their rituals. At the beginning of this study there was no membership list, initiation rite, or oath-swearing to identify people as members; rather, an informal process of mutual identification of belonging took place. By the end of the study, an oath was composed and sworn by nine members at Winterfinding in 2019, and core members not present when this occurred expressed intent to swear the oath publicly when the group next met. Participants range in age from young children to grandparents, with the core group spanning twenty-somethings to forty-somethings. At least four of the original core group were raised Pagan. At least five participants are nonbinary or trans. Most are not exclusively heterosexual, and some are polyamorous, meaning they may be in committed relationships with more than one person at a time.

The Heathens of Raven's Knoll overlap in these characteristics with Vindisir. Some members of Vindisir are quite active in the Raven's Knoll community and are often integral to ritual events there. Other Heathen groups that are active in Raven's Knoll events include Runatyr Kindred, based around Ottawa, Ontario; Golden Birch, Lokabrenna, and Nine Mountains kindreds in Quebec; and a number of hearths (family-based groups of Heathen practice). Individuals who are not attached to any particular group also participate at Raven's Knoll. The Heathen community of Raven's Knoll is somewhat amorphous and can most easily be quantified by participation in its largest Heathen event, Hail and Horn Gathering, which attracts around one hundred participants each year.[19] Like Vindisir, the Heathens of Raven's Knoll include people of various sexual orientations and gender identities, some of whom serve in prominent leadership positions, such as Vindisir gythia Jade Pichette, who is a nonbinary femme.

The Heathens of Raven's Knoll and Vindisir identify themselves as "inclusive" Heathens, meaning that they welcome people of all backgrounds to participate in their events so long as they do not exclude or discriminate against others.[20] Previous literature on Ásatrú and Heathenry following Jeffery Kaplan (1996) notes a divide between racist and nonracist practitioners, often characterized as "folkish" and "universalist," respectively. The Heathens of Raven's Knoll use the term "inclusive" to distinguish themselves from "folkish" and racist practitioners. The Heathens of Raven's Knoll generally do not use the term "universalist" to identify themselves. However, they repeatedly emphasize that all are welcome at their events, and they consistently reference support for the value of inclusivity in their rituals. Inclusion is a higher standard than tolerance: it requires welcoming diversity and making space for differences.[21] In the words of the Canadian Pagan Declaration on Intolerance, inclusion requires people to "look to not just tolerate, but to welcome LGBTQ, Black, Indigenous, and people of colour in our own communities, and the communities in which we live."[22] The aim is to create a community culture in which all feel welcome and able to participate.

The Heathens of Vindisir and Raven's Knoll are not representative of all Heathens with their high regard for the value of inclusion. Some Heathens are racist, some white supremacists use Heathen symbols and identify as Heathens, and some are much less inclusive of women, nonbinary, and trans folk than are the Heathens of Raven's Knoll and Vindisir, although Heathens in general are more progressive in their values and politics than Americans typically are (Berger 2019, 38, 126). Racism in Heathenry has been a focus of much previous research.[23] As American Heathen scholar Joshua Rood (2020, 83) observes, the "racist fringes" have been "portrayed in vivid detail, while the remainder of the Asatru movement was neglected," though he notes a few more recent studies in Europe that give alternative views. American Heathen sociologist Jennifer Snook (2015, 14) lamented the focus of previous research on racism but, in her recent study, found that it continues to be a problem in American Heathen practice. Often research on racism in Heathenry centers on the United States. German professor of modern Scandinavian literature Stephanie von Schnurbein's study of modern Heathenry *Norse Revival*, covers more territory, ranging from the early Romantics to present-day practitioners in Europe and America. She negatively associates any holistic account of a Germanic past that presents a unity of place, language, and history with racism and finds most reconstructions of Germanic Paganism to be problematic at best in the uninformed use of pro-Nazi sources (von Schnurbein 2016, 17), but inclusive Heathens indicate that racism need not be part of their religion.

The Heathens of Raven's Knoll and Vindisir are not complacent about racism, and, as a researcher, I do not want to minimize issues of white supremacism in Heathenry, but I also want to be clear that most Heathens do not endorse white supremacist views. Heathens are significantly more likely to identify their political orientation as "progressive" than is the general population. In conjunction with my ethnographic research, I conducted an international survey of Heathens and other Pagans in 2017, via Survey Monkey, and I found that Heathens are no more likely to identify as alt-right than other Pagans or the general population.[24] About 2% of all samples, including a random sample of Canadians, identified their political orientation as alt-right. While the term "alt-right" may have quickly faded as a self-identifier, it was current at the time of my survey. Heathens identified as liberal at about the same rate as other Pagans (20% and 19%, respectively), with the largest percentage of Heathens identifying their political orientation as progressive (30%, compared to 25% of other Pagans), significantly more than in the random sample (2%). While it is possible that more people support far-right views than are willing to say so even in anonymous surveys, the available statistics indicate that Heathens are more likely to hold progressive rather than conservative views. Yet there is a persistent, vocal minority of Heathens who are both very socially conservative and active proselytizers.[25]

The Heathens of Raven's Knoll and Vindisir encounter racist Heathens online more often than in person, but, when first meeting people face to face who want to join local kindreds, they screen people carefully to keep racists out.[26] Inclusive Heathens take a clear stance against racism because they feel strongly about differentiating themselves from Heathens who endorse white supremacy. Of course, practitioners in the wider Heathen community do not always sort themselves neatly into categories but span the political spectrum of possibilities from participating in acts of overt racism, to variations on constructing an ahistorical identity of whiteness or European heritage that may or may not entail excluding people of color from their groups, to ethnic traditions in specific European countries, to apolitical Heathens who do not want to think about race and/or want to separate religion from politics, to passive unreflective supporters of the status quo, to progressive Heathens who advocate for inclusion, and to Heathens who are actively involved in anti-racist politics. The Heathens of Raven's Knoll and Vindisir intentionally situate themselves on the inclusive end of this spectrum and welcome practitioners of all ethnicities.

While most participants at Heathen events at Raven's Knoll appear to be white, some Indigenous people and people of color participate regularly.[27] Half of the group that facilitates the organization of Hail and Horn Gathering have some Indigenous heritage, in that one of the women, Maryanne Pearce, is part Mohawk, and the other, Chantal Layoun, is French Canadian, Lebanese, and Anishinaabe, but they did not grow up in contact with Indigenous communities. Their partners, who make up the other half of the facilitators, are Austin Lawrence, who is Danish Canadian and British Canadian, and Erik Lacharity, who is French Canadian. Participation in Hail and Horn does not show any obvious gender divide, attracting about equal numbers of men and women. All Raven's Knoll events are open to new participants who must sign an agreement accepting the inclusive nature of these events and the prohibition of discrimination on the basis of the items included in the Ontario Human Rights Code, which are "age; ancestry, colour, or race; citizenship; ethnic origin; place of origin; creed; disability; family status; relationship status; gender identity or gender expression; receipt of public assistance; sex (including pregnancy and breastfeeding); and, sexual orientation."[28] Participants who violate this agreement can be asked to leave without refund, enforced by volunteer staff for the event.

Practitioners' self-identification as inclusive and agreements to uphold the ideal of inclusion do not, of course, mean that there are no problems with inclusivity in this community. It is a publicly stated value and an ideal pursued in practice, if imperfectly achieved. The 2017 #HavamalWitches social media campaign, for example, drew attention to sexism in Heathenry. It originated among the Heathens of Raven's Knoll, initially with the gythias Brynja Clark and Jade Pichette, and was mostly oriented toward the online behavior of Heathens extending beyond the local Heathen community, although some criticisms were directed within the Raven's Knoll community. Brynja and Jade expressed frustration with men speaking over women and the sexist stereotyping of the goddess Freya. They created some memes and aired some grievances online with the hashtag "#HavamalWitches," which subsequently started trending internationally on social media.[29] I found it noteworthy that what was evident in discussions at Hail and Horn Gathering was largely self-criticism.

The Heathens of Vindisir differ from the wider Heathen population in that the original core group of Vindisir were almost exclusively women or femme identified, and participants in their events usually include significantly more women than men. In common with Vindisir, Heathens and Pagans responding to my survey include more people who identify their gender as nonbinary or gender fluid than the general population. Heathens and Pagans are more likely to have an immanent sense of divinity in nature or see nature as sacred, are more likely to engage in ritual practices, and are more likely to prioritize ethical concerns when making economic decisions than the general population. Heathens fit the general profile more so than other Pagans in terms of their income levels, but, like Pagans more broadly, they tend to be more highly educated than the general population. My findings regarding income levels differ from surveys on Pagans that do not count Heathens separately, probably due to the higher numbers of men in my Heathen sample since men tend to earn more than women.[30]

The Heathens of Vindisir and Raven's Knoll are less concerned with fidelity to historical sources than are some Heathen reconstructionists, and they regard archeological studies and period writings as sources of inspiration more than something to be emulated. While they are interested in developing accurate historical knowledge, they are quite clear that they are developing a living tradition in the present which cannot and should not try to reenact all aspects of historic traditions.

Positionality Statement

Just as I needed to introduce myself to the Heathen community, I also need to introduce myself to readers of this work to be clear about my purpose and position as a researcher and a practitioner. I became Pagan more than twenty years ago, when I was first a graduate student. I completed my first doctoral study (Davy 2003) and *Introduction to Pagan Studies* (Davy 2006), among other works, more than a decade ago, so I was already both a scholar and practitioner before beginning this work. I became Heathen when I found my research community upon being welcomed at Raven's Knoll and by members of Vindisir.

I am a Heathen and a scholar, but do not "straddle two worlds." I am a scholar practitioner and speak with one voice that varies in tone. Switching voices is not always noticeable to me because it is common for me to shift between these tones of voice, both of which are part of my whole self in relation with others. It does not feel like a switch to me because both inflexions are my voice. I like to think of this in terms of traversing the world like Skaði. Skaði is the *dís*[31] of the mountains and snow, who traverses the land on what have been variously termed skis or snowshoes. As gothi (male ritual leader) Austin Lawrence taught in a workshop at Hail and Horn Gathering, Skaði wears the traditional accoutrements of her home terrain, which were more like one snowshoe and one ski. The ski enables one to slide over the snow, while the snowshoe enables one to push oneself along as necessary. So which one is the academic foot and which the practitioner? It does not really matter. They are both me, and together allow me to tell this story. The story I tell is from my point of view and describes how my kindred and community present themselves to me. Another researcher would tell a different story because they would see and hear from their unique perspective and people would tell them stories relevant to their interests.[32]

I do not speak for all Heathens, not even within my kindred, let alone the wider Raven's Knoll community, or for Canadian and international Heathen communities. I am not fully representative of the demographic identified by my survey. My views are not necessarily in accord with other Heathens. I do not regard "belief" in divinity as important, for example. While many Heathens identify themselves as "hard" polytheists, perceiving the gods and goddesses as unambiguously real beings, I approach divinity as if they are real in ritual and consider questions about the reality of deities to be unimportant. My views on gifting and reciprocity are not identical with other practitioners in Vindisir Kindred or the Raven's Knoll community. Other practitioners more often use the language of direct reciprocity, repeating that "a gift demands a gift," whereas I argue both within my academic work and as a practitioner that the best form of reciprocity is indirect. Society, just as life, is sustained by delayed and indirect reciprocity, by giving in turn, rather than giving back. We weave a stronger cloth by carrying the threads across multiple strands, rather than just going back and forth over the same patch.

If I think about what propels me, the snowshoe is my commitment to pushing modern society toward a more sustainable path. The ski is my commitment to my community that eases my passage through the world, providing me with a sense of belonging and sense of meaning. Both drive me academically. The point of my research and writing is not only to produce knowledge, but also to help work toward sustainability. I also aim to produce a description of Heathen practice that will be recognizable to other practitioners and be perceived as an accurate representation of their practices by the people of Vindisir and Raven's Knoll. This is a matter of "relational accountability" (Wilson 2008), maintaining right relations with people in my life. My goal in sustainability is to work toward right relations with the larger social ecological systems within which I am entwined. These right relations have an ethical orientation toward the rest of the world as well as a practical orientation toward ecological sustainability. By "sustainability" I mean maintaining the capacity to continue to adapt to changing conditions, not just for humans to be able to continue using nature, but to be able to continue co-evolving with other species.

In interpreting the results of this ethnographic work, I situate myself reflexively, being open about my positionality as a Heathen practitioner, as part of Vindisir, and as an ecologically committed person.[33] I try to be clear about when I am describing views that I think, as an academic, represent Vindisir, represent "Knollians" (a self-identifier for those who frequent Raven's Knoll), or represent Canadian Heathens so far as I am familiar with them, and when I am expressing my own views.

Self-Reflexive Participant Observation and Evaluating Ritual

To describe how ritual inspires a pro-environmental orientation or disposition may sound prescriptive and shade into what some may see as theology. Describing how rituals generate pro-environmental orientations and dispositions in practitioners requires interpreting meanings implicit in the practices. The articulation of this in explicit terms sounds prescriptive when it comes from someone within a tradition. As ritual studies scholar Ute Hüsken says, in ritual often "implicit values or beliefs become conscious only in the process of discussing and explicitly evaluating a ritual" (Hüsken 2007b, 339). To assess the efficacy of a ritual is evaluative and to ask if Heathen ritual practices are pro-environmental is an evaluative question. It requires engaging in what Grimes calls "ritual criticism."[34] If I am to assess how well or to what degree Heathen ritual is pro-environmental, then what I write will be necessarily prescriptive because evaluation and assessment requires judgment about what should be. If any tendency toward prescription is taken as theology, this restricts the study of religion to what "is" and cannot help move us toward what "ought to be." It results in the rejection of any assessment of ethics from the "scientific" study of religion. If study is only descriptive and not evaluative, then we remove the motivation to remedy environmental and societal problems.

For readers of this work who may be skeptical about the effects of ritual, I invite you to take the cognitive risk of considering what happens when we take ritual effects seriously—not necessarily in terms of believing in gods and goddesses, but in understanding how ritual can inspire feelings of obligation and nudge people toward ethical behavior. Getting get caught up in trying to figure out whether religious claims are true or false may lead us to miss what religion does—that is, the consequences of ritual, as religion scholar Adam Seligman and his colleagues (2008) argue. To understand the consequences of ritual, skeptics need to be open to new experiences and take an "as if" approach to practices and interpretations of practices. Part of the bracketing of beliefs should be to take the cognitive risk of considering that ritual might work. Taking cognitive risks is part of doing science, to consider what is real and what effects are possible. Assuming people participate in ritual only because of false beliefs makes ritual seem dispensable when, instead, it may play a significant part in forming and maintaining ethical relations between humans and between humans and nonhumans. Ritual is not a dispensable relic of a credulous past but an often-overlooked ongoing influence in our lives, and it may be a crucial means of passing on values and generating conscience through an embodied knowledge of how to relate.

Overview of Chapters

The following three chapters each begins with an ethnographic vignette describing a ritual event. The chapters then situate these rituals in relation to historical and related current practices, interpret them, and comment on their role in conscience formation. Chapter 1, "Wyrd Relations," focuses on the social psychological effects of gifting in the Heathen rituals of sumbel (a ritual of sharing drinks, making toasts, and, in "high" sumbel, giving gifts) as observed at the Hail and Horn Gathering at Raven's Knoll. It describes the relational ontology of Heathen practitioners and the gift ethic this relational ontology supports and is generative of in a feedback loop. Heathen understandings of wyrd provide rich metaphorical descriptions of relational ontology, envisioning human relations within the world as a web woven by all things in social ecological systems through processes of interdependent and overlapping relations.

The Heathen gifting rituals of sumbel and making offerings illuminate the origins of ethical sensibility, the basic motivation of ethical behavior. We feel obligated when we are given a gift—giving a gift creates a debt (Mauss 1990 [1950]; Offer 1997, 455). Obligation is directly related to *oblation*, the ritual practices of giving gifts etymologically and in practice. As has been demonstrated in a large body of literature on the psychology and social psychology of gratitude, felt obligation is prompted by gratitude for gifts received, and the experience of gratitude increases pro-social behavior in general.[35]

Chapter 2, "Becoming Ancestors," describes Vindisir Kindred's celebration of Dísablót, a ritual of giving offerings to female ancestors, and situates it in the context of ancestor veneration more generally in the Heathens of Raven's Knoll and Vindisir. The Heathens of Raven's Knoll and Vindisir venerate not just their blood ancestors, but also imagined ancestors and others of the past that they identify with, as well as ancestors of place, which overlap with landvaettir, understood as *genius loci*, or powers of nature. Practices of making offerings to ancestors help practitioners develop an inclusive moral community that extends into the more-than-human world, including nonhuman others, in gifting relations as well as into the future, with a sense of obligation to future generations.

This is probably intensified by the frequent occurrence of *death primes* in ancestor veneration in Heathen practice. Venerating ancestors likely functions as a death prime, so applying terror management theory to rituals of ancestor veneration suggests that the values raised in conjunction with ancestor veneration are likely to be operationalized. Death primes may function somewhat differently in the context of relational ontology, and other priming effects may also be in play in Heathen practices of ancestor veneration.

Chapter 3, "A Procession of Reconnecting," discusses Heathen practices of giving offerings as part of the annual procession of Nerthus at Well and Tree Gathering held at Raven's Knoll. Well and Tree Gathering includes Pagans of various types but is run by Heathens and prominently features the Heathen figure Nerthus. Participants conduct a reconstructionist revival of the Procession of Nerthus based on Roman historian Cornelius Tacitus's (1970) description of such events in first-century Suebi tribes in Germania.

The procession of Nerthus and the giving of offerings at this event inspires in practitioners feelings of reconnection, community belonging, inclusion, and generosity. The sacrifice to propitiate Nerthus was historically a human sacrifice, and human mortality is forcefully made salient at Well and Tree Gathering. A "Breadman" is sacrificed in the place of a human being, but the event includes discussion of the historical procession of Nerthus described by Tacitus as well as a retelling of what transpired at the first Procession of Nerthus at Raven's Knoll, in which one of the participants nearly drowned. Offerings to Nerthus at this event make the values of generosity, sharing, and gratitude for all that the Earth provides for us salient, and the rituals of making offerings to Nerthus include powerful stimulants of mortality salience in conjunction with raising these values.

Chapter 4, "How Pro-environmental Are These Heathens?" provides a qualitative description of what sort of pro-environmental actions are evident at Raven's Knoll and in Vindisir Kindred. I did not gather quantitative data or track practitioners' political activities because my study focuses on ritual practices. This afforded some interesting results in seeing how activities that did not seem on the surface to be pro-environmental can have pro-environmental effects. While these Heathens do not necessarily self-identify as environmentalists, their ritual practices support an ecological lifestyle.

Lifestyle choices may seem like insignificant personal choices, but they may be an important part of shifting toward a more sustainable way of life.

The final chapter, "From Here to There and Back Again," reflects on my experience in conducting this research and my findings in terms of the potential and limitations of Heathenry and ritual practices for generating social change and suggests some directions for future research.

1

Wyrd Relations

Welcome to High Sumbel

I would like to start by welcoming you to be a virtual participant at high sumbel at the annual Heathen event called Hail and Horn Gathering at Raven's Knoll.[1] It might be a long journey to arrive in eastern Ontario just off Highway 60, not too far from the easternmost point of Algonquin Park. There is a big white sign with black lettering saying "Raven's Knoll" to mark the turning (see Figure 1.1). We follow the sandy dirt road into the trees, mostly pines with spruce, balsam, poplars, birch, maples, linden, and a few remaining ash and elm. We pass through a sort of gateway flanked by two ravens and wind our way past an old house and barn, down into the campground, toward the Bonnechere River. A banner greets us with the words "Welcome Home."

If it is not too late, we check in with registration. We set up camp, often in the dark after a long drive, most of us in tents but some in trailers we have brought or rented on site. There is a communal campfire in the evenings, with stories and songs to share, and various activities over this July holiday weekend, but for now I would like to welcome you to experience sumbel.

After we have had a big meal together and cleared away and washed the dishes, we return to the large "U" of picnic tables set up around the Keyhole firepit near the Standing Stone (see Figure 1.2). It is the end of a long, hot, summer day.[2] Cicadas buzz, and the air is resinous with fallen pine needles, soft and orangey underfoot on the sandy soil. Decorations devoted to Skaði, a female figure associated with winter and snow-capped mountains, provide an ironic counterpoint to the heat. The tables are covered with snow-white cloths. White netting and strings of white LED lights hang on the awnings covering the tables, making a sort of marquee, almost a tent enclosing us, but open to the inside of the arranged tables. Banners of various kindreds are set up behind where each has grouped themselves around the tables, and snowshoes and animal pelts also adorn the back walls. Some kindreds have brought animal skulls or pelts not just as decorations, but as visitors to the feast and sumbel (see Figure 1.3).[3]

Wyrd Ecology. Barbara Jane Davy, Oxford Univesity Press. © Oxford Univesity Press 2025.
DOI: 10.1093/9780197804957.003.0002

Figure 1.1 Sign at entrance to Raven's Knoll.
Photo by author.

Figure 1.2 Keystone firepit, Raven's Knoll.
Photo by author.

Figure 1.3 Table at sumbel.
Photo by author.

A lot of people are gathered, perhaps as many as a hundred, sitting around both sides of the tables. Many are wearing ritual "garb," dressed in various interpretations of historically accurate clothing of the Viking era. Quite a few men sport long hair and/or beards and utili-kilts (something like a cross between a Scottish kilt and cargo shorts). Some people wear camping clothes or their usual clothes, which in some cases show a certain amount of goth flair. The bottom of the U of the tables serves as a "head table" where the Witan sits. As a newcomer, the Witan welcomes you to sit with them. The Witan is comprised of Austin Lawrence and Dr. Maryanne Pearce, stewards (and legal owners) of Raven's Knoll, and Erik Lacharity and Chantal Layoun (see Figure 1.4). They comprise the council that facilitates the gathering.

Austin, more commonly known as "Auz," sounds a horn to get everyone's attention and welcomes us to sumbel. He hands over the proceedings to Erik, who serves as thule, or "hall keeper." Erik welcomes us and introduces the byrele, the woman who is honored with serving as "horn bearer" for this

Figure 1.4 The Witan, from left to right: Dr. Maryanne (MA) Pearce, Erik Lacharity, Austin (Auz) Lawrence, and Chantal Layoun.
Photo by author.

sumbel. Auz and a few others help her fill Friðdrifa, Auz's large ceremonial drinking horn (see Figure 1.5). This takes a few minutes because the horn holds three full bottles of wine or, in this case, mead (wine made from honey). The Hail and Horn program (2018, 12) indicates that

> The name "Friðdrifa" embodies the intent and action of what takes place at an inter-group symbel (sumbel). The name is an Anglicized compound of two Norse words "friða" (frith) . . . loosely translates as "relations free from conflict" or "a balanced state of being." It is a much more active state than the modern English word "peace."

"Drifa" refers to an accumulation of a substance, as in a snowdrift. Thus Friðdrifa is an accumulator of frith, a vessel for holding and creating it between participants.

Erik briefly reiterates how the sumbel will proceed, saying that all who wish to speak may do so, but each is limited to three "stand-ups," whether

Figure 1.5 Friðdrifa, Auz's large, silver-rimmed ceremonial drinking horn used for sumbel, and his short-handled hammer.
Photo by author.

for giving thanks through verbal recognition in toasting people, in making boasts, or in giving gifts. He cautions us against making oaths since words spoken in sumbel reverberate in the Well of Wyrd and would bind all who are present. Part of his job as thule is to witness any oaths, or, more likely, refuse them if he thinks it unlikely they can be fulfilled. If anyone accidentally says something that could be interpreted as an oath he will ask the person to rephrase their words. Auz hallows (blesses) Friðdrifa with his short-handled hammer, saying it "is our well for tonight," and Erik hails the goddess honored by the blót held as part of the gathering for the first toast. He then directs the byrele to offer the horn.

Starting on the Witan's right, she begins to offer the horn to each person present in turn so that they may speak over the horn, recognizing worthy deeds of people in the community or making boasts of their own deeds. Some people pass over their chance with the horn, but many share deeply moving stories about what others have done for them, and tears fall freely from men and women alike. Each speaker takes a drink from the horn (or simply raises it or kisses it if they do not wish to drink alcohol) and finishes with a "Hail!" answered enthusiastically by the others in a loud chorus shouting "Hail!"

Many of the toasts are given in the form of what Auz calls "b'toasts" or boast and toasts combined that include a boast but boost others in recognizing how others have supported and enabled their accomplishments. Boasts include creating a program supporting library accessibility for those with vision problems and swearing of an oath to Freyr for beginning a new government job (noting that Canada now allows people to be sworn into such roles by making their oath to the deity of their choice). A person recounts her struggles with pregnancy loss, having a child, and experiencing postpartum depression while working in a healing profession. She discloses that, like many others who work in these fields, she worked past the point of burnout and became suicidal. She shares that the fact she is still here is a boast and thanks Ewan for faer[4] role in helping her through this. Jordan tells the story of dying and being revived after complications following his tonsillectomy and toasts Eir, goddess of healing, saying he recognizes now that it was she who grabbed him by the shoulder to say he was not done yet and sent him back.

Fireworks can be heard in the distance, in early celebration of Canada Day, and, at one point, Maryanne, known as "MA" (pronounced em-eɪ), announces that there is a bear at the other end of the campground near the place designated for smoking cannabis (now legal in Canada), so those using it may do so at another location nearer the camping area (where hopefully we are making enough noise to keep the bears away). Some toasts are accompanied by performances (cleared with Erik before sumbel began). These include a buffalo song, beautifully sung and drummed for us by a First Nations man, in thanks for all that MA, Auz, and the community at the Knoll have done for his sister, who is part of the Raven's Knoll community. People offer toasts to the community and thanks to those who volunteered in running the event. Brynja gives a boast on behalf of R. for having been personally involved with the rescue of a total of 12,000 dogs and cats. Another boasts of his new job as a paramedic and thanks Auz and MA and their family for the support they have given him through welcoming him into their home while he completed school.

Auz playfully works in a plug for bringing the god Tyr into the Vé (an outdoor Heathen sacred space)[5] in 2020, which prompts the response "I can't believe I said nice things about you!" from one who has long campaigned for "Bragi 2020."[6] Good-natured banter between supporters of Bragi and Tyr continues throughout the weekend. Chantal's toast recognizes the source of the apples for the much loved apple flesh served each year at the húsel feast preceding sumbel.[7] She tells us the story of how she used to see her neighbor's apples going unpicked and, at her children's prompting, asked him if they could pick them. He was happy to oblige them, saying his children are now grown and he cannot get out to do it anymore. Now Chantal and her kindred pick the apples each year, they all get used, and she gives her neighbor food prepared from the apples, such as preserves and cakes, in thanks. A number of newcomers speak over the horn, expressing joy, wonder, and thanks for the community they have found through participating in the events of Hail and Horn, and many respond with spontaneous shouts of "Welcome home!" Auz gives a mini memory ale naming those who have passed away over the previous year, including a man who had mentored some in the community, a woman who was a much-loved partner of a community member, and a prominent member of the community who was a personal friend of his, which brings many to tears.

The byrele refills the horn as necessary, so that everyone who wants to speak may do so and raise the horn in a hail. Her stamina in carrying this horn while carrying a toddler on her back is impressive, and she is relieved only briefly by Ewan when necessary to care for her child. Doing this while carrying a toddler is, to me, emblematic of modern Heathen women in this community—strong and capable in their expression of all that women can do, and fierce, especially when she raises the horn herself at the finish of the round of toasting. She admonishes us, saying "Skaði is angry!" We as a species, she says, are not acting responsibly toward the rest of the world. She directs us to do all that we can, through actions small and large, saying that the extreme heat over the weekend is a message that we need to change our behavior to avert climate change.

The heat abates a bit as night falls. Bats swoop above us catching mosquitoes. The stars come out, and we take a short break before beginning the gifting round. Loon song drifts in from the water, and fireflies blink around the edges of the surrounding bushes. Erik invites us to reconvene, and we sit for another round in which people give gifts and drink from the horn. The gifts are accompanied by words of thanks and expressions of hope for building relationships, and, again, each is followed by a hearty chorus of hails. The servers of the feast and other volunteers are recognized for their help, and some are given gifts as tokens of appreciation. Chantal, who organizes much of the cooking on site for the feast, is thanked for her work. Various people are singled out for particular services to the community or for help given to individuals, sometimes with emotional accounts of what people have done for them, what it meant to them, and what they want the community to recognize and witness. Groups and individuals offer gifts to other groups and individuals, expressing thanks for gifts already received or making new overtures of friendship.

Many heartfelt gifts are given in recognition of the worthy deeds of the recipients. Jordan gives Genevieve a beautiful throwing axe, thanking her for introducing him to the community and his girlfriend. Jade gives gifts to three people, thanking them for work they have done in support of trans and LGBTQ+ people in the Pagan community. I give MA a healing salve in recognition of all she does to comfort others, in the hope that she might use it to care for herself. Kára gives J. a wonderfully "pimped out" bike on behalf of the Sisters of the Hunt in recognition of all she has done for this group of women dedicated to supporting women and femme-identified folk. Kára also gives Harry a Skaði dagger for his showing of strength in vulnerability in "the emotional party car" they have shared in many trips to the Knoll, saying he is a model for modern Heathen masculinity. Brynja gifts Erik and Auz dragon-headed arm bands in recognition of support they have given her in growing together in their Heathenry. She also gives one to Auz's son in recognition of his words of help to her. There are many expressions of love, group hugs, and tears shed.

Finally the Witan present their gifts and offer thanks, and they invite us to suggest names for people to appoint to the Doughty, a chosen group of the worthy recognized by the community. They are honored with the gift of arm bands. New silver arm bands are crafted each year with some of the funds provided by registration fees for the event by metalsmith Jeff Helmes, who is a member of the community. The Doughty were originally chosen by the Witan, the council hosting the festival, and then selected by existing members of the Doughty, adding two new members each year. This year the people present are invited to submit three names each, by ballot, to provide the Doughty with a list of nominees to choose from. We take a brief break while the Doughty deliberate, then reconvene to give the arm bands and hail the two new members chosen by the Doughty.

Erik closes the sumbel a bit after one in the morning, and most people retire, but some of us meet up with Auz around the Keyhole Firepit to toast those who could not be named in this sumbel according to rules set by the thule because they are not allies of the Æsir group of gods. These include jötunn such as Thiazi (Skaði's father, who Auz theorized may have had a legitimate reason to fight the Æsir, perhaps being the one who was cheated out of magical items in another story), Hyrokken (the only one strong enough to push Balder's funeral pyre out to sea, signifying strength to deal with grief), and Loki (who may have been demonized in later sources of the lore, and many have found to be helpful in addressing mental health issues). This round of toasting wraps up after 2 AM, and some people continue to hang out by the fire sharing drinks for a while after, but the mosquitos are voracious. I hear others down at the river enjoying a swim as I go to bed, and perhaps you would be tempted to join them to soak the itch of bug bites away, but I was too tired.

Interpreting Sumbel

It may sound simple, but this ritual of shared drink and giving gifts encapsulates a Heathen understanding of how we should relate with others. Sumbel is not just a model for right relations, but an experience that gets "deeply into the bone," engendering nonpropositional or tacit knowledge of gifting relations and a lived gift ethic. Gifting is fundamental to Heathenry as it is practiced at Raven's Knoll. What distinguishes high sumbel as a ritual is the presentation and reception of gifts with the understanding that those gifts are tangible tokens of the relationships their giving and receiving sustain. When one receives a gift, this creates the desire give in turn. Gifting relations create mutual indebtedness in an overlapping system of delayed reciprocity—ideally, I argue, mediated by third parties in indirect reciprocity. This provides a model of how we should relate with others to sustain ourselves ecologically through a gift ethic.

It is perhaps not immediately obvious what sumbel has to do with ecological conscience formation. Examining the social and psychological effects of gifting in sumbel shows how it contributes to sustaining social webs of relations and models ethical relations between all that exists, not just humans. Gifts given in sumbel support the human social web of relations, but gifts given as offerings at other times extend this web beyond the interhuman. This is implicit in Heathen understandings of relations in wyrd, but more directly evident in practices of ancestor veneration such as Dísablót and rituals honoring gods and goddesses and generative powers of the land, such as the procession of Nerthus discussed in the following chapters. Sumbel conveys and enacts an understanding about the right way to relate with others, which for Heathens in this community is to participate in gifting relations. In my interpretation, high sumbel at Hail and Horn enacts a relational ontology. Heathens describe these relations in terms of "wyrd." To translate this Old English term simply as "fate" distorts a rich tapestry of meaning into an unduly narrow interpretation.[8] The meaning of this term is explored in depth below, showing how it is related to sumbel and how a Heathen understanding of gifting and relatedness pervades our way of life.

Sumbel in Historical and Comparative Context

Sumbel appears to have historical roots in a ritual structure that ratified law in pre-Christian northern Europe. Snorri Sturluson's *Heimskringla*, in Hákon's saga, includes a description of "ritual banquets" that required participants to share in a ritual of making toasts.

> It was an ancient custom, when a ritual feast was to take place, that all the farmers should attend where the temple was and bring there their own supplies for them to use while the banquet lasted. At this banquet everyone had to take part in the ale-drinking. . . . There would be fires down the middle of the floor in the temple with cauldrons over them. The toasts were handed across the fire, and the one who was holding the banquet and who was the chief person there, he had then to dedicate the toast and all the ritual food; first would be Óðinn's toast—that was drunk to victory and to the power of the king—and then Njǫrðr's toast and Freyr's toast for prosperity and peace. Then after that it was common for many people to drink the *bragafull* ("chieftain's toast"). People also drank toasts to their kinsmen, those who had been buried in mounds, and these were called *minni* ("memorial toasts"). (*Hákonar Saga Góða* chapter 14, para. 167–168; Sturluson 2016, 98)

Icelandic folklorist Jón Hnefill Aðalsteinsson (1998) persuasively argues that this saga shows that partaking in the feast of an animal sacrifice was required to ratify the law, but the saga indicates that sharing in the toasts was also required. Aðalsteinsson documents how participants swore an oath on an arm ring blooded with an animal sacrificed and eaten communally as part of lawspeaking events that put laws into effect.

The penannular shape, like the letter C, of historical arm rings is echoed by those given to members of the Doughty at Raven's Knoll and used to oath people into the Vé at Raven's Knoll. To enter the Vé, itself arrayed in a penannular shape in the wooden posts that define it, requires swearing an oath to someone already oathed into the space to venerate none but the Æsir group of deities and their allies within it and to treat the ritual space and those within it with respect, refraining from spilling any bodily fluid on the ground or committing any violence within the space. This arc or partially open circle motif is found in the material culture of pre-Christian archaeological sites in northern Europe and recurs at Raven's Knoll. The U shape of the tables at Hail and Horn's sumbel and the open circle layout of the posts that circum-scribe the Vé echo the horseshoe shape of *Thing* sites found in archaeological sites in Iceland and other parts of Scandinavia (Price 2020, 182). A Thing was a meeting for local governance at which agreements and alliances were made and disputes between family groups were resolved (Price 2020, 183), which seems to have developed out of the historic "ritual banquets" that ratified law. I see the penannular motif as a symbol of welcome in frith, negotiated alli-ance, and community agreement that is consecrated in ritual.

Some aspects of sumbel may seem reminiscent of wedding speeches and toasts, which preserve features of past tradition in Christian and secular Euro-American practices. It may be familiar from the story of Beowulf, and, indeed, Heathen understanding of sumbel is in part derived from this early-English story, particularly as it has been interpreted by Paul Bauschatz (1982) and Stephen Pollington (2010 [2003]). Pollington's description of sumbel is largely derived from Beowulf and reflects early-English tradition. Sumbel has become one of the most widely practiced rituals in North American Heathenry and is practiced in Iceland in a somewhat different form as a cen-tral part of blót (see Strmiska 2000). Diana Paxson (2006, 107), a prominent American Heathen associated with the Troth, an American-based inclusive Heathen organization, asserts that sumbel is "the ritual that is most basic to heathenry and most widely practiced." Calico indicates that Bauschatz's *The Well and the Tree* has been a key influence on sumbel (Calico 2018, 351). He suggests that while Michael Enright's *Lady with a Mead Cup* (1996) and Pollington's *The Meadhall* (2010 [2003]) have also been formative, they have not had the same degree of influence as Bauschatz (Calico 2018, 351).

Bauschatz found that sumbel is frequently referenced in Old Norse sources but little described (Bauschatz 1982, 50).[9] It was probably familiar enough from shared practice that no description was necessary. Bauschatz (55) notes that sumbel is not necessarily religious and that the gods have their own sumbels. It is often referred to as "sitting in sumbel," with references to passing a shared drink and making speeches. Bauschatz concludes that the central elements are drinking from a passed cup, speech making, and gift giving (51). The word "sumbel" continued in common usage more in Saxon and early English than in Norse sources, eventually giving us the words "assemble" and "assembly," and it consistently refers to something done in a group. Bauschatz (52) suggests an etymology of sum + ale, for "sumbel," making it a coming together for drinks, "ale" historically being a general term for alcoholic beverages (134). He finds that sumbel was generally an orderly affair not leading to drunkenness (51). It is not associated with physical violence in historical sources, which might be expected to be associated with drinking, but Bauschatz indicates that verbal assault appears to have been common (135), as evidenced in the "flyting" described in Beowulf and the *Lokasenna* in the Eddas (135). Flyting, a competitive "exchange of insults" (Larrington 2014, 65) is not part of contemporary sumbel in my experience, although some forms of verbal banter may approach this, such as exchanges over the merits of Tyr versus Bragi at Raven's Knoll and in American practice (see Gundarsson 2007, 421). Drunkenness at sumbel is frowned upon in contemporary practice, a point that is made explicit at Hail and Horn and also noted in popular American sources instructing participants to know their capacity (Gundarsson 2007, 421; Paxson 2006, 171).

Not all sumbels in contemporary practice are "high" sumbels. Sumbel can be a group of people sitting around someone's living room sharing a drink or standing around a backyard fire pit, but the importance of the occasion is marked by the use of a ceremonial drinking horn or other special vessel and "speaking over the horn." This speaking most commonly includes making toasts recognizing the worthy deeds of friends or family members, present or not, or ancestors and gods and goddesses, but it may also include boasts of worthy activities of one's own and, less commonly, oaths promising future activities (and possibly dedicating them to the service of a group, ancestor(s), or deity/ies) as offerings. "High sumbel" is a somewhat more formal occurrence of sumbel that includes the giving of gifts as well as words spoken over the horn.

The Hail and Horn Gathering 2018 program indicates that this group's high sumbel is modeled after Pollington and Bauschatz, and it differs from the common America-style sumbel. High sumbel at Hail and Horn does not use circular seating nor a three-round structure of first hailing the gods, then the ancestors, and then heroes, and anyone may request to speak over the horn. It also differs from American sumbel practices in terms of the social relations modeled in the ritual, with significantly less social hierarchy and little deference to the sumbel leader. In describing American sumbel practices, Calico says that "Usually, participants do not leave without permission from the warders and do not enter without their consent and direction" (Calico 2018, 359). While sumbels under Erik's direction have been more formal in the past, those I have attended have no warders, and permission to leave is not required. However, there is a certain amount of social expectation not to leave once sumbel begins, evident in discussions about the logistics of getting a portable toilet nearer the Keystone firepit for use during sumbel at Hail and Horn Gathering.

Sumbel at Hail and Horn differs from Pollington's description in a number of ways, including being held outside in a campground rather than inside, protected from "the wilderness" (Pollington 2010 [2003], 22). It also differs from Pollington's (2010 [2003], 43, 44) description and from American practice as described by Calico in that seating at Hail and Horn does not affirm a social hierarchy, or at least the Witan tries not to have seating arrangements show this by inviting new participants to sit at the head table with them. Calico observed that at American sumbels "The host occupies a high table at the front, while other participants are seated in hierarchical order from front to back, often according to kindreds led by a chieftain" (Calico 2018, 357). Upon reflection, I am not sure I would describe the "head table" as being at "the front" at Raven's Knoll. It is the bottom of the U of the tables, and the shrine to the gods and goddesses honored at the event is at the top of the U. The Witan invites newcomers to sit with them at the head table, articulating this aloud and in the program by explicitly saying: "All folk who are new to the gathering are invited to sit with the Witan during the húsel [the feast immediately preceding sumbel], if they wish." People usually continue on in the same seat for sumbel as they sat for the húsel. One person I spoke with noted that they did feel the seating reflected a ranking. In my experience, there is a certain amount of jockeying for space, but it is not to sit at the head table so much as ensure that all members of a kindred may sit together. I was unsure where I might sit the first time I went to Hail and Horn, but, over the multiple courses of the meal preceding sumbel, I felt welcomed by members of Vindisir.

There is a notable absence of ranked "chieftains" sitting at sumbel at Hail and Horn.[10] By my reckoning at least half of the groups that participate are led by women and femme-identified or nonbinary folk, such as Jade Pichette, Jessica Kelly, and Ewan leading Vindisir Kindred, Brynja Clark leading Lodestone Hearth (as well as presiding over Well and Tree Gathering at Raven's Koll), and Jaime Cadorette leading Golden Birch Kindred in Montreal, and other women leading Lokabrenna Kindred in Montreal. Some groups, such as Nicole Butler and Aesc Adams's Hwitan Hund (White Dog) Hearth in Napanee, are jointly led by men and women. Runatyr Kindred in the Ottawa area is led by gothi Erik Lacharity, and there are groups in Toronto and Montreal that are led by men and that participate in Heathen events at Raven's Knoll. Erik presides over sumbel as thule, but he is a host of the gathering as a member of the Witan rather than as a lord or jarl.

Terms such as "jarl" and "chieftan" do not apply in modern society. The Hail and Horn program (2018) specifies that "At the Hail and Horn Gathering we are each our own jarl," and "The Witan are merely the focus of advice and action for the folk that put on and attend this event. . . . [Hail and Horn Gathering] is an event of the folk, for the folk."[11] The Witan refer to themselves as "focalizers" or "organizers," and Auz and MA refer to themselves as "stewards" rather than owners of the land. Historically a witan was a council of advisors to the jarl, "chieftain," lord, or lady. At Hail and Horn they organize scheduling in cooperation with those who want to participate in putting on the event. There is some hierarchy in terms of experience and time of involvement with the event, but the Witan attempts to maintain a fairly horizontal social structure. The manner of gifting in high sumbel at Hail and Horn appears to encourage this, making it not about reinforcing social rank or hierarchy, but instead community building and alliance building between groups.

At Hail and Horn all who want to say something over the horn or give a gift may do so—the horn is offered to everyone in turn for each round of the sumbel. The cup is offered by the byrele, who is usually a woman or femme-identified person at Hail and Horn. Pollington (2010 [2003], 47) refers to byrelas as cup-bearers who refill the horn but does not identify the one who offers the cup as a byrele. Instead he refers to her as "the lady," who is the hostess of the event. She offers the drink first to the host, he says, "to underscore and re-affirm his power and prestige as the leader," continuing, "The drink should be offered in a splendid drinking horn, rather than the normal cup or beaker; horns were a status symbol at public events" (45). "The lady" serves "all those who are entitled to be served" from "the lord's cup" (47).

At Hail and Horn the cup is Auz's horn (and it is splendid), and he is the host, after a fashion, but Erik runs the sumbel and chooses a new byrele each year. In the United States, this role is often referred to as a "valkyrie"

(Calico 2018, 355; Snook 2015, 136), a term that carries rather different connotations in popular imagery of beautiful women serving mead to warriors in Valhalla. At Hail and Horn, the byrele is chosen for her strength of character, dedication to community, and reputation. It is an honor to be chosen because it shows that the community entrusts their words to the byrele since she carries the horn that represents the Well of Wyrd. In Erik's words, "Because they are carrying the horn around, they are carrying the words of those spoken . . . that's the quality . . . strong women who have that ability to carry around the words and the hopes and the dreams and the aspirations of the community, and that people trust them to do that as well" (interview February 13, 2019).

Speaking over the Horn

The sharing of words in speaking over the horn at sumbel is itself a gift. It is a speech act that creates intimacy and deepens relations. Listening to the words people speak in sumbel is an act of witnessing that allows the sharing of burdens and for community members to support one another. Speaking in sumbel is a distillation of thoughts that brings together a conjunction of speech acts of giving words and listening acts of witnessing that together generate a strong sense of community.[12]

Sharing words in sumbel creates an intimate atmosphere and produces a powerful sense of community. Auz explained that speaking aloud in ritual allows people to open up about feelings that usually remain private.

[A]t Hail and Horn Gathering you can see the rich interior emotional life of others when they approach the gods, or when we're at sumbel. It's an intimacy that you don't usually get with people who are acquaintances or strangers, and you often even rarely get with your loved ones or friends. . . . You bare it all at sumbel and at blót, and what this does is it forms social bonds between the people who are there, but it also allows you to think that you are not alone in the universe. (interview July 23, 2018)

Practitioners open up about their personal struggles in sumbel and blót, which invites others to empathize with them and be open to sharing their troubles and seeking help. This helps the community grow together because people realize that others experience similar problems. In relating their words, people form deeper relations with one another and a common sense of belonging.

Some of the stories shared when people speak about the challenges they have endured are painful to hear. Allison, an eclectic Pagan who attended Hail and Horn as part of her role in the larger Pagan community at Raven's Knoll as the Huntress in 2017–2018, recalled that she found some aspects of sumbel quite difficult because some of the stories of people's struggles were so moving. This was not a bad thing in itself, she said, because those stories are important to share in community. "It's important to hear everything, not just the good," she explained, because otherwise people tend to gloss things over and pretend everything is okay. Doing that lets people hide their vulnerability, but when they share their stories it inspires empathy because we see deeper than the false front people project to protect themselves. With the stories shared in sumbel, Allison said, she gained "compassion and sympathy and understanding for people, and the reasons why they are the way they are." This helps people grow deeper connections "because then you're not walking around in your community with this 'rose colored glasses' type of view" (interview November 2, 2018). Hearing the good and the bad helps people to know one another better and find a sense of connection.

While hearing about difficult things that have happened to others can be painful when people empathize, it is also a source of strength in community building. Aiden Solar said that one of the things he likes about Heathenry is how community support is mobilized when people share their stories of vulnerability in sumbel. It is meaningful because when people share their pain, the community responds (interview September 4, 2018). When people listen and respond, this is an act of witnessing that allows the sharing of emotional burdens as well as gifts. It spreads the emotional load and enables the community to help those who need it. Auz explained that doing this in the social context of ritual is crucial because "it solidifies those practices for yourself" and deepens religious experience. Witnessing each other's pain together and speaking aloud about it in rituals such as sumbel matter because it makes it easier to understand the interior life of others, and this understanding carries over into other contexts (interview July 23, 2018). Sharing words of thanks and appreciation for others while openly acknowledging personal struggles helps develop empathy within practitioners that extends beyond the community in their interactions with others.

Speaking aloud is also important because words attach meaning to gifts. When people give gifts in sumbel, the words they say lift people up by acknowledging the worthy things people have done. Everyone gets to hear the reasons why the person is being gifted and add their voice in community response by shouting "hail" in return. Allison said that "hearing people lift other people up and gift other people and acknowledge their deeds and their life was incredibly meaningful and important to me" (interview November 2, 2018). Giving a gift in thanks for help received is made more meaningful for everyone present through the words said along with giving the gift as a token of appreciation.

Choosing what words to say aloud clarifies our purpose and intentions. When I asked Allison about speaking over the horn, she said that doing this out loud in a ritual setting makes us deliberate in our choice of what we want to be heard, not just by the people sitting around the fire but also the gods. Maybe the gods can hear our thoughts, she said, but speaking aloud sorts through the chatter of our minds to speak what matters most to us.

> When you speak those words, you're actually putting together what's most important that you want the gods to actually know. And so that's the significance of speaking over the horn for me. It's taking the chaos of our human monkey brains and [laughs] putting it succinctly for the gods. (interview November 2, 2018)

When we speak aloud in ritual we choose what thoughts we want to share with the community and to be witnessed by the gods as well as other practitioners.

The Meanings of Wyrd

Heathens say that words spoken over the horn in sumbel resonate or accumulate in the Well of Wyrd. To speak in sumbel is to deposit the words witnessed in the Well of Wyrd. Erik describes this in terms of words falling like pebbles into the Well.

> [T]he words that are said in sumbel, they are words that, you know, they're those pebbles in the Well. They drop, they ripple, and there's something very powerful about them because they are usually deeply personal and deeply emotive, so what's important about that to me, and what I get from that is that in that space and in that time, . . . you get to hear the holy

words of people, to see their holy selves, and that kind of pulls together the worshipping community. (interview February 13, 2019)

Effectively, the words people speak over the horn are amplified in being witnessed by the gods and community in ritual. From a practitioner point of view, the words spoken over the horn create waves in the flow of wyrd.

When Heathens speak of wyrd, they use words connoting fluidity and connection, with metaphors of ripples and threads. Auz drew these together, saying "Our own ripples only exist with a uniqueness for a few circles. Because I know that I am not all that unique, I'm just threads of a wider reality, that I have pulled together in my own life, that's still going to keep taking place" (interview May 2, 2018). Ripples convey the flowing nature of wyrd, and threads connote the network of relations of wyrd.

Wyrd History

Wyrd is a deep metaphor. For Heathens it evokes the fluid upwelling of creation, birth, coming into being, and turning into what we are becoming, with associated imagery of spinning and weaving threads of connection. Wyrd is the upwelling of life in all its diversity and interrelatedness. It is the coming into being and the spinning out in relatedness of all that exists. In Norse mythology, wyrd is associated with the Well of Wyrd (Old Norse Urð) called *Urðarbrunnr*. Literally, this means "rill of Urð," referring to a natural spring where water wells up from the ground. Eventually it came to be associated with the structure built to enclose the water rising from the spring: "The idea of the *brunn-* came then to include the enclosure, the water within it, and the powerful, active force that allows it to fill" (Bauschatz 1982, 20).

The sense that the horn carries the words spoken over it to the Well of Wyrd comes to contemporary practice via Bauschatz's interpretation of sumbel in Beowulf. Bauschatz notes that the cup contains an extraordinary liquid, like an enclosure that allows water from a natural spring to accumulate into a well. He explains that these elements repeat the act of the speaking of the Norns that sets our lives in motion. The Norns are female figures somewhat like the Greek Fates. In Norse mythology, they sit at the Well of Wyrd and spin our lives into being. Wyrd is the name of one of the Norns, and the Well of Wyrd is her well. The words spoken over the horn in sumbel "disappear into the drink; as it is drunk, the speaker of the speech, his actions, and the drink become one, assuring that all now have become part of the strata laid within the well" (Bauschatz 1982, 53). Bauschatz discusses how Beowulf's swearing of an oath in sumbel is understood as something that must happen because it has been spoken into the Well of Wyrd. The oath compels action, it creates *sculan*, meaning "obligation," because of the flow of wyrd (Bauschatz 1982, 75). Sculan would appear to be related to the name of third Norn, Sculd, meaning "what will be" or "must be." These connections between the words spoken over the horn in sumbel with the Well of Wyrd are echoed in popular American sources such as Gundarsson (2007, 418, 422) and Paxson (2006, 108) as well as at Raven's Knoll.

Associations between the well and spinning are more apparent if one is familiar with how linen is made. In the *Völuspá* (17–21) of *The Poetic Edda*, the Norns take water from the Well of Wyrd and place a white substance from the well on Yggdrasil, the world tree. Snorri Sturluson's *Prose Edda* describes the water as so holy that everything that touches it becomes as white as the inner membrane of the lining an egg (*Gylfaginning* 16). I suspect this story may have a material connection with linen production from plant fibers such as flax. Flax is one of the earliest fibers spun, long before sheep were domesticated (Barber 1994, 53, 97, 103; Kvavadze et al. 2009). Flax grows in boggy areas, and when stalks are left to sit in standing water the outer part of the plant comes away (a process called retting), leaving long strands of white fiber in the water that can be hung to dry and then spun into thread and woven into cloth. Flax retted in water produces better quality and lighter-colored fibers without any bleaching required, whereas dew-retted fibers are darker and of lesser quality.[13]

To modern ears, well imagery and spinning may sound unrelated, but for Heathens they are similarly aspects of wyrd. Rills, little streams of water welling up from the earth in natural springs, thread through the land and are related to standing pools of water in the way that threads are spun out of layers of plant fiber. When flax is spun, it is sprinkled with water to make it easier to spin. This action appears in a number of Heathen ritual practices of asperging, such as blessing people during blót offerings and waking god poles or other embodiments of deities. These practices echo the story of the Norns who sprinkle the water of the Well of Wyrd on Yggdrasil, the world tree, to preserve and nourish it. Similarly, in the story of the first humans recounted in the Eddas (*Völuspá* 17, *Gylfaginning* 9), Ask and Embla are created from pieces of driftwood endowed with life by Odin and his two brothers by giving them breath, life, and blood in sprinkling them with fluid. In Heathen practice, the fluids of water, blood, and mead are all symbolically connected so that each can stand in for the other in ritual. The sprinkling of these fluids wakes the living being and tells them what they are turning into, and it sets them in relation with others by placing them in the flow of wyrd, the ever-changing web of relations.

Bauschatz says the Well of Wyrd contains not necessarily water; what matters is that it is fluid, which makes metaphorical sense. He speaks of the "flow of wyrd" (Bauschatz 1982, 56–57). It is something that can transform, turn into something else, an active and life-giving power.

> [T]he wells beneath Yggdrasil contain "water," but it is not the chemical composition of water or idea of water that is important. Rather, it is the idea of "fluidity" inherent in liquid, of which water is the most common type, and its relation to "flow" and "movement" that is repeated and becomes distinctive. Other configurations may significantly replace water with blood or intoxicant; indeed, any item or action expressive of "fluid motion" or "liquid activity" will contain the same iconic quality." (Bauschatz 1982, 9)

The drink in the shared horn is a liquid, like that in the Well of Wyrd. The flow of words builds frith, and the alcohol helps make social relations fluid by relaxing people.

According to Norse mythology as recorded in the Eddas (*Völuspá* 20–21 and *Gylfaginning* 15) the Norns speak the fate of people as they are born. This fate is shaped by the strands of wyrd of our circumstances of birth, our genetic and other material inheritances, and the familial relations we are born into, but also all the other relations we are embedded in our social ecological systems as we grow and influence those relations in turn. Barber (1994, 236) speculates that the association of spinning and speaking fate with birth may have arisen from women spinning as they waited for labor to progress and talking about the prospects of the child being born. Because spinning with a drop spindle, which was women's work, took so much time, it was likely to be taken up at any spare moment, including in the birthing chamber. This sort of spinning, when done well, can be described as a "fluid motion" as in Bauschatz's discussion of the associative qualities of the water of the Well of Wyrd, and some may find that it induces a trance state of mind.[14]

Wyrd Etymology

There are additional connections between wyrd, the Norns, birth, and spinning. Babies spin through the birth canal as they emerge, with a cord that stretches like a lifegiving thread into the womb. The first two Norns' names, Urð (Wyrd) and Verðandi, ultimately derive from the same Proto-Indo-European root *udero, which means "belly" and gave us the Latin term "uterus," adopted into contemporary English. Urð and Verðandi both have the same Indo-European root *uert, meaning to "turn, spin, rotate" (Bauschatz 1982, 18). These are the same roots that give Middle High German *wirtel*, meaning "distaff wheel" or "spindle" (Bauschatz 1982, 22), and also "whirl" and spindle whorl, the round weight that helps a spindle spin (which is referred to as the "dis" by contemporary spinners). There are multiple layers of meaning connecting wyrd with women's activities of spinning and birthing. Spinning is profoundly connected with creation, coming into being, and birth in this tradition. The Norse goddess Frigg, associated with domesticity and motherhood, is typically portrayed with a distaff, the tool used in spinning to hold layers of fiber ready to be spun. Distaffs have been found in ancient burials of women who scholars identify as "völvas" or seers (see Heide 2006, 250–253; Price 2019, 338–339) and have been adopted as ritual tools by contemporary gythias (see Figure 1.6).

Wyrd is cognate with Urð, the Norn whose name translates into English as the verb "to be." Old Norse *verða* means "to be" in the sense of what has already come into being (that which was) and what is now coming into being (that which is becoming). Urð and Verðandi are the past and present conjugations of the verb *verða*. The third Norn is Skuld, whose name means "what must be" or "what should happen," which conveys a sense of necessity, debt, and obligation. In Bauschatz's (1982, 79) interpretation, Urð's well is the *ur-well*, the ultimate well and the originating well of all, the arising of the world, the emergence of the everything into its unfolding interrelations. My interpretation is that "wyrd" means "what we are turning into," the ongoing emergence of being and passing away back into the well. It is also what is given, in the sense of what the past gives to us and all we are given, and the obligations that follow from this. Figure 1.7 shows etymological connections between wyrd and other terms.

Wyrd means to spin out of the belly/well, to come into being not just as a separate individual but as connected in a dynamic web of relations.

Figure 1.6 Gythia Jade Pichette, holding ritual distaff.
Photo by author.

The snipping of the umbilicus signifies the setting of fate by circumstances of birth but does not end the shaping of ourselves through our relations with others. In Heathen tradition, the placenta is called the fylgja, which means "follower" but also refers to a familial or protective entity that is a female guardian and often perceived in animal form. We might think of the fylgja as the primal layers of oneself that stretch back into our ancestors through the connections sustained in our mothers' wombs. Family and community shape us, but we also grow into those relations and shape them in turn. We grow together like trees with roots entwined with what we emerge out of and with branches making threads of interconnections with others. Wyrd also gives us the term "worth," which means "relational

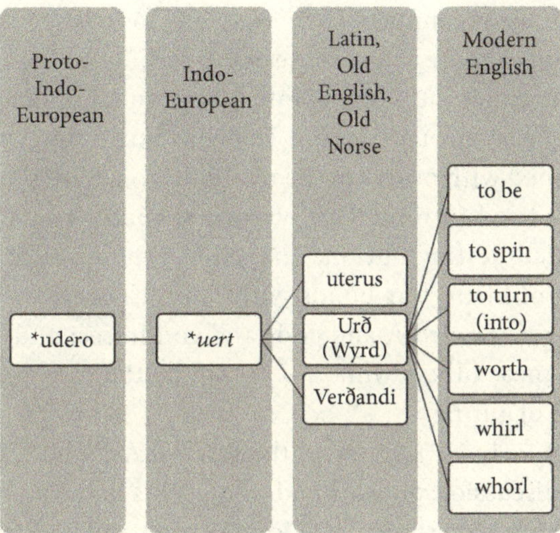

Figure 1.7 Etymology related to "wyrd."

value," signifying how we are always already indebted to others as well as how others are obliged to us. It refers to our situation in the web of wyrd, our web of relations.

Poetic Wyrd

"Wyrd" is not fate in the sense of a predetermined destiny, but means what we are turning into and the threads that connect us. It is hard to define the word discursively without drawing on references to many other things. It is a poetic metaphor, a deep metaphor for what it means to exist in a Heathen understanding of the world. Wyrd means well/web of relations/relational value/fate—probably originally in Owen Barfield's (2010 [1923], 73) sense of poetic speech, in which the word means all of these at once and was only later differentiated into multiple meanings, which we now interpret in terms of metaphorical allusions. Our understanding of the meaning of being has changed over time as ontology has changed. The modern sense of being is as a noun rather than a verb. In my view, wyrd gives a more active and relational sense of being as turning into, evident in the meaning of Urð, "to twine, to twist, to spin, or to turn (into)." This gives a more active sense of the verb "to be" as always turning into something, emerging, coming into being (and, implicitly, unwinding into something else through death). To be is to turn into what we are becoming, entwined with others in the world. Who we are is not unidimensional and not fixed in time. Our wyrd is shaped by our relations, not a future-oriented destiny but one shaped by where we come from; our circumstances of birth; our bonds with family, ancestors, and community, with place, *landvaettir*, and gods and goddesses; and it is bound by obligations to these others while supported by their obligations to us in ongoing cycles of gifting.

Calico (2018, 231–232) draws on the story of Ask and Embla (*Völuspá*, 17–18) in his discussion of wyrd and örlog. This is the story of the driftwood that washed up on shore, that Odin, Hoenir, and Lodur (*Gylfaginning* 9, says "the sons of Bor": Odin, Villi, and Ve) found and turned into the first humans, giving them blood, breath, and "fate." They were *ørlöglausa* when the gods found then. Calico (2018, 232) suggests this means they were without a past and that the gods gave them a past to make them individuals, but I take it to mean they were without relations. They were not tied to others, had no past that would lay down their connections with others, no one to draw upon for help, and no obligations toward others. They were not yet entwined in wyrd.

Orlog, variously spelled in contemporary practice, is interpreted by practitioners as the "primal layers" or "original law" (LaFayllve 2018, 101; Paxson 2006, 137). I think of orlog in terms of the layering of fibers on a distaff for spinning into thread but also as the layering of strata in the Well of Wyrd. In weaving on a warp-weighted loom, such as those used in Old Norse society, the work proceeds from the bottom up, and orlog could be understood as the first layers set down or woven into our existence. These are the "primal layers" of our connections to others set by the circumstances of our birth, what we are made out of, that shape how we turn out as the Norns spin our wyrd. Rightly or not, I also associate it also with the "original instructions" in Anishinaabe or Ojibwe traditions. These are teachings about how to live within the regenerative capacity of the land, woven into relations with nonhuman others rather than thinking we are above them or "on top of the blanket" or fabric of reality.[15]

Wyrd in Practice

For a least some Heathens, myself included, the sense of wyrd as the gifting relations between us includes the more-than-human world. A number of Heathens responding to my open-ended survey question "What is your connection to nature, what would you like it to be, and how does it matter to you?" explained their connection to nature in terms of wyrd and gifting relations. One respondent said that everything on Earth is interrelated, "woven together in Wyrd" such that "all that I do reverberates in the web." This respondent feels that

> [i]t is my duty, and that of my co-religionists, to live well on, and especially *with* the Earth. To live well with our local environment, to prevent harm where we can, heal it where it is unavoidable, and to do better by each generation, building up knowledge on how to live well with the Gods and vaettir [wights, or other-than-human persons]. It is our duty to live in right relationship with Nature, including our fellow humans, wherever we can. (survey response)

Another survey respondent specifically indicated that their "connection to nature is the gift exchange cycle" and that this gifting cycle is "central to heathen culture." They explained that "The Earth and the landwights give us the gifts we need to sustain our people. In return, we gift them through sacrifice and good husbandry of the land and livestock" (survey response). Another respondent said that they "have always felt a deep connection with the land and water, and with the creatures that share them with us" from growing up hunting and working on farms. They explain that it behooves us to acknowledge that what we receive from the Earth puts us in debt and that we need to be worthy of what we are given. They also noted the connection between gifting and our relations with nature, saying "Heathens believe in a gift for a gift, and the gifting cycle is the foundation of our spiritual practice." This respondent noted that they use a ritual refrain "From the gods to the Earth to us" and "From us to the Earth to the gods," which they explained means that humans should participate in the gifting cycle not just by giving back to the Earth but by giving in turn: "To acknowledge the bounty we are given, and when we give in return we complete the cycle. . . . We do not offer our sacrifices to the gods; but rather we show our respect for the bounty the gods have given us through the Earth by giving in return" (survey response). In these examples, wyrd is not individual human fate but the whole living web of relations in which we are embedded in gifting relations within the world.

At Raven's Knoll, Heathens associate the Well of Wyrd with what they call the Sacred Well, a natural spring at the campground. Gythia Brynja Clark, who leads the procession of Nerthus at Well and Tree Gathering at Raven's Knoll (featured in Chapter 3, "A Procession of Reconnecting"), describes this well as a repository of offerings, words, and intentions. It is a place where things accumulate rather than wash away (interview July 31, 2018). The Well holds the accumulating layers of intentions, words spoken in ritual, and oaths made, and it accrues them into being. Words turn into deeds. Just as spun thread is an accumulation of fibers wound together, making bonds and weaving connections, words spoken into the Well accumulate and sustain relationships.

Auz describes wyrd in terms of the many strands of fiber or threads that make up our interrelations, saying, "in Norse tradition we're a weaving, a tapestry." Each life is a bundle of threads, he says, that gathers threads that already exist and binds them together. These threads extend into the past and the future, and "those threads are bound up differently by different people. You're taking one of those threads by this interaction we're having. My children take many, many threads from many interactions and the biology I share with them."[16] The threads that make up the web of wyrd are "all like a gift," Auz says (interview May 2, 2018). In my view, this is because the web of existence is sustained by what we give each other, both socially and ecologically. Life cannot proceed without our exchange of breath with plants, those we consume as food, and those who consume our wastes.

Wyrd Ontology and the Gift Ethic

The deep associative meanings of wyrd are made salient in high sumbel and other rituals of gifting. Giving offerings (gifts given to ancestors, deities, or landvaettir), and giving gifts in high sumbel provide nonpropositional, embodied experiential knowledge of how to live in the world. These ritual actions can inspire a sense of what Levinas called "ethical subjectivity" in practitioners. Relational ontology fosters a sense of obligation that necessitates ethical if not political action because ethical sensibility is inherent to it. This is implicit in Heathen ritual practices of giving offerings and experienced by practitioners as a sense of felt obligation that they express as gratitude and a desire to give in turn. In this work, I am making the ethics that emerge out of Heathen gifting rituals explicit in consciously articulating them. Writing about what makes sense in terms of relational ontology and Heathen practice amounts to creating a prescriptive account of what should follow from Heathen ritual, but the point of my work is to show how a felt sense of ethical obligation emerges through practice.[17]

Gift giving enacts knowledge of how to be in the world through participation. Sumbel is a ritual that sustains this understanding of wyrd relations. A psychosocial consequence of meaningful participation in these rituals is a sense of connection, gratitude, and obligation.[18] Sumbel supports relational ontology and creates it in a feedback loop, sustaining mutual obligations in overlapping cycles of gifting. For practitioners the web of wyrd is the structure of the bonds between us, the threads of connection between us that are at once limits on our actions and what enables us to act upon others. In my view, these threads of relation are sustained through gifts given and gifts received, whether those are molecules of water, the air we breathe shared back and forth between plants and animals, or more obvious gifts given in sumbel.

Gifts given in a ritual context can be seen as illustrative of the origins of ethical sensibility. Gratitude for gifts received inspires in participants a desire to reciprocate. This is not a matter of intentionality, as though giving a gift "in principle" aims to generate reciprocity, but is instead a matter of felt experience. Giving offerings makes practitioners aware that all of life is a gift. We have nothing to give that we have not already received, including our own lives. If I pick a flower to give to you, it was already a gift to me from the plant, and indirectly from the sun, soil, and rain that grew it. In an animist world of *vaettir* or agentic other-than-human persons, every gift given is a gift already received. Each person who participates in gifting sustains the network of wyrd. Figure 1.8 shows a simplified synoptic model of how gifting inspires gratitude and the desire to give in turn, with each color representing a person in relation. Adding in the effects of gifting on each person creates a larger honeycomb structure, an interconnected network of relations experienced as the web of wyrd in Heathenry.

This larger structure, in which we find ourselves embedded in wyrd, entails a way of relating that can be described in terms of relational ontology.

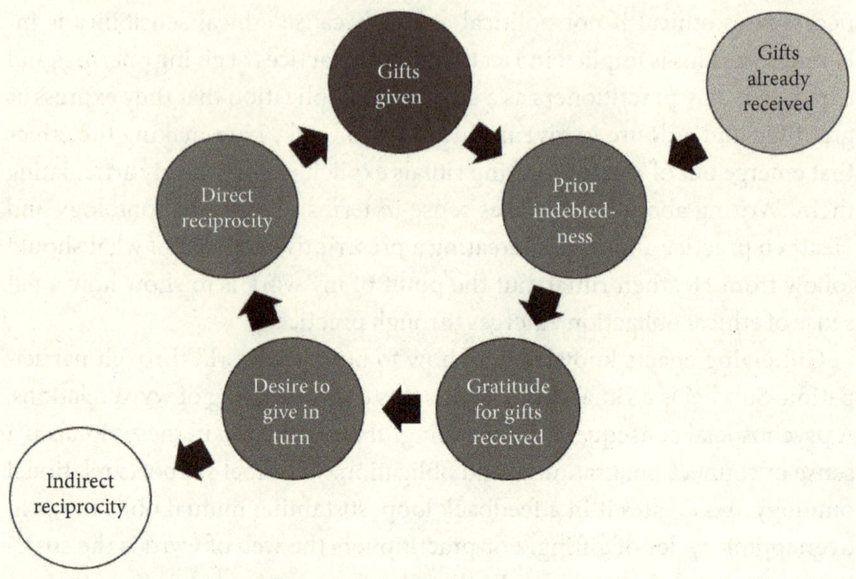

Figure 1.8 The relational ontology of gifting.

Calico suggests that reconstructionist traditions such as Heathenry entail "a re-Paganization of the mind" (Calico 2018, 44), but it is more than the mind that is changed. It changes both our perception of relations in the world and our manner of relating with others. It is not just a different model for thinking about the self but one that also gives a sense of being obligated, in being connected with multiple others. We can think about this in terms of having a different sort of self, as in Levinas's (1998) description of ethical subjectivity as "otherwise than being" but described relationally without a focus on subjectivity or selfhood. Calico finds what I call relational ontology in the American Heathens he studied, saying they construct "a dissenting vision of the human self. In contrast to the atomistic conceptions of individuality arising from the Enlightenment, Heathens are working on a more ecological understanding of the self, of an individual connected to sublime powers, the living past, ancestors, and other divine beings" (Calico 2018, 46). However, this is not just a different sense of the self but a different way of relating with one another—not just constructing "virtuous" Heathen selves (Harmsworth 2015) or magical selves (Pike 2001), not just crafting a different sense of "personhood" (Harmsworth 2015, 259), but a different ontology as a way of relating. This ontology is not willfully constructed as a model of the self but emerges from Heathen ritual practice as a way of relating.

Heathen Relationality

In discussing the Heathen sense of self, Calico says Luhrmann's analysis of Pagan magical practice is right in the sense "that magic involves a re-making of the self" (Calico 2018, 378). Building on other work in Pagan studies, in particular that of Sarah Pike, and Helen Berger and Douglas Ezzy, Calico says that magical practices create a new identity and a new sense of self in practitioners (Calico 2018, 386). Pagan ritual practices in general inculcate a different perceptual world that is more than human and more than what is verified by modern science through magical practices, but Heathen gifting relations and understandings of wyrd seem to me to go beyond this, sustaining a relational ontology and gifting relations.[19]

Calico suggests that an alternative sense of self facilitated through the practice of magic serves "an important therapeutic role as practitioners use its tools and techniques to reconstruct holistic selves out of the fractured individualism of modern life" (Calico 2018, 387). However, restoring the fractured individualism of modernity requires more than therapeutic self-help; it requires going beyond a new sense of self to change our patterns of relations. A new identity changes oneself, but a new ontology involves a broader shift in patterns of relation. It necessarily involves a way of relating with others (not just self-image) and a sense of obligation toward others.

Harmsworth, who studied some of the same people I have spoken with, suggests that Heathens have a fragmented sense of self (Harmsworth 2015, 263) and that they are trying to construct "authentic" or "virtuous" Heathen selves. I see this not so much as trying to be authentic, as live in frith. This may be partly from changes in how practitioners have understood and presented themselves over time, or it may result from our different lines of questioning and research foci. But relational ontology may look fragmentary if you are expecting a unitary sense of self from a perspective of individualized ontology. Relational ontology should facilitate a multifaceted sense of self in relation with others. Continuity of self-identity may be of less importance in relational ontology than in individualized ontology. When values are held in common across facets of the self, a coherent worldview is possible through a constellation of values in which different ones come to the fore depending on context or one's position in the web of relations. Harmsworth describes Heathens creating an expanding web of frith as "an expanding matrix of ethical, cosmological sites" (196) and describes Heathen understanding of the web of wyrd as an "associative web" of intertwined fate, in which the actions of each impact those they are connected with (200). This sounds like relational ontology and is evident in Heathen understandings of the consequences of breaking sumbel oaths. Such oaths implicate all present when they are made because they become embedded in the shared wyrd of the group. Harmsworth (202) notes the negative impact of a kindred member's behavior on the shared wyrd of Runatyr Kindred as felt by other members.

Calico corroborates that this understanding of the embeddedness of self in relations of wyrd is common with Heathens more broadly. Describing practitioners in the United States he says "Heathens reject the modern notion of the individual as an autonomous human being bound in time and space" (Calico 2018, 238). He interprets the web of social relations as integral to their sense of self (243) and discusses the Heathen understanding of a multiple soul in terms roughly compatible with my understanding of relational ontology: "For Heathens, the soul complex is more like connective tissue, connecting the individual to the past, to entities and powers beyond itself, sustaining the individual by drawing nourishment into the present" (242). "Individuals," he says, "are supported, strengthened, and enhanced by a shieldwall of the various relationships and powers to which they are connected as parts of their selves" (263).

Jenny Blain (2016, 17) notes that "Numerous writers within Heathenry or Asatru have commented that the concept of a body/soul dualism is not present in the literature." She explains that, instead, "there is a complicated interweaving of many processes of body, soul and mind, or body, mind and spirit." Her description of "'being' or 'self' constructed within communities and relationships" fits animist, relational ontology. In Heathenry, vaettir or "wights" are active agents in wyrd, whether humans, other animals, gods, or forces of nature (Blain 2016, 1). Sometimes vaettir is translated as "spirit," but, in keeping with reinterpreting such understandings in terms of the new animism, there is no need to categorize them as something with supernatural connotations. Vaettir are other persons in relation. As Strmiska (2000) suggests of Icelandic understandings of *huldúfolk* (the hidden people, sometimes referred to as "elves"), vaettir are not supernatural but deeply natural.

Historically in Norse literature, the sense of self includes not just the body and mind but also what anthropologists sometimes term a "composite soul" comprised of four (or more) parts: a changeable outward "skin" or shape (*hamr*), a mind (*hugr*) that resides in the body but can travel from it, one's "luck" (*hamingja*), and an ancestral guardian (*fylgja*). Archeologist Neil Price suggests that the hamingja could be perceived as the "personification of a person's luck." It "also had independent will and in extreme situations might even choose to leave its person" (Price 2020, 61). Fylgja is usually said to be "a guardian—a protector—but also the embodied link to one's ancestors" (Price 2020, 62). We might think of these four parts as differential relations and expressive of relational ontology. I think of hamr as the form I present that varies depending on who I am with and what I am doing, hugr as variable with my attention, hamingja as the changing configuration of my connections with other living beings, and fylgja as my connections to my ancestors. Together they describe how I am entwined in wyrd.

Heathen relationality is not exclusively human in that the hamr is variable, with the capacity to shift into animal forms, and the fylgja typically is perceived in animal form. "Hamr" literally refers to the skin or hide, and to put on the hide of another animal in some sense enables the person to become that animal. Literature scholar G. V. Smithers relates hugr to Huginn, "Thought," one of Odin's ravens, based on *Grímnismál* 20 in the *Poetic Edda* and the text fragment *Malskruþfrœþi*, explaining that hugr is the part of the self that can fly away, travel, or be projected in sleep or trance to act at a distance (Smithers 1959, 14–17). Fylgja, he says, often appear as birds: birds of prey for men and swans for women. The hamr is the shape; the fylgja the part of the self that travels, so one's hugr in the shape (hamr) of an animal is the fylgja seen by others (Smithers 1959, 19).

That contemporary Heathens share this sense of having a "composite soul" is most evident in esoteric rites, although the terms "hamr," "hugr," "hamingja," and "fylgja" came up often enough in conversation during my fieldwork that I had a clear sense of their historical meanings before finding textual references. At esoteric rites at Raven's Knoll some participants hamr-shifted into animal forms, with several "wolves" playfully chasing a "deer" on one occasion, and another esoteric rite featured the hamr-shifting of a participant into a "beast." Esoteric rites such as *seiðr* can include possession of the gythia by deities such as Odin, or other entities such as "norns," who did not seem to be distinctly differentiated from fylgur and dísir in the Vindisir's Winterfinding esoteric rites I participated in as part of this research. Who is manifested when gythia Jade Pichette conducts such rites is not always obvious to participants, and Jade does not necessarily remember what was said through them afterward.[20] Relational ontology would seem more easily to make shape-shifting and possession possible because persons and bodies are perceived as permeable, intraconnected, and not restricted to human form.

The "composite soul" can thus be seen as another way of describing relational ontology in Heathenry—the "self" here is fundamentally relational, with a singular inner sense of continuity (hugr), a variable outer appearance to others (hamr), connections to living others characterized as "luck" (hamingja) and to ancestors in fylgja. The self is embedded in relations of wyrd through their hamingja and ancestral guardian (fylgja) and is responsible for what they do through all these aspects. This gives a sense of the person as both singular and intraconnected with others.

Shifting Ontologies

Some readers may doubt that contemporary Heathens have relational ontologies and suppose that other ways of relating are an irretrievable part of pre-modern understandings of the world. Price, in his study of Viking worldview, mind, and magic, says that

> [o]bviously, in many respects the Vikings lived lives just like our own, experiencing the fundamental needs. . . . On the other hand, we seem reluctant to acknowledge that aspects of these and many other facets of their lives come to us filtered through a world-view that most of us would find incomprehensibly distant, unpalatable, even terrifying. (Price 2019, 2)

There are many undesirable aspects of pre-modern life that would feel quite alien to contemporary Heathens, but practitioners' descriptions of wyrd suggest that relational ontologies are supported within contemporary ritual practice. While the disembedding of economy from society has entailed changes in ontology, pre-modern lifeways of oral tradition and relational ontology are not incomprehensible and irretrievable. Individualized ontology has not overwritten relational ontology but submerged it. Carlo Ginzburg describes a somewhat alien seeming understanding of the world through an account of a sixteenth-century man accused of heresy, yet, he says, this account is appealing to modern readers because aspects of the account "render it instantly comprehensible even for those of us who live in a time far removed from his: the interweaving between oral and written culture, and his challenge to authority, both political and religious" (Ginzburg 2013 [1980], xiii).

As Bruno Latour (1993) argues, "We have never been [fully] modern." We have never become completely individualized nor are our economies completely disembedded from social obligation. Shifting from individualized ontology to relational ontology is not so much like a futile attempt to unlearn how to ride a bike as it is to remember that our original and still primary way of movement is walking. Owen Barfield (2012 [1979], 51) comments on the difficulty of trying to change what counts as common sense, saying "Try learning *not* to ride a bicycle!" but he also says it is not impossible. Tacit learning embodies knowledge in a way that is hard to ignore, but that is precisely how ritual can reshape ontology. Ritual instills tacit knowledge through embodied practice. Tacit skills become personal knowledge in Michael Polanyi's (2015 [1958]) sense. The knowledge becomes part of oneself, all the more so when we are talking about knowledge that becomes part of one's sense of identity. In this passage, Barfield overemphasizes thought, discussing the difficulty of changing ingrained thoughts, but ritual practices can change thought habits through processes of what sociologist Tanya Luhrmann (1989) calls "interpretive drift." Knowing how to ride a bike does not prevent us from walking. For some things bikes are better, such as going faster, but for others, such as getting around inside, they are more of an impediment. Similarly, individualized ontology is good for pursuing rights, but relational ontologies are good for recognizing responsibilities. Knowing we have rights need not preclude us from recognizing that we also still have responsibilities. Knowing how to ride a bike should not make us think that it is our only mode of being or that we cannot step off it.

Individualized ontology is dominant in modern society, but it does not render us into "five severed fingers" that can never again be a hand. Daniel Quinn uses this analogy in his novel *Ishmael*, in which the title character, a gorilla, says

in Africa I was a member of a family—of a sort of family that the people of your culture haven't known for thousands of years. If gorillas were capable of such an expression, they would tell you that their family is like a hand, of which they are the fingers. They are fully aware of being a family but are very little aware of being individuals. Here in the zoo there were other

> gorillas—but there was no family. Five severed fingers do not make a hand.
> (Quinn 1995 [1992], 7)

Even in modern individualized ontology, we are not detached fingers. We might think we are, but this is a delusion of modern consciousness. We are still connected. We remain dependent on one another, not just our families but all our relations. Individualized ontology has not removed us from being raised in families and communities and dependent on ecosystems. We are always part of larger wholes.

In modern consumer capitalism, we have never been closer to becoming "severed fingers," but we have not actually been cut off from one another. If we were severed, we would be dead. We know (all too horribly) what happens to primates when they are raised without emotional contact. Individualized ontology is like a too-small piece of clothing that impairs our movements and prevents us from full enjoyment of life. We have been sold this too-small garment to gain admission into consumerist society, but it does not afford us all the connections available to us without it. It is a lie of consumerism that consumer capitalism is the only way to happiness and guarantee of human rights.

The veneer of individualized ontology does not prevent us from also being "dividuals" in Marilyn Strathern's (1988) sense, intraconnected with others in overlapping relations. Marshall Sahlins (2011a) argues that the "dividual" is not a universal pre-modern subject, but that we should instead speak of this in terms of kinship. He prefers to speak of the "transpersonal distribution of the self among multiple others" (Sahlins 2011a, 13). In my view, to describe the self in terms of relational ontology is to describe kinship relations, one's relations to all, and thus "cosmology" in Viveiros de Castro's (2015) terms. Sahlins hints that we may all have an underlying relational ontology: "as a general condition of possibility, partible and relational identities may characterize persons who are not 'dividual' kin persons—but perhaps [describe] even bourgeois individuals like us" (Sahlins 2011a, 13).

Sahlins prefers to speak of this in terms of kinship understood not in terms of human genealogy but in a wider sense rooted in a totemic understanding of kinship with all life. In totemism, kinship is based on membership in wider animal clans. Sahlins indicates that kinship was not originally about biological relationships, but about who you feel indebted to. This would include the nonhuman. Sahlins mentions that the word "totem" means "co-resident" in the Algonquin language it is derived from (2011a, 10). Kinship is about "ties of mutuality" (Sahlins 2011a, citing Smith 1981, 226), and what Sahlins terms "mutuality of being." Sahlins (2011b, 229) points to scientific evidence that humans are uniquely capable of mutuality. He describes mutuality in terms of being "intrinsic to one another's existence" and "members of one another" (Sahlins 2011a, 2). Rather than describing this in terms of mutuality, which connotes dyadic reciprocity, I would say we are intraconnected. We are variously indebted, not necessarily mutually indebted at any given time but in overlapping relations.

Sahlins (2011a, 14) says kinship is not about having a common substance but instead that which is shared: common affect and experience. I would emphasize that it is shared practices that generate shared affect. Kinship comes from a community of practice that produces an affective community. This can be on the scale of clan, shared identity as belonging to a religion, or other affective or imagined community (e.g., queer community, nation).[21] Sahlins quotes Émile Durkheim on how kinship ties can be formed not just through genealogical relations, but also through tattooing, shared eating practices, and contract. Through shared ritual practices Heathens are becoming kin and building extended kinship ties. We are not "severed fingers" that cannot form a hand, but are instead weaving together a mitten that keeps us comfortable and warm. We are not severed limbs of one being but living beings that have always depended on others.

Culture teaches us the limits of kinship, which would otherwise be unbounded. Following Roy Wagar, Sahlins (2011b, 230) suggests that humans have a natural propensity to attribute intentionality to others (not just other humans). We are natural anthropomorphizers. As Sahlins (2011b, 238–239) says we are still animists. We still personify things, even if we are more likely to attribute agency to generalized collectivities such as nations. In my view, we still have relational ontologies even if they become submerged under individualized ontology. We are not fully formed as *Homo economicus* by modern society. Latour is right that we have never been fully modern, just as Karl Polanyi was right to say we have never had fully free markets because society would collapse without counter-movements of social supports to protect people from market volatility. Individualized ontology is often assumed to be the norm, but humans do not act in rational self-interest all the time, nor have we ever. If our more basic ontology is relational ontology, individualized ontology can never be anything more than a veneer or overlay. Remembering our relations is not like unlearning how to ride a bike but stepping off the bike and remembering that walking is our first and primary way of finding our way in the world.[22]

Relational Worth

As Blain (2016, 19) indicates, Heathens come to a different understanding of self through esoteric rites and giving offerings: "Understanding of a multi-part soul comes by insertion into practices such as formal honoring of LandWights and ancestors, whether physical or spiritual, and (for increasing numbers of heathens) journeying and other shamanic practices within the cosmology of the Nine Worlds and their beings." Participants learn how to relate through giving offerings and other ritual practices. Because wyrd is shared and sustained through relations of giving and being given, relational ontology includes an inherent ethical sensibility. To the extent that contemporary Heathens experience relational ontology, they will be ethically engaged, but to what extent this is a lived experience in contemporary practice varies.

The sense of obligation arising from prior indebtedness that we feel to others when we recognize what we have been given is rooted in basic human psychosocial dynamics that arose through our adaptive needs as a social species in which we depend on one another for our survival. In societies without state formations, this would be more obvious in terms of exile being a death sentence, with the literal dependence on one's community as survival unit. Because we need each other to survive, we developed an adaptive psychological need to be needed, a need to feel that others recognize our dependability. We rely on others to supply us with esteem, or relational worth, through what economic historian Avner Offer calls "regard," which is shown most easily, he says, through giving gifts. Giving a gift communicates regard and entails obligation, a debt (Offer 1997, 452, 455).

What others think of us is crucial for our own well-being, our self-esteem or relational worth. Calico (2018, 228) describes Heathens' sense of worth as "relational virtue." As noted above, the word "worth" derives from the same roots as "wyrd." Heathens perceive esteem as a relational value that varies with the debts and obligations one has with others. It is not about differential wealth but relational worth. In the context of the relational ontology emergent from sumbel practices at Raven's Knoll, relational worth is based on how dependable others find one to be rather than a measure of social hierarchy based on wealth accumulation or capacity for redistribution. Esteem, at its most basic level, is about how others regard oneself and depends on how likely one is to give in turn when able to do so and how oneself is indebted to others and thus obliged to give in turn.

We get some sense of self-esteem from identification with our lifeways or worldview,[23] understood as that which completes our "unfinished" selves. As historian Yuval Harari (2014) says, humans are born unfinished in the sense that our instincts are not enough to guide our behavior to ensure our survival. We need to learn from the accumulated collective learning of our cultures how to relate with others in various environments (McNeill and McNeill 2003). We are born in need of socialization or enculturation into a particular ontology or way of life—into the lifeways of our society. In anthropologist Tim Ingold's (2000) terms, we need to grow our lifeworld. We take instruction from our parents, caregivers, and other community members, but we grow our own worldviews partially by imitation and experiential learning that is not necessarily conscious either in being passed down to us or in our absorption of it.

It makes us feel good about ourselves to act in accordance with the received values of our society. We also get esteem through feedback from others, such as the recognition of worth given in sumbel and made tangible with gifts. Our need for esteem prompts our sense of obligation to act in accordance with the received values of our society and to act such that others will value our actions. Peer recognition from community members, for example, is a better motivator of pro-environmental behavior than self-interest or economic factors.[24]

Tacit Learning of How to Relate

We co-construct our ontologies first in our childhood learning of how to relate with others, but we also participate in perpetuating and shaping them through our ongoing relations. Participation in ritual activities negotiates gaps between how we think we should relate with others and how we do relate with others. Ritual gifting practices such as high sumbel do not just model how we should relate in giving gifts but also negotiate and enact a shared sense of ethics through embodied practice.

We develop conscience as a skill learned through tacit knowledge. Michael Polanyi (2015 [1958], 55) described tacit knowledge as "unconscious" in a particular way, as "subsidiary awareness." This sounds somewhat like the description of "salience" in social psychology, which may start out conscious but subsides into unconsciousness, whence it continues to influence behavior. Tacit knowledge, Polanyi says, is "unconscious" in the sense that it entails rules not articulated but followed. He gives the example of learning to ride a bike. We learn how to balance on a bike through making a series of corrections (Polanyi 2015 [1958], 49–50). This describes a process of continuous adjustment to feedback, which is adaptation. Much like how we learn to throw a ball, this is a matter of experiential learning through trial and error rather than a discursive or consciously controlled process of plotting a trajectory.

As Polanyi says, this form of learning results in acquiring skills. While he suggests that *the aim of a skillful performance is achieved by the observance of a set of rules which are not known as such to the person following them* (Polanyi 2015 [1958], 49, emphasis in original), I would say not *necessarily* known. Attempting to apply knowledge consciously in using skill can interfere with physical performance, as with self-consciousness in his exposition (Polanyi 2015 [1958], 56), but not all skills are physical or impeded by self-consciousness. Tacit learning is not inherently or wholly unconscious but experiential and learned through participation.

Polanyi describes how tacit knowledge becomes embodied in us using the example of learning to use a hammer: "Our subsidiary awareness of tools and probes can be regarded now as the act of making them form a part of our body. The way we use a hammer or a blind man uses his stick, shows in fact that in both cases we shift outwards the point at which we make contact with the things that we observe as objects outside ourselves. . . . We pour ourselves out into them and assimilate them as parts of our own existence. We accept them existentially by dwelling in them" (Polanyi 2015 [1958], 59). Our attention (hugr) extends into the tool. Through the development of skill the tool becomes part of our sense of self. Similarly, values learned tacitly in ritual become part of us, and we defend those values as part of our identity, as our worldview. This describes how the values made salient in ritual get "deeply into the bone" in Grimes's (2000) phrase. Polanyi explicitly notes that our beliefs, "intellectual tools," and interpretive frameworks become "anchored in ourselves" much as hammers and other tools do through tacit learning (Polanyi 2015 [1958], 59).

We can see "worldview" as an interpretative framework, unconsciously held. Polanyi argues that "When we accept a certain set of pre-suppositions and we use them as our interpretive framework, we may be said to dwell in them as we do in our own body." He says we start to identify ourselves with our interpretive frameworks through a process of assimilation in which the frameworks become "essentially inarticulable" (Polanyi 2015 [1958], 60). Interpretive frameworks develop over time, and they structure how we perceive the world and relate with others.[25]

We become aware of the effects of our tacit knowledge through "the operational results achieved through their use" (Polanyi 2015 [1958], 61). Ritual practice is like this, too—giving gifts builds social bonds and entails feelings of obligation: it is the explaining of it that is difficult. And such learning tends to be perceived as not acquired but a state of affairs that just *is*. A framework of understanding then seems invariable, what is given, such that we do not make social rules but only re-enact them: "This is an action, but one that has always an element of *passivity* in it. . . . The act of personal knowing can sustain these relations only because the acting person believes that they are apposite: that he has not *made them* but *discovered them*" (Polanyi 2015 [1958], 63, emphasis in original). Thus ritual is often perceived as reenacting previously encoded meaning, as in Rappaport's (1979, 1999) understanding of ritual, but better described as an ongoing "negotiation" of a shared "as if" as Seligman et al. explain (2008), or grown anew in each person, as Ingold (2000) describes lifeways.

This "negotiation" is more negotiable at some times than at others. It can also be more or less conscious depending on the ritual and social context. We often are conscious of what groups we identify with and act partly consciously to maintain in-group status, which may include consciously choosing some actions as well as unconsciously following others. Ritual is one location in which tacit learning of how to relate can be a more or less collaborative and participatory process of construction and negotiation. Conscience is formed through our received worldview, which seems unchanging but undergoes ongoing modification as each person in a community grows into and modifies it, as shown in Figure 1.9. It is also influenced by the values implicit and/or made salient in rituals we participate in, whether we are aware of this or not.

The Role of Sumbel in Tacit Learning of How to Relate

In rituals of giving, we acquire tacit learning about how to relate explicitly through words spoken but also through the actions we participate in.

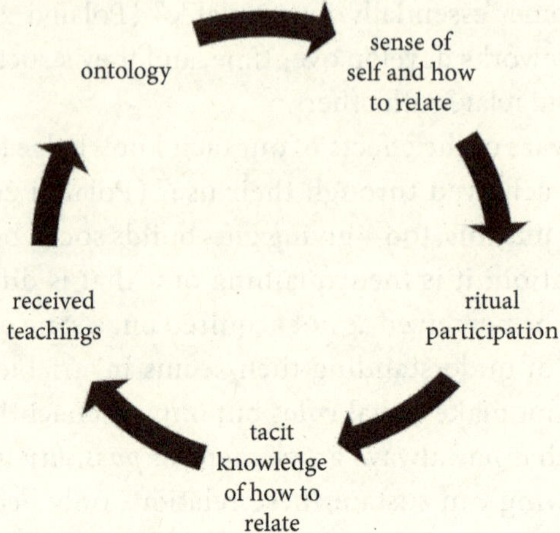

Figure 1.9 Tacit learning and conscience formation.

Auz likens Heathen gifting to "deep play." Participating in Heathen ritual, he says, "solidifies on an emotional level and a non-intellectual level" the gifting quality of how the world works. "I've gained this understanding," he says "because of the rituals I've experienced, because of Heathen ritual." Participating in high sumbel is a reminder that concretizes the perception that all our relations are gifting relations. Making gifting explicit in sumbel makes the ethics of gifting relations evident more generally. Auz explains that

> [t]he reason that we talk about it explicitly in sumbel is so that in other times, when we're not as pressed spiritually, we can also do it so that you can have the same worldview and reactions no matter where you're at. It's just that the religious experience … crystallizes it, and focalizes it, so that again, almost like a stone in the pond it ripples out in your life and other places as well. (interview May 2, 2018)

Through the gifting actions of sumbel participants acquire tacit learning of what our relations are and what it means to be in gifting relations, which influences our relations more generally.

Heathen rituals of giving gifts make the values of sharing, generosity, and gratitude salient, and, in conjunction with our evolutionary adaptive need to be needed, make participants feel obligated. Participation in rituals of giving gifts, such as sumbel and making offerings, inspires gratitude for gifts we have already received. Auz articulated this explicitly in saying that "One of the amazing things about the way Heathen worship is done is that it focuses gratitude. Gratitude for other people, gratitude for ideas, for virtues, values, and for ancestors, and for what ancestors have given us." He explained that when we are reminded what we have already received "when we realize those gifts, we feel richer, and we become better people because we focus on those gifts, and then those are the things that we start to give as gifts more often" (interview May 2, 2018). Participating in gifting rituals and giving thanks in ritual is a direct source of feelings of gratitude, which prompts participants to want to give in turn.

Gifts are tangible tokens of giving, generosity, and sharing. Giving gifts publicly in ritual marks relations and recipients as valued; it shows regard and confers relational worth. Participation in the act of giving/receiving matters, and related speech and listening acts matter. Public recognition and appreciation, giving thanks and expressing gratitude in ritual do not teach rules of ethics to obey but instead enact ethics as internally held values that become part of ourselves. Ritual thus operationalizes the values made salient (Rappaport 1979, 92; 1999,121–123). Sumbel does not just communicate or model ethics but also instills ethical sensibility through participatory tacit learning of how to relate with others in gifting relations. It embodies a gift ethic.

Heathens are not entirely in discursive agreement about the importance of giving material things as gifts. For gythia Jaime Cadorette, the physical gifts given in offerings matter. She said giving something tangible matters because "It's a physical proof: I am aware of you, I am giving you something." The physical gift makes recognition of the relationship real, she says, in the way that speaking aloud makes things real in a way that thinking about them does not.

> You're making it a real, a tangible thing. . . . Talking in your head is not the same as talking out loud. Talking out loud makes something happen. It makes it real. So when you're giving a gift, you're making it real, if I'm actually giving you something. (interview September 25, 2018)

Giving tangible gifts is a clear and obvious way to show our appreciation for others. It helps make gratitude conscious, or at least salient, but words are also important, as Jaime's statement evinces. Giving something physical serves as an ongoing reminder of one's relationship with the one who gave the gift and attaches importance to that relationship.

The gift is a token of relation. Jason explained that "it's not necessarily about the gift itself. It's more like a representation of the relationship between those two friends" (interview December 8, 2018). Many of the gifts given in sumbel seem to have a symbolic importance, in that the fact of giving from one person to another matters as much as what is given, so that the public recognition of the relation between the people is what matters. "Oftentimes," Auz recounts, "you'll see a gift given in recognition of a social relationship, rather than an actual return for the gift, because the gift is often a token that represents something else" (interview July 23, 2018). It is not a physical gift that needs to be reciprocated, but the relation. Many gifts are given to recognize worthy actions of the recipients, such as volunteering time, particularly of the youth who help with cooking and other tasks at events. Some are for emotional support already received, and some are more like overtures of friendships that people want to deepen.

Sometimes gifts are material but not tangible. Alex Vandermeer noted that Jason made a financial donation to the Humane Society of behalf of MA. There was nothing tangible to see in this gift, but it has a material effect. Finding "forever homes" for dogs at shelters such as the Humane Society matters a great deal to MA, and Jason's gift allowed him to publicly recognize and celebrate MA's quality of character, thus conferring relational worth. As Alex said, "There's a point of giving somebody a gift and then somebody acknowledging what kind of person you are publicly, and I think that's exactly what that gift session was, was acknowledging what kind of person that you have in your community" (interview March 15, 2019).

Heathen practitioners at Raven's Knoll are quite conscious of the social functions of sumbel in sustaining community, creating and maintaining alliances, creating debt in others, and relieving debts owed. Some have read extensively in anthropology (Auz, for example, has a master's degree in this) and are quite familiar with the social functions of gift economies. Erik explained that giving gifts puts people into the gifting cycle that historically structured relations between communities. Gifts were given with marriages in the form of dowries, but gifts also cemented other sorts of relations with "chosen family" and "blood brotherhood" in the past. In his explanation, "a gift always demands some form of reciprocity to the gift, so the gifting cycle is those gifts being given to and fro, back and forth continuously building and pulling those bonds tighter and tighter together." He described it as being "like lacing up a shoe: each side has a lace, and you keep lacing and lacing, then you pull taut, you wrap a bow. By the time everybody is dead they're remembered as being fast friends and kin" (interview February 13, 2019).

The articulation of reciprocity in terms of direct or delayed reciprocity is common among the Heathens of Raven's Knoll, expressed frequently with the refrain "a gift demands a gift" or "a gift for a gift." Some practitioners' thinking on this is influenced by Druid Kirk Thomas's book *Sacred Gifts* (2015). However, it is usually reciprocity with divinity that practitioners have in mind when they talk about direct reciprocity. Jaime Cadorette, for example, explained her understanding of reciprocity to me in terms of getting the attention of the gods.

> [I]f we want their attention, well, it's like that Janet Jackson song, you know? "What have you done for me lately?" . . . I think it's entirely important that we make offerings, and we make ourselves known, and we talk to them. Because why else would they bother answering? Because, as humans . . . people look at the gods and say me me me me me, and the gods are like "qui toi?" Like what have you done for me lately?

If people want a relationship with the gods, she says "it's imperative that you make offerings and you speak to them. Otherwise, why will they care?" (interview September 25, 2019). In this view, if you want to be able to ask the gods for something, you need to have maintained good relations with them through making offerings.

However, gifts given in sumbel are more likely to be instances of delayed or indirect reciprocity than the direct reciprocity implied by the phrase "a gift for a gift." (See Figures 1.10–1.12 for diagrams of these different forms of reciprocity.) Gifts are given asynchronously, with a year or more between receiving a gift from someone and giving them a gift in return. Often there is not an expectation of a return gift because people are giving gifts to express thanks for things people have done for them. Kára, also known as Pegacorn in the community, indicated that when people give gifts in sumbel, the gift draws the attention of the gods to what people do for one another.

> So the gifts nowadays though, in sumbel, it's people who you want the gods to recognize that they've done something for you. They've done a lot for you, or ultimately you want them to be recognized by the community that they've done a lot for you, or you've done a lot for them. (interview October 3, 2018)

Figure 1.10 Direct reciprocity.

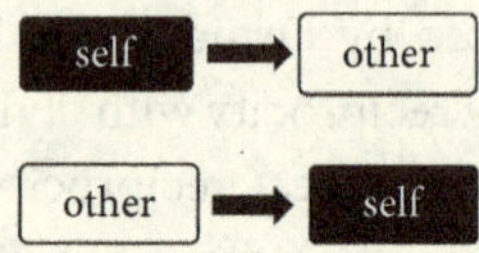

Figure 1.11 Delayed reciprocity.

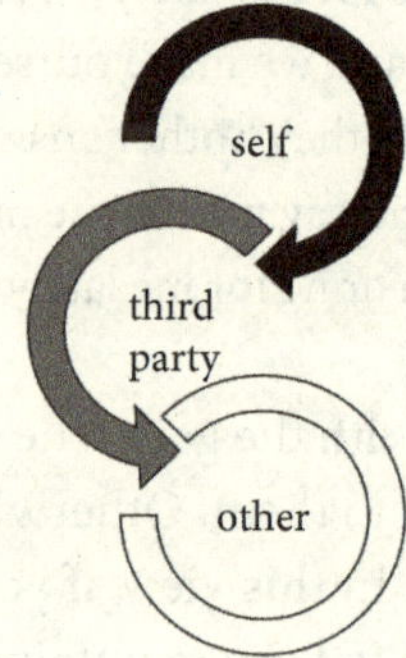

Figure 1.12 Indirect reciprocity.

Giving gifts confers relational worth in the community, witnessed by those present, including the gods. It is not a simple transaction of direct exchange.

My feeling is that we weave a stronger fabric of society (and social ecological systems) by giving in turn rather than giving back and forth over the same relations. It is all too easy to restrict reciprocity to direct exchange and maintain interhuman relations, notably within one's own in-group, at the expense of all else. Sumbel at Raven's Knoll operationalizes delayed reciprocity and indirect reciprocity rather than direct exchange. In sumbel, people do not trade gifts directly. Often gifts are given as a thank-you for support already received, and sometimes gifts are given indirectly. When Jason gave money to the Humane Society as a gift on behalf of MA, this embodied generosity through indirect reciprocity, in which he gave to the Humane Society so that they could give help to animals on behalf of MA. This is also the form of giving idealized in the Heathen survey respondent who said they give to the gods so that the gods can give in turn: "From the gods to the Earth to us" and "From us to the Earth to the gods."

The ideal embodied here is not that I should give so that you give back to me, but I give so that you can give to someone else in turn. It is through this delayed and indirect reciprocity of giving through third parties that larger systems, such as society and social ecological systems, are held together. Expanding on Levinasian ethics, the third party does not only create the need for justice (Levinas 1969, 88; 1998, 157), but also creates the possibility of justice. Levinas distinguishes between ethics, in which I owe everything to the other in a face-to-face encounter between oneself and another, and justice, in which a third party also inspires ethical obligation and necessitates a comparison of competing claims. In my view, it is through gifts given in turn that ethics extends beyond dyadic interpersonal relations, beyond our inner circles of friends and family, and beyond the interhuman to weave together our social ecological systems in distributed networks of indirect reciprocity that can create justice. In this way, relational ontology should, ideally, sustain social ecological systems through a gift ethic as gifting inspires the obligations that sustain the intradependent webs of ecological relations. This does not mean it is effectively doing this in practice, but that this is an ideal implicit in ritual practices sustaining relational ontology.

In modern society, we are accustomed to thinking of ourselves as autonomous individuals, each with our own rights and accountable only for our own behavior. This leads to a view of self–other relations in binary terms, as oneself over against the other. It steers us toward a skewed understanding of reciprocity in binary terms, but wyrd and sumbel show us a wider relational context in which everyone and everything is made up of gifts received from others and what we give in turn. While Levinas was highly critical of conceiving of ethics in terms of reciprocity (see Levinas 1989), his understanding of ethical relations epitomizes an idealized form of completely asymmetrical reciprocity. He emphasized repeatedly that in ethical subjectivity I am more guilty than all the others, and I owe everything to the other, saying, for example, "I am responsible for the Other without waiting for his reciprocity, were I to die for it" (Levinas 1985, 98). In ethics, for Levinas, the other is always in a position of height above oneself, obligating oneself. His concern was that direct reciprocity would reduce ethics to transactional exchange. But sumbel illustrates how giving gifts inspires obligation and infuses a relational ontology in which we can support one another in overlapping gifting cycles that sustain an extended network of delayed and indirect reciprocity and embodies the generosity of asymmetrical reciprocity.

Without involving third parties, giving gifts can degenerate into making bribes. This became clear to me in an accidental exchange I precipitated. When traveling to a conference in Boston, I stumbled upon a mead seller and spontaneously decided to buy a bottle. I realized only as I was in the process of checking in at the airport that I would have to pay to check my bag because I would not be allowed to bring that much liquid in my carry-on luggage due to American regulations. I mentioned my dilemma to the airline staff, who suggested I sneak off and drink it before boarding. Deciding that was not a good plan, I inquired about the fee to check my bag. Since it was more than I had paid for the mead, I decided I would just give it to the airline staff. I intended this as a gift freely offered without expectation of return yet I found myself bumped to first class when showing my passport to confirm my identity at the gate. While I was grateful for the additional leg room and other perks of first-class travel, I felt guilty at the possibility that someone else might have been displaced; this experience was the impetus for thoughts about why it is better to give in turn than to give back directly. It also prompted me to consider the effects of direct reciprocity negatively applied in revenge, as in "an eye for an eye" which, of course, we can apply until the whole world is blind. The positive action of giving in turn through indirect reciprocity expresses an ideal of justice that does not entail retaliatory punishment and considers a wider context that can take equity issues into account without being blind to competing interests, one's own included.

The ideal of indirect reciprocity is operationalized in sumbel by making the value of generosity salient. How this value should be enacted is under negotiation in current sumbel practice, evidenced by stories Heathens told me about problems with inflation and "flattening" or over-gifting. Gifting in sumbel is based on reconstruction of past tradition but is in ongoing processes of reinterpretation and reinvention in contemporary practice. Erik explained to me that gift giving in historical tradition was "asymmetrical" such that "you would always try and re-gift a little more value than what you originally been gifted." This sustains a gifting cycle because nobody wants to be the one who does not give a gift of good enough value (interview February 13, 2019). Over time, back and forth gifting of this sort can lead to inflation, which has led to some changes in sumbel gifting at Raven's Knoll.

Erik now reminds participants in his annual sumbel workshop at Hail and Horn that gift givers should consider the capacity of others to reciprocate when they are giving gifts so as not to "flatten" the recipient, who will likely feel obligated to give in return. He repeated in interview a story he tells as a cautionary tale in the community about how gifting can get out of hand. He had been giving gifts back and forth with someone at sumbel rituals for over a decade, and the value of the gifts escalated to the point that he gave the person a wolf pelt. The recipient had not expected such an extravagant and powerfully meaningful gift, was overwhelmed, and felt "flattened." They had to take extra time to be able to give a gift of similar "weight" in terms of monetary value, but also meaningfulness. Erik says, "This was not a cycle that they necessarily wanted to keep on . . . as it was very heavy. At some point there is only so much you can give." He realized that with the gift of the wolf pelt he had reached the maximum of what they could give to one another. When he was considering what to give, he was thinking of all the things he had received over the years, and he had taken "time to get this really nice big gift" but had not thought about what might follow if the recipient wanted to be able to give a return gift of comparable value and significance. Receiving a gift places an obligation on the recipient that can become too much to bear. Receiving gifts in sumbel for "some people," he says, "really scares the shit out of them . . . because they'll have to return it" (interview February 13, 2019).

Giving "heavy" gifts can also result in the inflation of social status of recipients, which is actively resisted in sumbel practice at Raven's Knoll, but still happens sometimes when people want to initiate more relations than some recipients can maintain. Jade indicated that at the previous two Hail and Horn sumbels they "felt flattened by community, such that I could never repay the community to that extent. But the thing that people keep telling me is that, 'Oh no, you've already given your gift, it's just been through your actions'" (interview October 9, 2018). Auz also receives a lot of gifts in thanks for what he does for the community, but he cannot always reciprocate in the way he would like. He related that sometimes gifts are disproportionate to people's existing social relations and, may inflate the receiver's status or result in hurt feelings if the gift is not reciprocated. Anyone who participates in sumbel can give Auz a gift, and many do so because of his generosity in providing the place for Hail and Horn and other events at Raven's Knoll. Like Jade, he also receives gifts because of his generosity with his time and expertise. These things make him highly regarded in the community, and people give him gifts to confer relational worth, but he only has three opportunities to give gifts at sumbel, so he has to carefully consider who he gives to. "You can give roughly three gifts, you're allowed three 'stand-ups,'" he said, "so you can give three main gifts, but you can receive many more than three gifts because you can have many people give you a gift." Extra gifts can be given if people are recognized as a group, such as when Auz and MA give gifts to people who have helped out with food preparation for the feast. This counts as one "stand-up" even if several people receive gifts. Auz sometimes gives gifts at other times, too, but he noted that doing it publicly in sumbel matters because part of the point of gifting is "to have it witnessed" (interview July 23, 2018).

The three-gift limit was set in an attempt to rein in over-gifting. Jade explained that when Hail and Horn started there was no limit on the number of gifts people could give. Some people participated quite enthusiastically, giving gift after gift. Jade said that between them and Erik and Auz in particular "it became a bit too much" because of the number of gifts and the expense. This became a problem "especially around issues of other people's finances and being 'flattened' and because people with more money are able to give sometimes bigger gifts that you feel like you can never repay, and then you feel in debt to that person" (interview October 9, 2018). Because of this experience, the three-gift limit was instituted.

Gifting Community

Heathen gifting practices are forming an incipient gift economy in the community, in which gifts initiate and maintain social bonds. Participants say that participating in gifting practices in sumbel generates community. The words "connection" and "community" came up repeatedly in interviews. A sense of community is produced not just through physical gifts, but also through the recognition of the worth of recipients through the words of praise offered in sumbel. Erik said that this is what he likes best about sumbel, because when people give gifts and share words of praise "That's really what stitches together a community. Sumbel is about community building" (interview February 13, 2019).

Giving gifts as offerings also brings the community together. Erik explained that hearing the words people say when making offerings "helps with that whole stitching together the community. When you hear the words of those you're sharing worship with aloud and you kind of see where they are in their relationship with the deity, or where they are in their personal life" (interview February 13, 2019). Hearing what others say when they give gifts in sumbel and offerings at other times inspires empathy and draws people together. Similarly, Auz indicated that sumbel is one of the most meaningful parts of Hail and Horn Gathering for him because of how it recognizes the spiritual bonds people share and "the spirituality of community" (interview July 23, 2018). This sense of community at Raven's Knoll is highly valued by participants. I frequently heard articulations of giving back to the community, such as Kára's statement "I like helping . . . everything I do, I do because of the community and I help out people because I enjoy that giving back" (interview October 2, 2018).

Community building through gifting is accomplished not only through the giving of gifts among friends, but also through more or less overt political maneuvers that create debt in less-liked others in the broader social community to build alliances as well as to build frith through making amends and extending overtures of connection, friendship, and inclusion. Jaime was quite forthright in acknowledging the political nature of sumbel gifts, recalling that historically "We know that that's how communities would make ties together. 'Keep your friends close, and your enemies closer,' right?" Gifting was a way to maintain community by putting others in one's debt. "If you keep everybody in debt, in this debt cycle of 'I owe you,'" she said, "it keeps a community going. That's how it was done historically, and that's how they're reproducing that whole concept of the gift cycle." She explained that this is how positive social relations were maintained between clans in the past and said that "on a larger level, that's just how community works. I give to you so you'll give to me." She is amused to see people who do not necessarily like one another at sumbel give gifts in order to create debt. With a chuckle, she said "They are doing it to create debt. I kind of get a kick out of that to be honest" (interview September 25, 2018).

Giving gifts from one group to another builds community by initiating and maintaining alliances. Jade explained that giving gifts recognizes enduring relationships between people, showing respect for recipients and their contributions, but is also a means of building new relationships. Vindisir has given gifts to groups in western Canada and in Montreal to build relationships with them and received gifts as a kindred as well. Brynja, gythia of Well and Tree Gathering and Lodestone Hearth, gave Vindisir a drinking horn called Wolfmaker. Jade said that using that horn "during our ceremonies, because it was gifted to us . . . it means that bond between us and Brynn's hearth is always there. It is always there through that horn" (interview October 9, 2018). The gift of the horn recognizes the value of the relationship between Vindisir Kindred and Lodestone Hearth and makes people mindful of this relationship when it is used in ritual. After receiving Wolfmaker Vindisir used the horn at Winterfinding and filmed a short video to share with Brynja, which also served to deepen relations between the groups.

Kára said that sumbel gifts can also be used politically if someone wants to mend relations, for example, if they have broken an oath. A gift can be offered as part of an apology, saying "I still want to foster a better, maintain a better, relationship with you.... Let's foster a working environment together. Here's a gift" (interview October 2, 2018). Giving a gift can be a gesture of making amends. Jade told me of a man in the Raven's Knoll community who had argued with them against allowing Skaði into the Vé at Raven's Knoll. Each year at Hail and Horn Gathering a god pole is erected in the Vé and offerings are given to the deity evoked into the pole and whose likeness is carved into it. Including Skaði had been a somewhat divisive issue in the Raven's Knoll community, with some people feeling quite strongly that as a jötunn she should not be allowed into the Vé, which is set up to honor the Æsir group of deities allied with Odin. Some Heathens regard the jötunn as outsiders and negative forces. Others, including Jade, countered that because Skaði married Njord, one of the Vanic gods allied with the Æsir, she could be regarded as a goddess and welcomed into the Vé. Skaði is one of three dís particularly celebrated in Vindisir Kindred and by other Heathens in the Raven's Knoll community, in part because she is a symbol of women's empowerment, but also of the value of inclusion. According to Norse mythology (*Skaldskaparmal* 1 in Sturluson 2005, 82–83), after Skaði's father was killed by the Æsir she dressed herself for war and demanded recompense. As part of the settlement she negotiated with them she was allowed to choose a husband from among them by looking at their feet. She chose Njord, god of the sea and fishing, but he could not abide living in the mountains with her, nor could she stand to live by the sea with him, so they divorced, yet she maintained her kinship status as an ally of the Æsir. Jade and Kára each took time to help the man understand why it was important to them to welcome Skaði into the Vé. Jade said,

[h]e was so against Skaði going in, and he talked to Kára about it, and he talked to me about it. I actually did an hour-long Skype call with him

explaining the merits of why Skaði should be in the Vé, from an archaeological perspective, from a philosophical perspective, from a lore perspective, just went at it for a full hour explaining why she should be in the Vé. And by the end of that conversation he agreed.

Jade recalled, "he had bought these really beautiful Skaði pendants," and he gave one to each of them to thank them for their time and effort (interview October 9, 2018). Such gifts can forge stronger relationships after arguing.

Gifts can also extend new overtures of friendship and connection or express the desire to form new relationships. Kára, for example, gave a jar of honey to Runatyr Kindred at sumbel, saying "I want to get to know you guys better, because I think you're awesome people and I want to spend more time with you" (interview October 2, 2018). Runatyr subsequently invited them to participate in events with the kindred, and they have gotten to know Chantal and Erik better.

Sumbel gifts can also be a way of enacting the value of inclusion. Auz and MA do this in giving gifts to those who have not been well integrated into the community. Auz noted that "Sometimes it is to encourage and incorporate marginal people into a network of social relations" (interview July 23, 2018). Sometimes he and MA give gifts to people who are new to the community, especially if they have come from far away. This way, they initiate contact with those who may not yet have any relationships in the community. Giving gifts can forge new relationships, deepen existing relationships, mend faltering relations, and invite reconciliation. Giving gifts includes people in the social ties of wyrd in the community.

Wyrd Conclusions

Sumbel inspires a gift ethic, encouraging a relational ontology through the giving of gifts, expressions of gratitude and giving thanks, public recognition of the worthy deeds of others, and making the values of sharing, generosity, and inclusion salient in ritual. These values become part of the participants' way of life, or are affirmed as part of their way of life, through tacit learning of how to relate in sumbel. Speaking over the horn and giving gifts brings wyrd relations into being through public recognition of gratitude for gifts already received and inspires the desire to give in turn. Sumbel supports a gift ethic feedback loop, weaving participants into the extended and overlapping cycles of indirect reciprocity that sustain patterns of giving and a sense of connection and community.

These relations in wyrd extend into the more-than-human world through Heathen practices of giving offerings. The feelings of relatedness that extend beyond the interhuman, supported by Heathen understandings of wyrd, should promote pro-environmental behavior, sustaining larger social ecological networks. Studies in the sociology of religion find that feelings of connectedness promote pro-social and pro-environmental behavior (Taylor et al. 2016, 342–343). Heathen practices of giving offerings may not perfectly enact a gift ethic that includes the more-than-human world, but this ethic is implicit in their ritual practices and influences the behavior of practitioners. The next two chapters of this work examine how Heathen rituals inspire a gift ethic beyond the interhuman, including ancestors in Vindisir's Dísablót and other inclusive Heathen practices of ancestor veneration and powers of nature such as Nerthus at Well and Tree Gathering at Raven's Knoll.

2

Becoming Ancestors

Welcome to Vindisir's Dísablót

In mid to late January of each year, Vindisir Kindred gathers at the home of one its gythias, Jessica, to celebrate Dísablót and honor our female ancestors.[1] This is a fairly relaxed event, in which the kindred gathers as "chosen" family and enjoys a cozy atmosphere akin to an extended family gathering. Children and pets intermix with older relatives, romantic partners, and family friends that vary year to year.

Jessica welcomes my husband, our child, and me into her home, offers us drinks, and helps us get settled. We carry the food and drink we have brought to share into the kitchen and catch up with people we have not seen in a while as other participants trickle in. Newcomers are introduced, and we get acquainted over drinks around the fireplace, in the kitchen, and around the dining room table. The house is a beautiful old home with gorgeous wood trim and floors and is filled with oddities and collections curated by morbid fascination. Animal skulls are everywhere, and shadowboxes display every kind of curio you might hope to find in a hidden old attic or an out of the way antique market of lost things.

A complete human skeleton named Aloysius (pronounced "AL-oh-WISH-əs"), sits at their dining room table (see Figure 2.1).[2] On the table in front of Aloysius, affectionately known as "Wishes," sits a wooden bowl, ready to receive offerings for the *dísir*—understood as female ancestors in this context[3]—from the food and drink we have brought to share. An altar is set up on the table, featuring images of Freya and Skaði, bird skulls, and Wolfmaker, the kindred's drinking horn gifted to us by Brynja Clark of Lodestone Hearth.

While sitting around the fireplace, some of the kindred give gifts. Ewan gives Jade a chainmail necklace that fae has made, featuring a cat vertebra; Joan a necklace that fae made with the feet of the chicken sacrificed at the previous blót[4]; and Jessica a vulture skull that fae recently found. These gifts are appreciated, and they thank faer. Joan gives a serpent necklace to

Wyrd Ecology. Barbara Jane Davy, Oxford University Press. © Oxford Univesity Press 2025.
DOI: 10.1093/9780197804957.003.0003

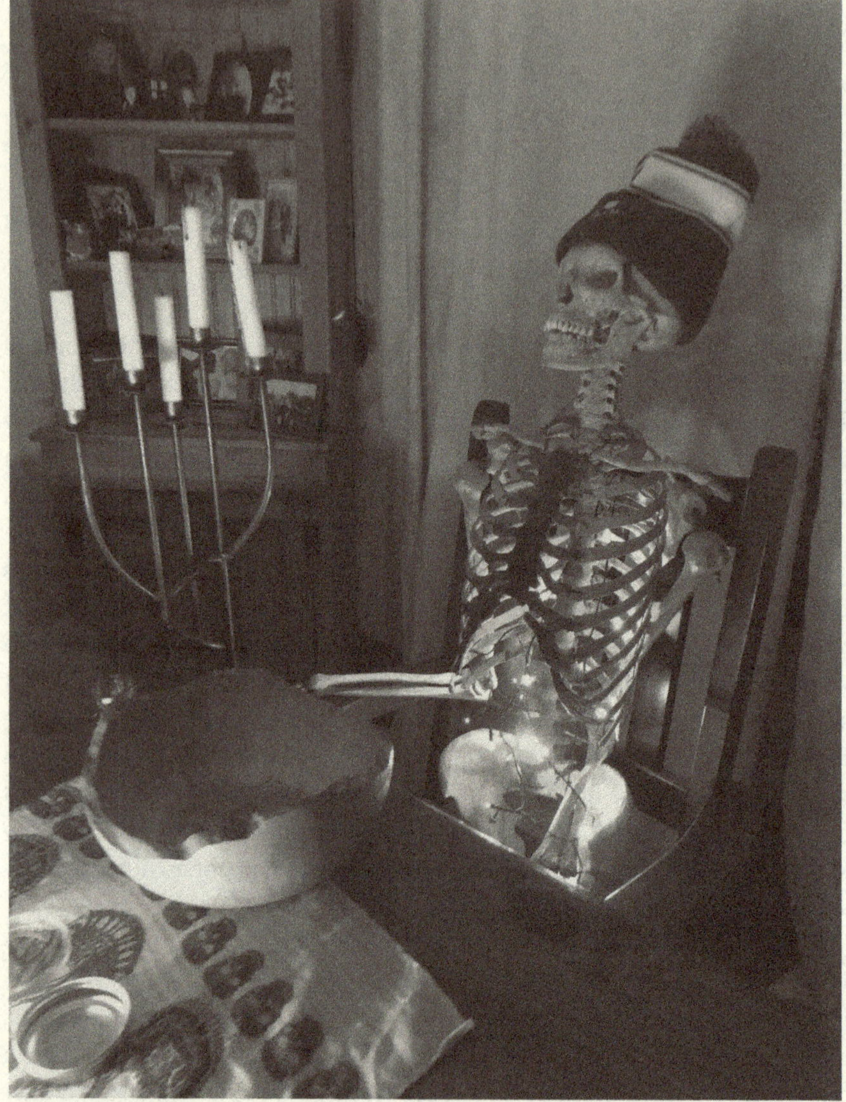

Figure 2.1 Aloysius with offering bowl.
Photo by author.

my child and me a jar of relish she has made, as well as three old "skeleton" style keys on a big ring. This latter gift is significant to me since keys are associated with Frigg, a goddess important to both of us as mothers and keepers of the home. We had had a conversation about Frigg's power while we plucked chickens at the previous blót. As Joan noted, Frigg is the only one who orders Odin around. She is not just a "housewife" but an ancient power to be reckoned with. It is a thoughtful gift, and I am quite touched by it.

Once everyone has arrived, Jade opens the blót with a brief address to the group, beginning with their characteristic hearty shout of "Hail!" to focus everyone's attention. They remind us that the Dísablót is to honor our female ancestors. Jessica interjects that we also honor women who have gone before who are not our biological ancestors. Jade responds with a smile saying, "Yes, I was getting to that." They note that kindred members have told the stories of their female ancestors in years past, and that we need now to "feed the ancestors in ourselves." They explain that so many of them, particularly the ritual leaders (Jade, Jessica, and Ewan), have given a great deal to their communities and need to step back from that a bit.[5] Jessica adds that they need to look after themselves so that they have the resources to sustain the work they are doing into the next generation, gesturing to the children in the group. Jade raises the horn, drinks, and pours a libation in the offering bowl; she then passes the horn on to circle through the group, indicating that we may each drink and that there is no need to speak over the horn at this time. (At times Vindisir's Dísablót includes a sumbel at this point in the event.)

Jade dims the lights and explains the next portion of the rite, which varies from year to year. They then proceed to narrate a story within a story throughout the remainder of the ritual. The measured phrases and intonation of their voice sets a trance-inducing tone, and the story serves as a sort of guided meditation, making us ready to invite our dísir to be with us for the evening. They tell us of how Frigg, who knows more than she says, spent her time while Odin was wandering, how she tried to protect her son Balder by securing promises from all the world but mistletoe to do him no harm, and his death and descent into the underworld.[6]

One by one we go into the kitchen and receive a candle, along with some words of wisdom from Ewan. In the dim light, fae is a shadowy hooded figure. Fae presses a candle into my hand and asks me if I know the tarot card "Temperance." Fae describes the image of a figure pouring water from one vessel into another and notes that it is a finite amount. I am not sure in the moment what that might mean, but I go directly into the dining room.

An altar is set in the middle of the table, and I light my candle from the large red candle there and place it on the table in the growing pool of light with the others' who have come in before me. I then briefly sit with Jessica, who is seated at the foot of the table. Like Ewan, she is hooded. Her eyes are closed, and her hands cradle an old-fashioned tea cup on the table. The saucer of the cup holds the tiny bones of birds (see Figure 2.2).[7]

I invite my grandmother Anne, and it seems Jessica embodies her holding the cup so similar to those in which my grandmother used to serve tea to her sisters. When I was very young, each week my grandmother had tea with her five sisters, and my mother often brought me to Grandma's house when "the Aunts" were there for tea, sharing finger sandwiches, cookies, and tea in bone china cups. These were my great aunts, and I suppose in some sense they signify the dísir to me. At the time, my grandmother was the only one of them to still have a spouse. All of the other men of that generation had died, including the Aunts' four brothers. We had less contact with my father's kin, and the Aunts meant family to me. They were the matriarchs that organized family events, sniped about each other endlessly, gossiped about everyone across two counties in a sometimes overwhelming cackle, and loved all of us with an intensity I came to understand only after starting my own family.

Figure 2.2 Tea cup with bird bones used in Dísablót ritual.
Photo by author.

It is strangely easy to imagine them turning into valkyries after death, trading their very proper attire and manners for blades and armor to defend their descendants, as some imagine the dísir. They embodied the folk wisdom passed on in the phrase "Don't let a wishbone grow, dear, where your backbone ought to be." I feel a sense of comfort from contact with them, reminding me of the child I was, but also giving the sense that I am one of them and have things to do in the here and now. I am their hands and arms in this world. We are the spinning moment of action, gathering fibers of the past into the threads of our lives, which then spin out again. Each of us is like the rune gebo, an X in the ancestral lines that gather into a configured point and flare out in our descendants.

After writing an account of this for my fieldnotes, I looked up the meaning of the Temperance card that Ewan mentioned and found that it parallels that of the gebo rune in some ways. Temperance, according to Eden Gray's (1960) interpretation of the Rider-Waite tarot deck, refers to the tempering of the person from the mixing of the waters of life. Like the X shape of gebo, the card represents the union of male and female, and the shaping of the stream of life from the past, through the present, and into the future. Gebo means "gift," and I take this to mean that we are each a gift from our ancestors, to be given in turn to our descendants. To me, this is the true meaning of reciprocity, giving in turn rather than giving back in direct exchange. Through gifting, we shape the web of wyrd, each of us a gathering point of connection supporting others.

After we all have a chance to invite our dísir to join us, Jade opens the lights and invites us to make our food ready to eat. We place our offerings in the bowl before Aloysius and then share in the feast together. We have a potluck of cheese, fruit, and homemade pickles, freshly baked bread, salad, smoked salmon, hot and sour potato, shepherd's pie, cheesy cauliflower, smashed potatoes, and venison, with shortbread, apple crisp, and lazy daisy cake for dessert and hot apple cider, wine, and other drinks. As is usual for Dísablót, Jade had invited us to contribute food made from family recipes that have been passed down, with the added suggestion to keep various dietary restrictions in mind. Since one member is celiac, and some are vegetarian, some recipes were modified.

Joan brought the venison, beautifully slow-cooked with onions and carrots. She explains that this deer was gifted to her by those in charge of enforcing the tagging of deer to prevent poaching. Local officials in Ontario have discretion to allocate seized carcasses to people in need in the community. They knew she had bought a tag to hunt that fall but had not got a deer with her bow and also that she had recently lost her job in unfair circumstances, so they gave her the meat of an entire animal, fully processed for freezing, which they had seized from poachers who had taken animals without tagging them (and thus were likely illegally overhunting). Joan explains that the mild taste of the meat indicates that this was likely a doe.

We enjoy a pleasant evening sharing delicious food and drink, with those of us who live in different cities catching up on what we have been doing since we last talked. We pass a horn of mead that a newcomer has generously brought to share, speak a few boasts, and share some meaningful stories about what matters to us. We visit late into the night, sharing drinks and stories, with some people enthusiastically singing along with recorded music. I treasure the time we spend together and am loathe to say goodbye at the end of the night.

Interpreting Dísablót

Ancestor veneration is a widespread cross-cultural pattern (Reuter 2014; Sheils 1975), presumably because it serves an adaptive need to pass on collective learning. This would encourage the emulating of elders and positive valuation of local traditions that have enabled people to live in various environments. Ritual has played a significant role in the self-regulation of social ecological systems in conjunction with gift economies (Davy and Quilley 2018, see also Berkes 2012 [1999]; Rappaport 1968, 1979). This provides a clue about how rituals of ancestor veneration such as Vindisir's Dísablót support relational ontology and can contribute to the formation of ecological conscience. Ritual practices of giving offerings to ancestors can change life goals from individual success to community remembrance, shifting ontology from an emphasis on self and a way of being toward a way of relating and maintaining the quality of ongoing relations with the dead. Because the ancestors overlap with the dead more generally, including other animals, and shade into a broader imagined community that extends into the past, future, and beyond the human into the whole web of wyrd, Heathen practices of giving offerings to ancestors supports a broad gift ethic that includes all our relations. Rituals of making offerings and giving gifts to ancestors thus nudge practitioners toward ecological conscience.

Vindisir's Dísablót, and ancestor veneration more generally in the context of relational ontologies, may initiate a process of interpretive drift toward attention to relational worth and gratitude, which may help mitigate modern affluent overconsumption by nudging participants toward a more relational ontology. Ancestor veneration may spur interpretive drift toward a more inclusive moral community by extending gifting relations beyond the human. Applying terror management theory to Heathen ancestor veneration suggests that the values made salient in these practices will be operationalized because death is made salient. However, Heathens cannot support themselves entirely through gifting, and the effects of their ritual practices are limited by the difficulties inherent in sustaining a tradition on the margins of dominant modern individualist society.

Historical and Comparative Context

In historical practice, the dísir appear to have been perceived not so much as named or personal female ancestors, but as powerful female entities more broadly, including other-than-human female guardians such as valkyries and fylgja, or other powers such as female jötunn or goddesses (Ellis 1968 [1948]; Ellis Davidson 1998; see also Gunnell 2000). It seems likely that the referent of the term "dísir" was historically less precise than modern scholarship prefers. The meaning of "dísir" has shifted over time, as have interpretations of the personages associated with the term. Treating dísir as female ancestors is a common, if disputed, contemporary North American interpretation. Calico indicates that American practitioners regard the dísir as "helping spirits" of the family line that may provide luck and guidance through dreams or guided meditation (Calico 2018, 260, 262), which is similar to the perception of the Heathens of Raven's Knoll and Vindisir and in keeping with historical interpretations of female guardians of family lines (Ellis 1968 [1948], 141; Gunnell 2000).

Vindisir's Dísablót is perhaps more like historical descriptions of Mother's Night than blóts to the dísir, but the term "dísablót" is historically no more precise than "dísir." The sagas recount dísablóts at the beginning of winter (mid-October) in *Víga-Glúms Saga* 6, in autumn in *Egil's Saga* 44, and the beginning of February in *Ynglinga Saga* 33. Folklorist Hilda Ellis (1968 [1948] 136–137), in her analysis of death in Old Norse society, notes evidence of offerings made to the dísir at the beginning of winter or later, at different times depending on geographic location and historical time period, not based on set calendar dates but local practice.[8] Philologist Rudolph Simek (1993 [1984], 60–62) indicates that the Icelanders seem to have associated dísablót with practices in Norway and Sweden by the time of the writing of the Sagas and Eddas. *Ynglinga Saga* 33, written by Icelander Snorri Sturluson, links dísablót with Disting in Sweden, an annual gathering at Uppsala, which is still held annually at the beginning of February.[9] Simek refers to the event described in *Egil's Saga* as a "banquet" for the dísir. It is not named as "dísablót" in Bernard Scudder's translation of *Egil's Saga*, and the glossary of Thorsson's edition of the *Sagas of the Icelanders* (1997) refers to such events as "Winter Nights," but describes the latter as a feast with offerings to the dísir at the time of slaughtering in preparation for winter, which included an animal sacrifice and sharing it in a communal feast. This corresponds more closely with Vindisir's Winterfinding blót, which includes animal sacrifice and honors the goddesses favored by the group, rather than the female ancestors as at Vindisir's Dísablót. *Gisli Surrson's Saga* 44 mentions a sacrifice to Frey at Winter Nights, which would seem to indicate that Winter Nights was not necessarily, or exclusively, a time of offering to the dísir. Folklorist and scholar of Old Norse literature Terry Gunnell (2000) speculates that Winter Nights activities shifted from late October to Yule over time and that similarities with dísablóts held in February or the beginning of spring may have been due to recognizing the beginning and end of winter in different areas with offerings to female powers. From the evidence he presents, offerings to the dísir at Winter Nights were typically semi-private events, while events associated with spring were larger events, such as Sweden's Disting.

While ancestor veneration is widely practiced in Heathenry, and honoring the dead is common in contemporary Paganism more generally, events honoring the dísir in particular, either as female ancestors or female powers, are somewhat less common. "Dísablót" in some contemporary American traditions refers to quite unrelated practices. Like Gunnell and other academic sources, American Troth Heathen Kveldulf Gundarsson notes regional variations evident in historical sources and suggests that Disting was a larger communal gathering, while dísablóts may have been smaller family-based events associated with Winter Nights to honor the "idises," the Germanic version of the term he prefers to "dísir" (Gundarsson 2007, 364). However, his chapter on Dísablót does not discuss the honoring of female ancestors or other-than-human persons but rather a ritual of "Charming of the Plough" from the early English Æcerbot charm to bless fields, with offerings for land wights placed in the first furrow ploughed in the spring (365). Somewhat confusingly, he also refers to dísablóts as feasts honoring ancestors as part of Winter Nights in celebration for the harvest they have aided. He likens the giving of offerings to ancestors at this time to Samhain, a Celtic feast of the dead held at slaughtering time (325–326). Calico similarly refers to Dísablót as a "Charming of the Plough" event associated with "May Day, or Walpurgisnacht" (Calico 2018, 464), but a few pages later indicates that Dísablót is a winter festival (Calico 2018, 466). There may be some confusion between Winter Nights and Walpurgisnacht (May eve) underlying this, in conjunction with the variable dates in historical sources, resulting in diverse practices and naming of events.

Paxson (2006, 8) indicates that "Honoring the ancestors, especially the *dísir*, the foremothers who guard the family line, is a core belief." Paxson discusses "Mother Night" as an event honoring the goddess Frigg and female ancestors held on December 19 and notes that there was historically a prohibition on spinning from this time until the end of Yule (Paxson 2006, 111), or Christmas. She also mentions Dísablót in discussion of "Idis-thing," held in February, saying that, if the dísir were not honored during Winter Nights, they may be feasted "when winter is beginning to give way to spring" (112), which in most of Canada would be not until at least March. Paxson associates Winter Nights with Winter Finding, which she sets at the first full moon after the fall equinox (109).

Jade described Vindisir's Dísablót as a "time to reconnect and honor the women who came before. . . . What it came down to was family coming together, having good food, honoring our ancestors, but especially the dísir in particular" (interview February 3, 2018). Usually this event includes sharing stories about female ancestors as well as sharing food and drink with ancestors, kindred members, and other guests. Ewan said that Dísablót is for "honoring our women ancestors, and those that came before us, and making sure that they are remembered" and added that when we honor the dísir in ourselves we are "continuing the story, for those who will be our descendants, and taking care of ourselves so that we keep our lines going." Fae explained that this is a way to "honor women ancestors, and our place in the line among them" (interview February 12, 2018). Jade suggested that Vindisir's celebration of Dísablót is somewhat unusual in contemporary practice because "there are not really that many people who are honoring the dísir. . . . Ancestral work and the ancestors that are less honored, generally, are the women" (interview February 3, 2018). Ewan similarly commented that Heathens who are more focused on "Viking revival culture" tend "to ignore the goddesses and the female ancestors" (interview February 12, 2018).

Mother's Night

Feasts in which offerings are made to female ancestors are historically attested in the Icelandic sagas as well as in related early English practices known as Mōdraniht, or "Mother's Night," held at beginning of the new year or Yule, and associated with the Germanic "matron cult" of the Roman era (Simek 1993 [1984], 61–62, 220–221). Vindisir originally held Dísablót closer to Yule, but some participants found this difficult due to family obligations and otherwise busy schedules at that time of year. Ewan recalled, "we actually started doing it more as a Mother's Night thing a few years ago. . . . but December is too busy for everyone, so we meet in early January" (interview February 12, 2019). Jade noted the historical variation of the timing of dísablóts, and explained that the timing for Vindisir is based on what fits the needs of the kindred. They said,

> Dísablót evolved out of our general Yule blót, so that was the timing that got built in for us. But we're also modern people who don't base our lives on the seasons as much. We do to a certain extent, but we don't in others. We're not sitting in longhouses where it's dark . . . this is the busy season . . . traditions evolve. (interview February 3, 2018)

Jade continues to celebrate Mother's Night in addition to Vindisir's Dísablót. They indicated that "one of the traditions that I have in my home and have had consistently . . . is Mother's Night" (interview February 3, 2018).

Some Heathens of Raven's Knoll give offerings to female ancestors for Mother's Night as part of Yule celebrations as well as more informally at other times. Aesc Adams of Hwitan Hund Hearth, who runs *The Heathen Underground* (a popular Facebook page) with Nicole Butler and their daughter, said that he and his family celebrate Yule by giving small gifts over the course of twelve nights leading up to Mother's Night. For Mother's Night, the family honors their mothers, grandmothers, the "divine feminine," and the "ancestral feminine" (interview May 7, 2018). Auz informally honors female and male ancestors in dísablóts and álfablóts, respectively, and sometimes celebrates Mother's Night with his family. He explained that because he and MA are so deeply involved with planning and hosting events at Raven's Knoll, their family-based practices "are really low key." By comparison with those large events, what he does for ancestors at home is more informal.

> At home . . . it's nothing elaborate . . . just me by myself, or one or two family members. What we usually do is raise a horn, and we speak generally about a male, or, for dísablót, a female line, and everyone will speak about one female ancestor, and then we'll speak generally about one topic or two if we feel like it. So it's very informal. Usually what it is, is a sumbel, almost a miniature sumbel on a theme without any kind of structure, so people do whatever they feel like, they just all know it's about the *dís*, the female ancestors. (interview May 2, 2018)

Auz's family does not have a set practice of when they do dísablót and álfablót at home, but they often do a dísablót sometime around Yule. Auz noted that often if they do a memory ale on the anniversary of the death of a loved one, this can spontaneously turn into something like an informal álfablót or a dísablót. The historical and contemporary meanings of *álfar*, those honored in álfablóts, vary, as do practices of making offerings to ancestors in Heathen practice. Taking a wider look at ancestor veneration in Heathenry illuminates the breadth of who the honored dead are and the social ecological consequences of making offerings to them.

Inclusive Ancestor Veneration

Ancestor veneration is common among Pagans and Heathens internationally (Ivakhiv 2005b, 228; Strmiska 2005b, 40) and among American Heathens (Calico 2018, 345). It is an important practice for many in Vindisir and the wider Heathen community of Raven's Knoll, both in community events and in day-to-day personal practices. Aesc indicated that, for Hwitan Hund Hearth, ancestor veneration "has every bit as much significance as the worship of the gods or any other otherworldly powers" (interview May 7, 2018). Similarly, Jade said that, for them, "It's central. I feel that ancestor veneration is a huge part of what I do, what I understand of my Heathenry . . . sometimes even more important than the gods" (interview May 7, 2018). Auz said that day-to-day ancestor veneration is somewhat less important to him because he dedicates so much time and energy to events at Raven's Knoll: "my Heathen practice does not involve daily devotionals. I know a lot of people do that type of ancestor work, but I simply don't" (interview May 2, 2018). However, he noted that sumbel always entails ancestor veneration for him.

Who is venerated, and how, matters for ecological conscience formation because it can expand people's sense of with whom they are in gifting relations and thus who is part of their moral community. For the Heathens of Vindisir and Raven's Knoll, ancestor veneration is not limited to biological ancestors. They understand ancestors in an inclusive sense beyond the biological, evidencing conceptual overlaps between different sorts of ancestors and a sense of kinship that transcends the human.

More than one way to categorize ancestors makes sense for this community. There are named ancestors recognized as individual family members who have passed on and collective ancestors whose names are not recalled. The dísir can be thought of in both these ways, as, for example, my grandmother and great aunts whose names I know, but also as all of the mothers who came before me in my ancestral line or all the women of my community (however imagined) who have passed on. Psychologist Daniel Foor (2017) provides another way of categorizing ancestors as ancestors of blood (genetic or biological ancestors), ancestors of affinity (those who one feels an affiliation with, such as historic role models), and ancestors of place (meaning those of the original peoples of the land who may or may not be biological relations). The Heathens of Raven's Knoll and Vindisir regard ancestors in an inclusive sense, recognizing named and collective biological relations, ancestors of affinity or imagination, and ancestors of place.

Blood Ancestors

Blood ancestors are those we identify as genetically related to us, and it is often these who are venerated by name by the Heathens of Raven's Knoll and Vindisir, although not always or exclusively. These are the ancestors to whom practitioners typically give offerings of food and drink, either at home or sometimes at burial sites. Nicole indicated that "For me, the ancestors that are important to my practice are my grandfather, and both of my grandmothers, my maternal and paternal grandmother. . . . I was very close to my grandfather, and I think I honor him more frequently than I honor my grandmothers" (interview May 7, 2018). Aesc said that he thinks named ancestors are more significant than those who are more distant and whose names have been forgotten, but he notes that even those more distant relations matter because without them "we would not be where we are today." Ancestor veneration is important, he said, because the ancestors "have a stake in you succeeding and living a good life, whereas the gods kind of don't. They're . . . not as personally invested in you as your ancestors are" (interview May 7, 2018). When I asked Auz what ancestors are important to his religious practice, he also mentioned known relatives, such as his "bestemor," the grandmother who was a household member when he was growing up (interview May 2, 2018).

Sometimes named or known biological ancestors are not the ones venerated, or people have reservations about venerating their ancestors for ethical reasons. Jade explained that although honoring their known ancestors is important to them, they struggle with the fact that those ancestors include French colonizers as well as some Indigenous people. Jade is careful to clarify that they do not identify as Indigenous because they were not raised in contact with an Indigenous community but that they do honor their Indigenous ancestors. They said,

> both of my parental lines, so my dad's mother's line and my dad's dad's line, both of them do have different Indigenous ancestry within them, to the extent that on . . . my grandmother's side there are sections of the family that actually have status [a legal designation as First Nations people in Canada]. But I've always been so disconnected from that that it is not something that I would personally claim for myself. But it does mean that when I do some of my ancestral practices I also honor that lineage. And the fact that . . . I'm standing on unceded Indigenous territory, and that those ancestors, even if they aren't my direct ancestors, are still here, they're still present, and should still be honored. (interview May 7, 2018)

Jade is uncomfortable with honoring their French ancestors that imposed colonization on their Indigenous ancestors, but they give offerings to more recently deceased relatives, such as their grandfathers.

American Troth member Patricia Lafayllve (2018, 63, 65) notes that the "deliberate forgetting of an ancestor" is appropriate for those who were abusive, which is a topic that has come up for discussion at Vindisir's Dísablót. Intergenerational discussion has in some cases prompted reevaluations of previous judgments of older relatives, acknowledging, for example, that parents have generally done the best they could, but there seems to be some agreement that ancestors who were abusive should not be venerated and are owed nothing in death.

Ancestors of the Imagination

For the Heathens of Raven's Knoll and Vindisir, community membership is not about biological ancestry, so it makes sense that not only biological ancestors are venerated. Nicole and Aesc spoke of including "chosen family" in the ancestors they venerate. Jade affirmed that ancestor veneration goes beyond blood, saying, "I also believe in the importance of recognizing people as your ancestors who aren't your blood ancestors." They explained that it is not only our blood relations who give us life and shape us. They gave the example of adoption, saying it fits within a Heathen worldview in that "If you are adopted into a family, you are family. Period" (interview May 7, 2018). This idea is present in Norse mythology, with figures such as Skaði and Loki who become part of the Æsir family of gods. For the Heathens of Raven's Knoll and Vindisir, chosen family, just as adopted family, become kin. Jade mentioned specifically including the partner of one of their former partners in their offerings, saying "I honor him as one of my ancestors because of the impact he had on me. We are not blood in any way, but he still had an impact on me, and so I still honor him as an ancestor" (interview May 7, 2018).

Jade also recognizes historical figures from other communities they belong to, such as the queer community, as ancestors: "I've done offerings to Sylvia Rivera and Marsha P. Johnson, who are the Latina and Black trans women who helped start the Stonewall riots in New York City, which led to the gay rights movement" (interview May 7, 2018). When I interviewed Jade, I mentioned Foor's idea of ancestors of affinity, and they agreed that this term fits their experience of who people recognize as ancestors within Heathenry.

Auz mentioned the importance in his practice of what he called "imagined ancestors" in differentiating between the veneration of ancestors known by name and remembered and more generalized ancestors. The Heathens of Raven's Knoll often give recently deceased relatives such as grandparents offerings of specific food and drink that they are known to have enjoyed in life, but Auz shared that although he sometimes makes offerings in this way and often makes toasts to them in sumbel, when he thinks of the ancestors, he more often thinks of them in a generalized sense of those whose names have been forgotten. For him, these collective ancestors of the pre-Christian period are more often what he thinks of as "the quintessential ancestor." Auz said he often does not speak with others about how his practices and beliefs about ancestors differ due to of his position as gothi of Raven's Knoll because he does not want people to feel that focusing on more recent ancestors is not also valid. However, he said "I think back to imagined ancestors in my actual spiritual practice or meditation a lot more than I focus on a known ancestor" (interview May 2, 2018).

Auz's linking of the idea of "imagined ancestors" of the pre-Christian period to romantic ideas about the past recalls political scientist and historian Benedict Anderson's (2016 [1983]) understanding of "imagined community." Anderson argues that "imagined community" is constructed through cultural convention rather than a consequence of biological kinship. Auz said that thinking about ancestors from the distant past allows him to put himself into that place and time and "romantically engage with it in the present as part of my spiritual practice" (interview May 2, 2018). In including ancestors of affinity and imagined ancestors in their practices of veneration, the Heathens of Raven's Knoll construct an imagined community that stretches beyond biological boundaries and into the past. When people give offerings to imagined ancestors, they become part of their imagined community and part of their moral community included in gifting relations.

Ancestors Beyond the Human

For the Heathens of Raven's Knoll and Vindisir, ritual practices honoring the dead go beyond the human, including other animals. When I asked Nicole and Aesc if the idea of nonhuman ancestors made sense, they agreed. Nicole said their dogs are part of their family, and it was actually the passing of one of their dogs, a white Husky, that led to the family becoming Heathen. Nicole had been Pagan for some time, but Aesc had been an atheist. After their Husky died, they buried him in their yard. Aesc found visiting his grave and talking to him spiritually moving, which led him to do research online, where he came across Heathenry. They named their hearth White Dog Hearth in honor of this dog. As they became inspired more specifically by English Heathenry, and due to fears that the name "White Dog" might make others think that they were white supremacists, they changed the name to Hwitan Hund, which is "white dog" in early English. They covered the dog's grave with stones, and this became their hearg, an outdoor altar made of piled stones. They regularly give him offerings of biscuits, dog treats, and peanut butter, which he enjoyed in life, on a flat stone there. They regard him as a protector and indicated that he is their *fylgja* (interview May 7, 2018). *Fylgjur* (singular *fylgja*) in Old Norse historical and literary sources appear as personal or familial guardians who may take animal form (Simek 1993 [1984], 96–97) and/or be perceived to be part of oneself as an embodiment of ancestral relations.

Jade similarly indicated that "for me it's ancestor worship whether they are human or not." Jade has various bones and animal skulls that are important to their religious practice. They have crow, wolf, and cat skulls on their bedside altar and periodically give offerings of blood to these as part of their caring for the bones (interview May 7, 2018). These skulls were originally found or thrifted items (bought second-hand) that they received as gifts from other Heathens in the Raven's Knoll community (personal communication December 7, 2020). They are part of Jade's honored dead. In this way, ancestors shade into the dead more generally, who may include other animals. Those venerated in this Heathen practice are the honored dead in whatever form, not just biological ancestors.

When it comes to ancestors of place, the honored dead overlap with *landvaettir* (land wights),[10] or powers of the land, in Heathen practice in the Raven's Knoll community. Landvaettir might be categorized as *genius loci*, or land "spirits," but I prefer to refer to these as "powers" or "forces" of nature because these do not indicate something incorporeal inhabiting nature but describe natural entities as themselves powerful.[11] Overlapping connections between landvaettir and ancestors are especially evident with álfar, who are variously understood as elves, gnomes, *nisse* (Danish for "gnome"), and *huldufólk* (Icelandic for "hidden people"), which might all be classed as landvaettir and sometimes as ancestors of the original inhabitants of a place. Some practitioners regard álfar as the masculine form of dísir. However, Lafayllve (2018, 60–61) indicates that, historically, there was no term for male ancestors. While she notes that some men are known as álfar (plural) after death, she indicates that "*álf*" (singular) does not always refer to the dead but can also refer to elves as other sorts of beings. Yet she does refer to álfar as "the dead in the mound," associated with a specific place where ancestors are buried. Blain (2016, 12–13) indicates that "*dökk-álfar*" the "mound-elves," have sometimes been confusingly translated as "dark elves," but these álfar were understood to be ancestors. Paxson (2006, 34, 109) equates álfar with "elves" and "ancestral spirits" in general. Calico (2018, 260), following his American Heathen informants refers to álfar as male ancestors.

The meanings of "álfar" and "landvaettir" are variable in historical sources. As folklorist Terry Gunnell notes (2007, 114), these terms originated in oral traditions that do not have fixed meanings in the way that written sources later tend to standardize terms and construct logically consistent accounts. In early twelfth-century Iceland, álfar and landvaettir were distinct. Originally álfar were associated with a particular geographic region in Sweden, and landvaettir were powers of the land in a collective sense; but, over time, and with the multicultural settlement of Iceland, álfar became equated with elves (116–120). "Álf," unlike "dís," seems to have originally referred to a named personage, possibly a circumlocution as the bright or shining one, associated with godlike beings who may have been euhemerized ancestors (127). Both landvaettir and álfar are other-than-human persons, and both may be associated with ancestors who either became powers of the land or gods in passing on. Blain (2016, 38) finds that "Ancestors can be found in the landscape around—those ones who have lived in the places where you now lived, and of whom the land bears traces" and that the boundaries between ancestors, álfar, and landvaettir are not clear.

Some of the Heathens of Raven's Knoll use "álfar" to refer to male ancestors, but acknowledge overlaps of meaning between landvaettir and ancestors of place. Aesc explained that, whether or not the álfar, or elves, are a type of ancestor or other sort of entity is debated among Heathens and scholars of Old Norse literature and folklore. He remarked, "I guess I'm agnostic on that. I don't know enough about it to really have an opinion. I don't know whether that's something that I believe as well" (interview May 7, 2018).

Auz explains the variety of interpretations as a historical development, referencing how, in Denmark, the nisse (stereotypically pictured somewhat like garden gnomes) were initially regarded as ancestors and much later as elves or gnomes that might be conflated with house wights (household "spirits") or landvaettir. When I asked Auz if there are animal ancestors, he gave an extensive explanation of this that included a detailed description of the transformations of biological ancestors to ancestors of the land, to powers of the land. These entities blend together because originally people venerated their known ancestors, but, as their names were forgotten and people continued to give offerings where they were buried, what the practice meant changed over time. Eventually those who were perceived to be

Figure 2.3 At Raven's Knoll, the "Gnome Home" serves as both an ancestor and landvaettir shrine, where ancestors of the original people of the land are honored.
Photo by author.

in the ground where the offerings were left came to be understood as álfar, understood as divine powers something like gods. But with Christianization the importance of these entities diminished, and how the people imagined them diminutized them such that they eventually came to be perceived as nisse, household "spirits" or small human-like entities that wear cute pointy hats (see Figure 2.3). People gave nisse cream and other food offerings in farm outbuildings for luck, a tradition that has continued into modern times in Danish folk traditions with the Yule-nisse, a gnome-like figure given porridge with a big pat of butter at Christmas. Auz had a secular upbringing, but the Yule-nisse was still part of it, and he has a particular fondness for gnomes because of this link to pre-Christian tradition and its enduring cultural currency. He points out that the nisse were not demonized or perceived as threatening, so they never really went away but instead changed over time. He explains,

nowadays there is just the back corner of the garden the Germans have for the gnomes that they don't cultivate. And then when you get back in time, and modern Norwegians, etc., if they have a household farm that has been in the family for generations they offer on a mound on the farm. And before that they would have actually offered to individual ancestors on that mound because it is a burial mound for a person. . . . So what we have is this known ancestor that you're putting into a mound, that you are burying in the earth, and then you start to venerate that mound, that place. And then eventually you forget the name of the ancestor, and eventually . . . they become almost like a tutelary spirit of the family . . . becoming almost like a valkyrie in certain parts of northern Norway. And they sort of get forgotten, the names, and you just get them as an álf or a dís . . . and eventually they become a gnome in your back garden. This is the transformation of an ancestor. . . . All those different ways along the path, I can relate to as ancestors.

Mound dwellers eventually became associated with ancestors of place, in part because when the Norse migrated to different places, they found what looked like what they knew as álf mounds. Auz speculates that

the Norse came in and found mounds . . . like the megalithic mounds, and then they started venerating there because "this looks like an álf mound so we're going to venerate at this mound" but it wasn't their [biological] ancestors that were buried there . . . it was just that sense of the imagined connection to a place, so they became ancestors of place. (interview May 2, 2018)

If the "ancestors of place" are not one's biological ancestors, it is easy to see how they can be associated with landvaettir, or powers of the land. This could happen even when the ancestors are one's biological ancestors, but their names have been forgotten. At Raven's Knoll practitioners have erected a Standing Stone for the ancestors to evoke links with this long-term development that has passed through veneration of named ancestors, to veneration of collective ancestors, to veneration of the powers of places at megalithic monuments that seem to have been religious centers in the past. Ancestor veneration shades into veneration of the landvaettir when those given offerings are imagined as gnomes or álfar, understood as elves. As Jade noted, there "There's a certain gray area between land spirits and ancestors . . . so I'll talk about and offer to the landvaettir, but sometimes even some of that practice is about ancestry and ancestral practice" (interview May 7, 2018).

There are also conceptual overlaps between ancestors and animals in that ancestors can appear as animals in dreams or visions, and landvaettir can refer to animals such as crows and squirrels that eat offerings left for ancestors and deities. The Heathens of Raven's Knoll and Vindisir say that when animals eat such offerings, this means that the offerings have been accepted. This understanding is historically based, evidenced by the tenth-century writings of Ahmad Ibn Fadlan, who was an attaché to a Muslim mission to the Volga River. Ibn Fadlan (2017, 33–34) described such reasoning by the Rus, who were a population that migrated from what has become Sweden into the Volga region of what has become Russia.

For the Heathens of Raven's Knoll, the spirits of place form an "ecosystem" of other-than-human persons. Auz explained that landvaettir and various wights, ancestors, and animals are all part of overlapping relations.

> Wights, and the spirits of place are also animals, and they become part of an ecosystem with those generalized ancestors, and when you offer to the landvaettir you're not just offering to one gnome. You're also offering to different kinds of wights that are there, which are animals, so you have that overlap. (interview May 2, 2018)

It is not always clear who receives an offering or who appears in a dream because ancestors can take animal form. Auz said that álfar and dísir participate in the same "spiritual ecosystem" and, like the gods, are shapeshifters. He said,

> they can take transformation and in dreams they are represented by animals. In visions they are represented by animals, and in that way personhood blends into animal, spiritness, when you get into the realm of the ancestors. . . . if you ask someone like myself about a vision and you say "was that an ancestor?" . . . well, it felt like it, but they didn't have a human face. (interview May 2, 2018)

In Auz's interpretation, patterns of practice indicate that, over time, the meaning of terms shifts, and what were perceived as ancestors become identified with the land they are buried in and, in some sense, are equivalent to or associated with the powers of place, as either house wights (household "spirits") or landvaettir (*genius loci*). Human ancestors become ancestors of place and identified with powers of the land, and they can appear as animals.

For the Heathens of Raven's Knoll ancestor veneration is about honoring ancestors of various sorts, not just biological ancestors. Ancestor veneration is an important part of their religious practice, but not all biological ancestors are venerated, and the dead who are venerated include those who are not blood ancestors and the nonhuman dead. All of these are included in gifting relations when practitioners give them offerings.

Complexities in Gifting Relations with Ancestors

The gifts given to ancestors and how they are venerated depends on who they are, despite conceptual overlaps between what sort of entities they are. There are differences in what Heathens offer to landvaettir, to álfar and dísir as biological ancestors, and to ancestors of place understood as the ancestors of the original inhabitants of colonized North America. Despite the conceptual overlap between ancestors and landvaettir, how the ancestors of the original inhabitants of the land are approached is somewhat different from how named ancestors are approached, even or perhaps especially when Heathens have known Indigenous ancestry. As noted above, Jade honors their Indigenous ancestors as part of their veneration of their collective ancestors, but because they were not raised in Indigenous community, she defers to those who were when it comes to giving offerings to ancestors of place and landvaettir if Indigenous people are present and willing to take on that role in ritual. When Jade had a house warming ritual, for example, they asked an Indigenous friend to give a first offering. They invited her to give the offering of tobacco that Jade had purchased, which she did in Jade's garden. Then Jade gave an offering on their porch (interview May 7, 2018). Jade indicated that "Before Indigenous spirits I'll always give some type of sacred medicine. So usually that's tobacco, but sometimes if I don't have tobacco on hand that might be cedar, or sage, or sweetgrass, depending on what I have." They also noted that they "won't buy cedar or sweetgrass or sage or tobacco that is for offering unless it's actually from Indigenous folks," saying "I actually consider that part of the respectful ancestral practice" (interview May 7, 2018). The obtaining of the offering by ethical means is part of the offering. Tobacco is the most frequent offering to ancestors of place that I have observed, but, as Jade noted, sometimes sage, cedar, or sweetgrass are given or burned for smoke cleansing at the beginning of rituals.[12]

Raven's Knoll and Vindisir events typically begin with a land acknowledgment, and, if an Indigenous person is present, they are invited to give tobacco or whatever they feel is appropriate to the ancestors of place and/or landvaettir. When no Indigenous person is identified, someone with Indigenous ancestry (by preference someone with local Indigenous ancestry) usually makes such an offering as part of a land acknowledgment. A land acknowledgment is a statement recognizing the Indigenous people in whose ancestral land the event takes place. Raven's Knoll is on Anishinaabe land, so if someone who was raised in an Anishinaabe community is present, they will be invited to make an offering to the land, or Chantal may give offerings to the landvaettir and/or ancestors of place since she shares some Anishinaabe heritage. If she is not there, MA will make the offering, acknowledging that her ancestry is Mohawk, so, although she is part Indigenous, her ancestors were not local to the land of Raven's Knoll.

The Heathens of Raven's Knoll and Vindisir indicate that showing respect for the original inhabitants of the land and giving them offerings such as tobacco and other sacred medicines that they are accustomed to receiving is important for having good relations with the land. They indicate that there are historical and structural differences between their relations with the land and Indigenous peoples' relations with the land and that the legacies of colonization cannot be ignored. Auz's description of how ancestors become álfar conveys a sense of how people can become attached to land in a process that takes generations and is facilitated by practices of ancestor veneration. Attachment to land in this sense is not a matter of proclaiming an identity of "blood and soil," but inviting and maintaining relationships with local ecosystem communities, ancestors of place, and powers of the land. In North America, there are preexisting powers of the land and ancestors of place, and, to quote Jade, "they are pissed" about colonization.[13]

Practitioners often want a tribal sense of belonging and to practice what would have been the Indigenous traditions of their ancestors, and part of the appeal of being Heathen can come from a desire to be Indigenous. But their ancestors are, as Jade described, likely a mix of oppressors and oppressed, and most Heathen practitioners in Canada benefit from systemic racism because of the European ancestry most practitioners share. The Heathens of Raven's Knoll are aware of this and self-critical in their desire to be inclusive. When I asked Auz if he thought ancestor veneration contributes to the development of racialized consciousness or racism, or works against it, he said that he thinks ancestor veneration can be a contributing factor. Racist ideology became embedded in folkish Heathenry through racist appropriations of folklore in nationalist agendas of the early modern era, and this, he says, leads people to overemphasize ancestry for a sense of validation. It appeals to people's desire for belonging and authenticity. Auz recognizes that a desire to feel authentic in one's religious practice may lead people to seek out Heathenry with an ethnocentric focus. People are drawn to it because they have a desire to adopt a pre-Christian religion and feel they cannot ethically appropriate Indigenous traditions. He explained that when people of European descent reject Christianity, pre-Christian traditions appeal to some as a politically correct alternative to adopting the religious practices of other cultures, which pushes some to adopt what they see as an ancestral religion: "But the strange thing is, then you are put in the place of racism. You're put in a place where ethnicity and race matter when you get into ancestor worship" (interview May 2, 2018).

Most people, Auz said, do not have an academically informed understanding of race and can unreflectively get caught up in a focus on biological ancestry. His mixed ancestry is important to his Heathenry, but, as for Jade, this does not mean his ancestry is an uncritical source of pride. His Danish background through his mother is the result of immigration following World War II, but most of his British ancestors participated in colonization because they arrived in New England with the Puritan migrations. He is also part Finno-Ugric through his patriline (identified by a Y-haplogroup genetic test), which may be the result of distant Sámi heritage or, as he says, a "proverbial Finnish milkman" somewhere in his family tree. He remarked, "you're never pure, and that's one of the things, being a person whose ancestors were oppressive, and a lot of the Heathen groups were oppressive. Look in my very self—I'm probably the descendant of a slave, oppressed by another ethnic group" (interview May 2, 2018). Auz was here alluding to the likelihood that his patriline test results showing Finno-Ugric ancestry indicate that he has Sámi ancestors due to the enslavement of Sámi people by his Danish ancestors. While he is pleased to have some Finno-Urgic genetic heritage, having Finno-Urgic ancestors does not automatically entitle him to claim a Sámi or another Finno-Urgic ethnicity and reminds him of the complex ethnic and moral relationships that existed between his ancestors and persist now in his relationship with them. As he says, none of us is "pure."

The supposition of folkish Heathens that their ancestors would have identified as white or had a sense of racial purity is anachronistic. Recent genetic testing of human remains from archeological sites in Scandinavia indicate that populations were genetically diverse, and Viking society was much more multicultural than racist practitioners believe (Krzewińska et al. 2018; Margaryan et al. 2020; Price 2020, 24, 408, 437, 440). Jade indicated that the "warped sense of ancestry" that folkish Heathens espouse comes from colonization. Before colonization the concept of race did not exist: "it was 'are you tribe or not.' If you're tribe, you're tribe, period." Alluding to stories in Norse literature that indicate positive interaction between different cultures, Jade remarked that "There's plenty in terms of the lore that directly counteracts racist ideology, but I don't think people look that deep" (interview May 7, 2018). Expressing anger and frustration with racist Heathens, Jade said that ancestor veneration is about more than Heathen origins. The colonial context of North America and practitioners' desire to be respectful of Indigenous traditions prompts the Heathens of Raven's Knoll and Vindisir to be very careful to try to avoid cultural misappropriation while also approaching the land and the ancestors of the original inhabitants of the land with respect in giving offerings.

In contexts other than land acknowledgments, the Heathens of Raven's Knoll and Vindisir give food offerings to landvaettir and, in Auz's case, sometimes coins. Auz gives coins to landvaettir and nisse for things such as when the family cuts a Yule tree at a tree farm, for the tree itself, the place, and the nisse, and he is more likely to give offerings of coins at the gnome home at Raven's Knoll than offerings of food and drink (interview May 2, 2018). This is partly to avoid attracting wildlife into the camping area nearby, but he indicated that "if I'm thinking of a human face, a human personage as that ancestor then it's always a food product, and for álf and dís, also food products." He elaborated that for human ancestors

> [i]t's usually what we're eating and drinking. It's exactly sharing what's at your own table. . . . Sometimes . . . I only give to them, I don't consume, but that rarely ever happens with ancestors. I almost always do—it's something that's shared. The only time I wouldn't do that is if I wasn't consuming alcohol for some reason. Then I might just pour that out because I'm not consuming it at the moment. (interview May 2, 2018)

When he gives these offerings of food and drink to blood ancestors at home he offers them first inside and then transfers the offerings to his hearg (stone altar) outside.

Collective ancestors such as the dísir are usually given food and drink and are more often recognized collectively at group events than in day-to-day practices. Jade noted that Vindisir's Dísablót is a service the gythias provide for the kindred that supports other people's connections with their ancestors and builds Jade's connection with the community, while their personal day-to-day practices are more important for developing relations with their own ancestors. Jade explained that working with the dísir in ritual at kindred events such as Dísablót "is intense ancestral work" that connects the community with their ancestors, but leading ritual requires a different sort of connection with ancestors than they get from their personal devotionals (interview May 7, 2018).

The Heathens of Vindisir and Raven's Knoll often give named ancestors offerings of food and drink in personal day-to-day practice. They share gifts of food and drink with ancestors as a way of honoring them and maintaining connections with them. Specific drinks may be offered to particular named ancestors. Jade recalled that "there are specific named ancestors that I do certain things for . . . my grandfather . . . once a year at sumbel . . . I will always give a toast to him, every single year" (interview May 7, 2018). For their great-grandfather on their mom's side, they offer whiskey because that is what he liked in life. Nicole also offers specific drinks to different named ancestors: "when we're pouring wine . . . and when we're choosing spirits or whatever, I think of who I'm giving to, so sometimes it's whiskey if it's my grandfather. I'll give wine if it's my grandmother" (interview May 7, 2018). Nicole and Aesc also regularly leave food offerings for the dog they honor (interview May 7, 2018).

The food that is offered to human ancestors is usually shared from what the family or individual is eating, but people are more likely to offer part of special meals to ancestors than from regular meals. Nicole indicated that "If I'm making a special dinner we definitely put some aside first and then take the ancestor bowl out" (interview May 7, 2018). On these occasions Nicole and Aesc also share whatever they are drinking. They have a special ancestor bowl for food offerings and two goblets they use for offering drinks and desserts. The first serving of special meals goes to the ancestors. Nicole recalled,

> they get the first serving, dessert and everything. If I make pudding,[14] we actually fill the goblet with pudding, and take two goblets out, one with wine and one pudding. It's kind of like Sunday dinner, and we invite the

ancestors and we leave the bowl on the table until the end and then we take it out [to their hearg] after we've all eaten. (interview May 7, 2018)

Aesc explained that their practice is much like traditions of setting an "empty seat at the table, a symbolic welcoming to ancestors except it's not the seat, it's the full meal that they are invited to join in with us" (interview May 7, 2018).

Calico similarly found that Heathens give food and drink as offerings to ancestors (Calico 2018, 259). Lafayllve mentions that food and drink are typical offerings to ancestors and indicates that the practice of setting an "ancestor plate," sometimes with an empty chair at the table, to serve them at feasts is adopted from "another tradition," which she does not specify (Lafayllve 2018, 64). I have also seen this in other Pagan traditions, with first servings of each dish offered to ancestors, much as is done within Vindisir at Dísablót and other events, in keeping with how Nicole and Aesc described their offerings to ancestors.[15]

Food and drink are frequent offerings to named ancestors and to collective ancestors, such as the dísir in home-based practices. Álfar are more diversely understood and may be given food and drink when practitioners imagine them as human, but they are more likely to be given nonfood items when practitioners imagine them to be gnome-like or elves. When they shade into landvaettir, practitioners may imagine them as gnome-like or as wildlife who might be given birdseed or shiny things such as crows like, but when identified with the ancestors of the original inhabitants of the land, the Heathens of Raven's Knoll and Vindisir are more likely to give them offerings of plants held sacred by the Indigenous peoples of the land such as tobacco, white sage, cedar, or sweetgrass.

Passing On

A big part of Vindisir's Dísablót is the food offerings that participants make from family recipes that have been passed down and share together in the potluck meal. This can strengthen bonds within families when participants ask family members to share recipes. Jade said, "historically a few people actually have asked their mothers and grandmothers for a family recipe that they were missing" (interview February 3, 2018). The lazy daisy cake that I usually make for Dísablót is from a recipe my mother gave me when I was getting married, as part of a book of family recipes she had my maternal relatives contribute to. I remember making the cake with my grandmother in her kitchen when I was a young child, and it is a favorite of my mother and me. Making this cake for Dísablót reminds me of these connections and helps me feel close to and appreciate my dísir.

Other members of Vindisir have similar stories about the food they make for Dísablót and for other ancestors. Jade told me about how their maternal grandfather loved to cook and that "Every Yule I will make his potato and leek soup, and that's an ancestral offering for me, is that practice of connecting with him by doing something that he loved" (interview May 7, 2018). Jade remembered when they sat with him as he was dying,

> he asked what I wanted of his and I said "your potato and leek soup recipe." That's the only thing I have of my grandfather's.... So every Yule, no matter what, I will make it. And I make it from scratch. It's one of the few things I make from scratch these days.... For me that's an ancestral practice that I do to honor him. (interview May 7, 2018)

Making specific dishes in memory of those who have passed on or that were particularly enjoyed by or with them passes on intergenerational knowledge. Making recipes passed down is particularly evident with Dísablót, but other skills are also passed on, such as gardening, foraging, wildcrafting, brewing, firekeeping, knitting, crocheting, sewing, metalworking, and woodworking techniques, sometimes using tools that are passed down. Some of this contributes to local knowledge that passes on collective learning of how to live in place. It shows a desire to pass on what is valued from ancestors, which can become adaptive knowledge transfer across generations, preserved in practitioners' appreciation for the skills passed on to them and that they desire to pass on in turn.

Calico found that practitioners feel connected to their ancestors through traditional crafts such as brewing and canning (Calico 2018, 259), particularly through the use of items passed down, such as a canner from grandmother to mother to daughter. Some think of such items as family heirlooms. Calico uses the term "ancestor relics" (Calico 2018, 261). Lafayllve (2018, 62, 65) describes practitioners' use of mementos as a sort of "show-and-tell" items in blót. Keeping and using what belonged to one's ancestors instead of buying new things may help reduce consumption. Jade treasures their paternal grandfather's hand-carved walking stick, valuing it beyond money. On such heirlooms, they said, "there can be no price tag" (interview

May 7, 2018). Similarly, I treasure the old wine press I inherited from my father that we used to make apple cider every fall when I was a child, along with the motor he built for grinding the apples. With these tools, and the knowledge of brewing that he passed on to me, I am able to make cider rather than having to buy it.

The keeping of knowledge passed down as ancestral work applies also to ancestors of affinity. Jade sees the preservation of knowledge of lineages of Heathen practice, archaeological research, history, archival work, and story-telling as part of this work of remembrance. They are concerned that if we do not retell or write these things down they will be forgotten, whereas sharing this information passes on recognition of the worthy deeds of others, which is part of ancestor veneration. Jade identified four lineages of Heathenry in Canada: Ontario and Quebec (Raven's Knoll), BC Heathens, Clearwater in Calgary, and Maritimes/East Coast. Auz was one of the earlier figures in Canadian Heathenry, after becoming a gothi with the American Vinland Association, which he describes as "a tiny non-racist, leftist sort of splinter" from the Troth in the United States, which he had been in contact with in the late 1980s and early 1990s (interview May 2, 2018). Jade explained that recounting such history and telling the stories of those who have passed on is part of ancestor veneration for them. In this respect, the work they did with the ArQuives, Canada's LGBTQ2+ archives, was particularly meaningful and significant as a queer person because "We usually have our histories erased in a lot of ways." Working at the ArQuives was a way to honor those whose stories might otherwise be forgotten and give something back to their ancestors of affinity. Jade noted that "even though those people and those stories and the like aren't direct blood ancestors I still honor them because I wouldn't be where I am today if it wasn't for them" (interview May 7, 2018).

Telling the ancestors' stories is a big part of Heathen practice. As Jade said, "The people that become known as ancestors are the people that are remembered" (interview February 3, 2018). A sumbel is often included as part of blót at Vindisir events, and the saying "what is remembered lives on" is a common response to toasts to ancestors as are retellings of the good deeds of the living within Vindisir and the Heathen community of Raven's Knoll. Jade usually hosts a "Fallen Heroes Sumbel" each fall honoring those who have served in the Armed Forces, and they share stories of their grandfather who served in the navy (interview May 7, 2018). Nicole explained the importance of telling such stories, saying, "Part of what lives on in everybody, the only thing that lives on are the stories that you have, the stories that your children and your grandchildren can tell." She and Aesc like to share family stories of their grandparents so their kids will know them. Nicole said,

> I'll tell stories about my grandfather in the war, or my grandmother in the war, or my other grandmother and how she came to the big city when she was fourteen and was made to leave her family, and that kind of thing, and the story of their lives. That will help them live on because then when [their daughter] is older she'll tell their story, and hopefully, if we have an exciting enough story maybe she'll tell our story, too. (interview May 7, 2018)

Aesc connected this desire to pass on stories of relatives to the *Hávamál* verse "Cattle die, kinsmen die, / But one thing that does not die is the honor of a life well lived," saying,

> "We very much take that to heart. Life is about impermanence, and that which survives you is your deeds, the tale of your deeds." (interview May 7, 2018)

Heathens have a notable desire for renown. Boasting is socially sanctioned in sumbel practices. People want their deeds to be known, and they want to be recognized by name for those deeds. This is evident in the desire of most participants in this research to be identified by their legal names. They want to be remembered by name, but with recognition that our worth comes from what we do and what we pass on. Aesc said, "that which survives you is your deeds, the tale of your deeds, and hopefully some concrete deeds that survive you and people can actually look upon and realize, that have changed the world for the better" (interview May 7, 2018). Nicole agreed, and she and Aesc indicated that the legacy they want leave is to be remembered well and to have made a positive impact that will extend into future. They both said they want their legacy to be "That we left the world a better place." Aesc spoke of a desire to become an ancestor who can look out from the mound of where they are buried.

> [B]eing an ancestor, you go to the mound, and from the mound you get to kind of view what all of your descendants are doing. And you get to contribute, if you are recognized, if you've done good deeds. If you were a good person, and they remember your name, they come bring you offerings so much the better. (interview May 7, 2018)

Auz expressed comfort with the idea of his name being forgotten and even a preference for becoming part of the generalized ancestors remembered collectively. He said he is okay with the inevitability of his name being forgotten. His family and religious community will remember him for a while, but those memories will fade and eventually there will be no one who remembers him by name. He will then be part of the ancestors. "The real magic," he said, is in becoming "an álf, about being that far back, but still the things that you did having meaning in the present even though you've been so forgotten that you are now a mythological being. I think I'd rather be one of those" (interview May 2, 2018). He indicated that renown matters, but not as an end in itself. What matters is what one passes on. He illustrated this by alluding to the meaning of giving arm rings in Norse mythology. "Renown," he said, "is important because in this life . . . the threads we have drawn together should be good ones, and we want more people to have those threads so that all of reality, all of nature, can work better together." It is good to be known for participating in good relations, "but it's not a good thing because you are special and unique and have to exist somewhere special and unique forever. That's avarice, that's being a dragon, that's collecting wealth." Like Smaug in *Lord of the Rings*, the dragon Fafnir in *Völsunga Saga* in *The Poetic Edda* sits on a hoard of wealth. But the ideal supported by Heathen gifting practices is not to hoard wealth but to give it away. This applies to things but also to words of praise. Auz said, "You need to be a ring giver to give it away. To be a ring giver, to be a true ring giver, you need to gain renown, but then you have to give it away." Ultimately, we need to cede our place in world, to accept that our memories will fade and that what remains is what we pass on.

Auz explained that doing good things matters, and part of ancestor veneration is recognizing what is worth doing, but what matters more is what remains of us when we have been forgotten. He said that the only real way to leave a lasting legacy is to contribute to things that you can make important to other people and that they also play a part in creating. Speaking of his contributions to running gatherings, he said

whether or not someone's going to remember it specifically as mine, I don't think that's that important because it lives longer if the people think it's theirs. If the next generation thinks it's theirs rather than someone else's it will live longer, because it is part of the fabric of their reality. So all the things that I might consider my legacy, I didn't create the idea of them, create this corporate structure, that thing, whatever, it's just the interactions of those things. So what I want is those good things to continue happening, and it's not going to be associated with my name, or a remembrance of my personality. It's going to be associated with their lives. (interview May 2, 2018)

This attitude, I think, is a key sustaining force of the strength of the community at Raven's Knoll. Tradition and community continue through passing it on, sharing the co-construction of it with others, and giving it into their care. This is how things of lasting worth are made—by allowing people to collaboratively invest themselves in the co-creation of tradition.

Giving Death a Seat at the Table

Making offerings to ancestors, giving gifts, and giving thanks for gifts received inspires a sense of gratitude for what the ancestors have given us and a felt sense of obligation to give in turn, in passing on. When the ancestors include the dead more generally, this supports the development of a system of delayed, indirect reciprocity with the more-than-human world, influencing practitioners to include them in a gift ethic.

Ancestor veneration inspires in Heathen practitioners a sense of indebtedness and a felt desire to give in turn, and it nudges people toward an inclusive sense of who is part of their moral community. Applying terror management theory and other priming theory provides an explanation for how ethics emerge out of ancestor veneration. Because this is an ethnographic study rather than a series of empirical tests, as in terror management studies, it cannot prove that death primes are causing pro-environmental behavior among Heathens, but applying terror management theory is helpful for understanding how ethics emerge in practice. Death primes make mortality salient, and this can help operationalize the values made salient in rituals of making offerings to ancestors and thus nudge participants toward inclusivity, sharing, generosity, and gratitude.

Nudges Toward Gratitude and Felt Obligations to Past and Future Generations

When the dead remain part of the community, we have ongoing obligations toward them that shape our interactions with others. In *Civilization and*

Its Discontents, Freud (1961 [1930]) argued that conscience is formed from an internalization of the voice of the father, creating the superego to check the selfish desires of the ego, invoking a mythic story of sacrifice of "the father" by the brothers of "the primal horde" that creates society by internalizing constraints on our behavior. But when ancestors are venerated and recognized as still remaining within the community, debts owed to ancestors are present. It is not some mythic sacrifice in the far distant past that creates society and enshrines conscience, but instead debts to ancestors "paid forward," giving in turn to future generations. Making offerings to ancestors prompts gratitude for all one has received from them and inspires in practitioners the desire to give in turn. Conscience then becomes, in part, the felt obligation to ancestors. Such debts can be repaid through caring for children, continuing society, and passing on a way of life that will sustain the community into the future.

Making offerings to ancestors can shift us from egocentrism to a more inclusive relational ontology that prioritizes family and community over self-interest. Aesc described how ancestor veneration changed his behavior in a way that shows a psychological process that is different from Freudian superego development. It is not "god-the-father" in this experience that becomes the voice of conscience, but the ancestors, some of whom are not human. After beginning to make offerings Aesc became aware of the ancestors' presence in his life as an ongoing background awareness. He said,

> I'm constantly aware of that. It affects how I act in my life. It affects how I make decisions. Because when you have that feeling that every decision that you make is being weighed and watched and possibly judged by your ancestors it changes how you decide things. It changes the decisions themselves.

He confessed that he used to be quite self-centered, but since becoming Heathen and making offerings to the dead, he finds that he wants to do more for his family, the community, and even for strangers. He said the reason for this is "in the back of my mind there is always that thought that 'what would my ancestors want me to do?'" His understanding of how people in communities in the past needed to support one another to survive also shapes how he thinks about this now. He said,

> there is a certain sense of obligation to the community because without that community fostering everybody's well-being, our ancestors themselves

wouldn't have survived. They were obviously part of tightknit communities that supported one another, and that was quite a revelation to me.

Thinking about how he will himself become an ancestor fundamentally changed his perspective.

> When that came to me, that I was living my life not just for me, but that when I became an ancestor myself, how would I like to be looked upon, how would I want my works and my words to be viewed—it was sort of a seismic shift in my perspective. (interview May 7, 2018)

Aesc's shift in attitude with taking up Heathen practices of giving offerings shows how adopting the practice of ancestor veneration can support a different way of life. Engaging in the ritual practice of making offerings to the dead changed his sense of how he should relate with others.

Priming Effects in Heathen Ancestor Veneration

The fact that ancestor veneration brings death to mind means that mortality is made salient to practitioners, which terror management theory indicates will make participants want to act in accordance with the values made salient in rituals of ancestor veneration insofar as those values are part of their worldview. At Vindisir's Dísablót, death rather literally has a seat at the table, in the form an actual human skeleton (see Figure 2.1). Leaving an empty seat or extra place setting, as Nicole and Aesc describe, or setting aside a portion of food and drink for ancestors makes them part of the community and primes death. Giving offerings to ancestors of place and landvaettir, with the inclusion of the nonhuman dead, may also activate other primes that nudge people toward pro-social and pro-environmental behavior.

Conscience and worldview modifications are aided by value salience in conjunction with mortality salience in rituals of making offerings to ancestors. These ritual practices include the tacit learning of core values that become embodied in conscience. Applying insights from terror management theory suggests that participation in rituals of making offerings to ancestors operationalizes the values made salient because mortality salience makes us want to act on the values that come to mind as part of unconscious worldview defense. Mortality salience in modern affluent society usually prompts consumerism because it is the dominant worldview, but some studies in terror management theory demonstrate that bringing other values to mind in conjunction with mortality salience operationalizes those values, provided they are part of the participants' worldview.[16] When diversity is discussed as an American value, for example, Americans are more likely to express tolerance than when it is not brought up in conjunction with mortality salience (Gailliot et al. 2008). Similarly, when helping is made salient, research participants become more helpful (Jonas et al. 2002). Heathen rituals of giving gifts and making offerings consistently bring the values of sharing, generosity, and giving to mind, instilling a sense of gratitude. Feeling grateful for gifts received makes practitioners appreciate what they have, which can generate a countercurrent to the desire to consume.

Giving to the ancestors illustrates how gifting instills appreciation for what one has already received and models an ideal of indirect and delayed reciprocity. Of course, this does not mean that Heathens always act ethically but that their practices of ancestor veneration support the ideals of indirect and delayed reciprocity. While practitioners recite the formula "a gift for a gift" and espouse reciprocity, they understand this in terms of giving back for gifts already received as an expression of gratitude. As discussed in the previous chapter, participating in gifting rituals inspires feelings of obligation in Heathen practitioners. When I asked Auz what the ancestors give, his response illustrated Levinas's sense of being already indebted in ethical subjectivity: "they've already given me something. That's the thing, the gifts have already been received, and they are blessings and gifts that have already been laid down" (interview May 2, 2018). Auz explicitly made a connection between Heathen gifting practices and the generation of gratitude.

When I interviewed members of Vindisir about Dísablót, they said that making offerings to the dísir makes them feel grateful for what they have and appreciate what they have been given. Ewan emphasized that thinking about how faer ancestors would have lived gave faer a sense of appreciation for the ease and comfort of modern life. Fae said,

> I think it's important to remember. For me, it's more about my roots. It's more about learning and remembering what it was like for those who have come before us, realizing how much easier it is for us than it was for my ancestors two hundred, or six hundred years ago . . . or longer than that.

Noting that fae walks a lot because fae does not drive or have a car, Ewan reflected on the effort that would have gone into producing warm outdoor clothing before modern manufacturing, saying

> I think about how many stiches went into this crocheted sweater I'm wearing, and the time. I think about how my ancestors would have prepared by spinning their wool, and constructing a garment, and how many garments it would take to be warm enough. And enough to clothe your family, and to feed your family with what you save from the harvest. And I think about how physically and emotionally taxing that would have been.

Ewan said fae is grateful that fae does not have to endure this. Fae indicated that fae thinks about it a lot, and it makes faer appreciate what fae has (interview February 12, 2018).

Ewan also indicated that participating in events such as Dísablót displaces greed. Fae explained that "coming together and sharing, bringing as much as we can afford to bring as an offering to the community and to your gods and ancestors . . . it's 'anti-greed.'" Fae said that when people come together and share food and drink, "there's that very physical nourishing on another level even if an individual has nothing to offer, the community can still provide." As in sumbel, there is an emotional aspect to this, too, in sharing words: "so if somebody is having a really rough time the other people are there to be depended on as well" (interview February 12, 2018). Sharing together in ritual confers a sense of relational worth that can lessen in practitioners the desire to consume.

When I asked Jade about how Dísablót relates to their values and ethical outlook, like Ewan they mentioned gratitude. Jade commented on the importance of honoring women in particular because it is relatively rare. They indicated that it makes participants "have gratitude for what we do have." Jade also mentioned that participating in Dísablót gives them the desire to give in turn through community building. After long involvement with various social movements, Jade regards community building as more important than direct action for generating long-term social change. Jade became politically active as a teenager and participated in and helped organize direct action campaigns using tactics such as "die-ins" (in which participants occupy a space by acting dead to attract attention to political issues)[17] and blocking traffic. While Jade found direct action to be effective and necessary in some cases, they found that "what actually builds stability, and builds actual change" is community building. They have shifted away from direct action partly due to chronic illness, but indicated that the capacity of religious groups for "building that community, having that space, having that support" is a vital capacity of religion in society. Jade said,

> it's one of the reasons why religion existed for so long, is that community space. The gods are important, the ancestors are important, the wights are important—and not to diminish any of that because it's one of the things that brings us together—but the fact that we come together, period, I think, is the most important piece.

Their religious community provides emotional and spiritual support that Jade said "feeds me when other types of political activism or the types of things that I was getting myself into before would consistently detract from." Political organizing, protests, and demonstrations can be exhausting and lead to burnout, but participation in ritual provides a community in which people "can come together, and bond, and become family" (interview February 3, 2018).

Jade seemed taken aback when I asked what the ancestors have given them. Their response was "life," which, as they said is obvious. They explained, "I mean, I don't think that they need to give me anything else at this point" (interview May 7, 2018). From a gifting perspective, we owe our parents and the ancestors everything, more than could possibly be repaid, but we often take this for granted in modern society. Ancestor veneration makes this debt salient. Jade said,

> I don't need to get anything back—it's just the memories that I already have … it just feels like what I should be doing. It's not necessarily about getting things back for me. I think I have more of that type of relationship with the gods and land spirits, those more *quid pro quo* type of "a gift for a gift" type of thing. But with some of my ancestors, they've already given me a gift and I'm just trying to repay it. And I probably never will, and that's okay. (interview May 7, 2018)

Gifts from ancestors are deeper than can be returned. Heathens in this community experience these gifts as creating a "debt that is always open" in Levinas's (1990, 152) sense. Offerings given to the dead are not about getting things from them, although relations with deities may be perceived in this sense. Jade indicated that organizing and leading events like Dísablót are important and powerful in their life because it is a way "to give back to my ancestors." They said, "I owe it to them because I exist" (interview February 3, 2018).

Offerings to ancestors function as reminders of participants' mortality while at the same time raising the salience of values such as gratitude, generosity, and sharing, which together make those values operational in the participants' lives as felt obligations. Gifting relations thus become second nature. After reading my fieldnotes on Dísablót, Jade commented that they had not thought of the kindred's actions at that event in terms of gifting but recognized that "we do gifting exchanges without thinking that we're doing gifting exchanges. We do this without thinking that we're doing that. It's just . . . it's not formalized in that same way because it's about just community and how we live" (interview February 3, 2018). Giving offerings to ancestors can thus generate delayed and indirect reciprocity through tacit learning and shape conscience.

Giving offerings to ancestors brings the recognition, as Aesc said, that one will become an ancestor. Auz expressed this in terms of becoming an ancestor as a process that begins while one is still alive.

> I'm already becoming an ancestor. . . . The more you experience life, the more of an ancestor you become until you die, until you have the title. It's not like living things aren't ancestors either. We just haven't been given the title yet because we haven't crossed that imaginative barrier, that barrier of consciousness yet, from the perspective of the others who will have it. (interview May 2, 2018)

Death primes in Heathen practices of ancestor veneration may have other effects beyond those usually observed with mortality salience, and some additional priming effects may be operative. Terror management theory takes individualized ontology as the norm, but the effects of mortality salience may be different in relational ontology. Most studies in terror management theory are in Western, educated, industrialized, rich, and democratic (or WEIRD) societies (Henrich et al. 2010), which has led some scholars to question the cross-cultural applicability of terror management theory (e.g., Bonsu and Belk 2003).

Cognitive scientists of religion Ryan McKay and Harvey Whitehouse (2015, 463) report that giving food offerings to ancestors primes "agency detection" in the Pomio Kivung, a New Guinea cargo cult. Ancestor veneration is not the same in this context—for the Pomio Kivung ancestors can "see into people's hearts and minds," whereas Heathens are more likely to think that they have to verbalize thoughts for nonhuman others to hear them, for example—but ancestor veneration may prompt participants to be more likely to perceive nonhuman others as persons. Religious people are more likely to detect agency after "supernatural" priming with words such as devil, demon, angel, god, and ghost, and "individual differences in religiosity and supernatural beliefs" show differential effects on agency detection (van Elk et al. 2016, 7). Religious primes need to match a relevant culture or worldview if they are to have an effect. It may well be that shifting toward a more relational ontology and giving gifts to other-than-human persons makes Heathen practitioners more likely to detect agency in nonhuman others. This sounds tautological, but van Elk et al.'s findings suggest that religious belief affects agency detection, and, if those religious beliefs are animist (or participants have a relational ontology), then they may be more likely to perceive nonhuman others as persons—and this matters for ethics.

Researchers of the cognitive science of religion theorize that humans evolved cognitive mechanisms to detect agency in others because it would be more dangerous to mistakenly assume that something or someone was not an active agent than it would be to mistakenly assume that they were an agent. It is safer, for example, to assume that a shadow in the bushes is a predator and avoid it than to dismiss it as nothing and get eaten. Thus humans developed what experimental psychologist Justin Barrett (2000) calls a "hyperactive agency detection device" (HADD) and related tendencies to attribute intentionality to nonhuman agents.[18] Barrett (2000, 2011) and cognitive scientist of religion progenitor Stewart Guthrie (1980, 1993) suppose that this evolved tendency to overestimate agency is associated with belief in supernatural agents. From the perspective of the new animism, this is not necessarily an overestimation and is not so much about "supernatural" agents as the perception of other-than-human persons.

Some terror management studies suggest that "there may be important differences between cultures (and individuals within cultures) that construe humanity as separate from versus part of the natural world" (Goldenberg et al. 2000, 214). Some of the literature touches on possible differences in effects of mortality salience in animists but assumes that nature is less threatening for animists because they see it in supernatural terms (Goldenberg et al. 2001, 433), taking a Tylorean view of animism. Ara Norenzayan, Ian

Hansen, and Jasmine Cady found that exposure to death primes made people less likely to anthropomorphize trees and volcanoes, whether participants were Christian or nonreligious (Norenzayan et al. 2008, 194). However, their study excluded religious people who did not identify as Christian (192), and they wonder if "Perhaps under mortality salience, individuals in animistic cultures would be *more* likely to anthropomorphize nature" (196).

It is possible that the effects of particular death primes may differ with ontology and perception of relations with nature. For Heathens who include animals in their practices of ancestor veneration, animal skulls may serve as a death prime. There is some evidence that mortality salience usually makes people want to distinguish themselves from animals as a repression of death awareness (see Goldenberg et al. 2001), but those with a more relational ontology who see animals as other-than-human persons may react differently. When animals are seen as potential persons, the social distance to them is decreased, and lower perceived social distance results in a stronger sense of social obligation (see Rigdon et al. 2009, 359).

Skulls can function as death primes but may also prime a sense of being watched. Several social psychological studies demonstrate that even subtle images of eyes give people a sense of being watched and that this stimulates pro-social behavior.[19] Levinas (1969, 66, 262) argued that it is the face of the other, and in particular their eyes, that inspires ethics in oneself. Watchful eye priming studies suggest that there is a social psychological basis for this and that it can be activated even by the subliminal suggestion of a face in three dots arranged in the triangular position of eyes and nose (Rigdon et al. 2009). Animal skulls and masks also may do this, priming a sense of being watched and stimulating pro-social behavior beyond the interhuman in Heathen practitioners. The Heathens of Vindisir frequently use animal skulls in ritual and include them in their practices of ancestor veneration. At Hail and Horn Gathering the Heathens of Raven's Knoll and Vindisir also display animal skulls and hides that sometimes have the head still attached. Sometimes these have taxidermied heads with life-like fake eyes inserted (e.g., the wolf in Figure 1.3), but more often if the head is still attached it is not taxidermied and they have empty eye holes (as can be seen in Figure 1.6). The empty eyes holes actually give me a greater sense of being watched than the fake ones, perhaps because, as a practitioner, this gives me a greater sense of the dead watching me.

The eyes on god poles and other deity images used in ritual, which practitioners may experience as embodying the deity imaged, are also potential watchful eye primes that are likely to give Heathens a sense of being in a watchful world and nudge them toward pro-social behavior that includes relations with the ancestors, the gods, and other-than-human persons more generally, which may include other animals. It seems likely that the evolved human tendency to "overestimate" agency, in conjunction with "supernatural" priming and watchful eye priming, will prompt Heathen practitioners to pro-social actions when they do ritual with skulls, whether they are human or from other animals.

Ben Raffield, Neil Price, and Mark Collard (2019, 9) discuss the effects of eyes on helmets in archaeological finds and suggest that these may have reminded people of the existence of the gods, engendered a sense that the gods may be judging people's actions, and thus spurred pro-social behavior, but it may be that just the sense of being watched makes people want to act on their values. It is not necessarily about having a sense of being watched by deities and fearing their judgement, but the psychosocial effect of the suggestion of being with others, in relation. It may be that animal skulls make Heathens feel watched by the more-the-human world. Anthropologist Richard Nelson describes how the Koyukon perceive the world in this way.

> Traditional Koyukon people live a world that watches, in a forest of eyes. A person moving through nature—however wild, remote, even desolate the place may be—is never truly alone. The surroundings are aware, sensate, personified. They feel. They can be offended. And they must, at every moment, be treated with proper respect. (Nelson 1983, 14)

Contemporary Heathens are not immersed in relational ontology to the same degree as Indigenous people such as the traditional Koyukon Nelson describes, but Heathen practices of ancestor veneration using animal skulls nudge them toward relational ontology and the inclusion of other-than-human persons in their moral community.

The Heathens of Raven's Knoll and Vindisir show some sense of plants requiring respect in practices such as Auz's giving a coin when he cuts a tree for Yule. When practitioners cut trees at Raven's Knoll for god poles, they first ask permission and seek omens about which trees to cut, and they give offerings in thanks for being allowed to take the trees. Similarly, when members of Vindisir forage for plants they ask permission, give thanks, and leave offerings. When bow hunting, Joan gives offerings and asks to be given an animal. This is not to say that relations between practitioners and the land are perfect. Relations with bears at Raven's Knoll have not always been good. Early on a "problem bear" was shot because it had become habituated to seeking human food in the campground. Practitioners were saddened by this and learned to be more careful with their food waste and food offerings in the Vé. Now food offered in the Vé is removed to the Sacred Well so that large animals do not come to look for food in the campground.

Heathen practitioners do not necessarily label themselves as animists, and, as I have said, they did not self-identify with the label "relational ontology" before I introduced the term. For some practitioners, gnomes may simply be cute garden spirits that are interesting and amusing to leave offerings for and tell each other stories about, rather than be perceived as powers of nature that require respect. Animal skulls could be seen as supernatural allies that have nothing to do with relations with living animals. Calico assumes that offerings to landvaettir are "supernaturally directed practices" (Calico 2018, 448) and thus finds only "incipient ecological possibilities" (Calico 2018, 449) in Heathen animism. Bron Taylor has suggested that Heathenry is not an example of what he calls "dark green religion." Dark green religion, Taylor says, entails having a sense of nature as sacred, with intrinsic worth, and for which practitioners show reverent care (Taylor 2010, ix). Calico quotes Taylor's comments on Heathenry from an interview in *Journal of Contemporary Heathen Thought*[20] saying,

> Perhaps to the disappointment of his interviewers, Taylor dismissed the idea that Heathenry might become a viable ecological actor: "I mean no disrespect to those who represent supernaturalistic forms of Paganism, but I think the naturalistic forms are the ones that will have the greatest long-term cultural traction." Taylor seems correct in his observation that while a religion might be dark green in its orientation to the earth, it very well may not be effectively ecological, simply because the adherent is oriented towards the transcendent dimension of the relationship. The act of offering food and drink to a nature spirit is not a straightforward ecological act. (Calico 2018, 448)

However, in Heathenry, the gods are not necessarily supernaturalistic. Natural versus supernatural is a distinction that does not necessarily make sense outside modern categories. Berger (2019, 75, 94, 111) found that Heathens are less likely than other Pagans to practice magic oriented toward some sort of supernatural realm and more likely than other Pagans to participate frequently in ritual activities, which may indicate a greater this-worldly focus.

Arguably, it is the separation of ritual practices of giving gifts from religious practice and economic relations that allows the development of the idea that the gods are something other than agents in the natural world to whom we have ethical obligations. But Taylor and Calico are in some sense right to say making offerings is not straightforward. My research shows a connection between making offerings as giving gifts and the experience of felt obligations, but if those to whom gifts are given are seen as having no material reality, there is no point in giving them gifts. If giving gifts to nonhuman others is important in maintaining a sense of obligation to them, giving to "spirits" or gods perceived as supernatural entities will not accomplish the same thing. Some Heathens may give offerings to gods they see as residing in Asgard, which they may understand as some sort of supernatural realm rather than the natural world, but the Heathens of Raven's Knoll and Vindisir have a more naturalistic sense of relational ontology in which the gods and goddesses live in the natural world or are natural forces in the world, and this sort of animistic perception is more likely to be ecologically sound. This is the sort of perception in which it makes sense to interpret offerings as received when they are eaten by wildlife, as the Heathens of Raven's Knoll and Vindisir do.

Conclusion

Applying social psychology and cognitive science research, the death primes and watchful eye primes in Heathen practices of ancestor veneration can be expected to make people feel watched, which encourages pro-social behavior and makes them want to act in accordance with their worldview. In conjunction with an inclusive sense of with whom we are in gifting relations, this nudges practitioners toward a sense of gifting relations with a larger moral community that extends into all wyrd. While the efficacy of this is limited by immersion in the dominant system of consumer capitalism, engaging in such practices at least episodically interrupts the economic frame and brings other values to mind.

Practices of ancestor veneration in inclusive Heathenry nudge practitioners toward a more relational ontology than the dominant individualized ontology of modern society. Gifting relations with ancestors and between kindred members are part of a larger incipient gift economy that supports ideals of interspecies reciprocity and generosity toward non-human others as integral participants in wyrd. Ritual practices of making offerings to ancestors foster a sense of being part of a community that extends beyond the human and in time into the past as well as the future. Gifting relations help generate a sense of obligation to that imagined community that can be fulfilled in passing on a way of relating to future generations. If we want a sustainable, diverse, and inclusive future, we need to become the ancestors who will be remembered for helping create it, and we must pass on those values in traditions that can endure even when our names are forgotten. In these practices of Heathen ancestor veneration, we can begin to see the formation of a gift ethic that supports a land ethic. Further tendencies in this direction are explored in the next chapter, which investigates a revived practice of the veneration of Nerthus, understood as a primal regenerative power of the land.

3

A Procession of Reconnecting

Welcome to the Procession of Nerthus at Well and Tree Gathering

It is the first long weekend of the summer in Canada, the May 24 weekend, so actually early spring. In eastern Ontario, in the area where Raven's Knoll is located, the ice has only been out of the lakes for a few weeks, and the trees are budding or newly in leaf. Daytime temperatures can be quite warm, but the nights are cold. It is the cusp of blackfly season. About fifty of us are here for Well and Tree Gathering, an annual festival featuring the procession of Nerthus.[1]

The ground is saturated with melt water, and camping is restricted to higher ground. The air is sweet with the smell of birch and poplar buds, and, if we are lucky, as night falls we will hear spring peepers start their nightly chorus that heralds the coming of spring. If we have had to endure the long drive from southern Ontario after work, we may have to set up in the dark. Those fortunate enough to live closer gather around the Keyhole firepit in the early evening to reconnect after a long winter, in which many of us have had little contact with one another apart from social media. Newcomers are welcomed to introduce themselves, and Brynja Clark, who leads this event, introduces herself and others to turn to for help in navigating the event.

Brynja, with gythia Nicole Butler of Hwitan Hund Hearth and their teenage daughters set up a temporary vé[2] for Nerthus around a poplar tree near the Standing Stone and Keyhole firepit. The tree is fairly small, growing up from the roots of a larger tree that previously had been a focus of this space. Poplars are not long-lived trees and tend to blow down when they die, so the tree that had been there was cut to avoid it falling on anyone. Logs from this tree are set upright in an open circle (penannular arc) to make the vé for Nerthus. Brynja and Nicole offer tobacco at each of these nine short posts, and the girls hook a rope around them to establish the vé as sacred space set aside in *frith* (peace, without arms) for honoring Nerthus. People continue to arrive later into the evening and, after setting up camp, join the group enjoying a communal bonfire at the Keyhole firepit nearby.

Wyrd Ecology. Barbara Jane Davy, Oxford University Press. © Oxford Univesity Press 2025.
DOI: 10.1093/9780197804957.003.0004

The next morning we gather around the fire pit, sitting at the eighteen or so picnic tables forming a large U around it. Brynja welcomes everyone and thanks Nicole for making the Breadman, a loaf baked in a human shape, which will be loaded with offerings and intentions and placed in the Sacred Well as an offering to Nerthus at the culmination of the weekend's events. Addressing the many children present, Brynja asks for a name for the Breadman. "Bob," a small voice pipes up. Brynja swallows hard and responds that this is a very appropriate name, reprising the name of the first Breadman offered to Nerthus at Raven's Knoll, and she recalls the tendency of offerings to "bob" around in the water of the Sacred Well when they are given.

Brynja notes that this event is a time to gather in honor of Nerthus "in gratitude and offering for the fertility of the upcoming year." She invites us to take slips of paper and write our thoughts on what we would like to grow in the coming year. We roll up our slips of paper and put them into the hollow Brynja has made in the Breadman's belly, along with seeds and some apple slices.[3] Then we decorate Nerthus's cart with flowers, shells, and stones, with lots of help from the young children present.

In a workshop later that morning, Erik Lacharity gives a history of the event of the procession of Nerthus, providing us with a booklet that he has prepared, titled *Holy Mother Nerthus Redux*. The reconstructed ritual of the procession of Nerthus at Raven's Knoll was inspired by the historical reference to such a procession in Tacitus's *Germania*, in 98 CE. Tacitus describes a procession of a covered representation of the goddess Nerthus, which he identifies as "Mother Earth," saying,

[t]hey believe that she interests herself in human affairs and rides among their peoples. In an island of the Ocean stands a sacred grove, and in the grove a consecrated cart, draped with a cloth, which none but the priest may touch. The priest perceives the presence of the goddess in this holy of holies and attends her, in deepest reverence, as her cart is drawn by heifers. Then follow days of rejoicing and merry-making in every place that she deigns to visit and be entertained. No one goes to war, no one takes up arms; every object of iron is locked away; then, and only then, are peace and quiet known and loved, until the priest again restores the goddess to her temple, when she has had her fill of human company. After that, the cart, the cloth, and, if you care to believe it, the goddess herself are washed clean in the secluded lake. This service is performed by slaves who are immediately afterwards drowned in the lake. Thus mystery begets terror and

pious reluctance to ask what the sight can be that only those doomed to die may see it. (Tacitus *Germania* pp. 53–54, para 40)

Erik indicates that Nerthus was carried through the countryside on a wheeled cart pulled by cattle or oxen, saying translations vary. He explains that the procession was a time of celebration, frith (peace and building respectful relations, with all weapons laid aside), and feasting. At the end of the procession, he says, the priest would have washed the representation of the deity with the help of slaves, who were then sacrificed to the goddess because none but her officiant could see her form without dying.

The inaugural procession of Nerthus at Raven's Knoll took place at the seventh annual Midgard Festival in 2010, which was the first festival held at Raven's Knoll. Erik was at that time in charge of scheduling for Midgard Festival and took Brynja and Jade's suggestion of a ritual dedicated to Nerthus as a favorable recommendation "to bring bounty and joy to the folk and the land for years to come" (Lacharity 2018). This first procession has shaped the development of the gythias and gothis and their relationship with Nerthus.

Erik tells the story of their first procession, with added comments from Brynja and Jade. Erik and Brynja served as priest and priestess—only they were to see the figure of Nerthus, procured by Brynja, which they carried on a palanquin covered with a dark blue linen cloth. Jade served as herald, announcing the procession. They set up a vé to represent the grove in which the goddess would reside during the festival and decided that the Sacred Well (see Figure 3.1), the natural spring at the Knoll in which offerings are deposited, would be the body of water to which the goddess would return at the conclusion of the festival. They did not prepare a sacrifice in place of the slaves historically given in this rite according to Tacitus's account. At the conclusion of the procession, when it came time to sink the image in the Sacred Well, she bobbed up to the surface of the water and would not sink. Brynja and Erik feared what might befall other visitors to the Well if they were to see her. Realizing that there must be an air pocket inside the image, Erik set out to retrieve it so he could break the bubble and allow it to sink.

Erik recalls,

we both instinctively looked at each other and thought the same thing, which is, nobody else can see the idol. . .. But it was still floating and

Figure 3.1 The Sacred Well, with veiled Nerthus.
Photo by author.

floating and it wasn't sinking. I . . . looked at Brynn [and] said, "don't tell my wife I'm doing this." I stripped down to my boxers and made my way into the bog to fetch the idol. Now, context: I don't swim very well, if at all. . . so as soon as I set foot into that bog, my legs immediately sank deep into the roots of the alders in that mire. I kind of sucked myself out, and flattened myself out, floated and waded out into the middle. Because of course the idol had floated to the middle. (interview November 21, 2018)

Brynja watched from the side, impassive to his plight as he slipped and sank beneath the water. She remembers,

I was sitting on the upper embankment of the Well area with my arms folded over my knees, at my chest, just watching. I watched him struggle, I watched him choke on the water. . . . I sat there, and I watched and I waited, and I waited and I watched. And when he finally dragged himself to the embankment and he was spluttering and coughing, and trying to compose himself, because, you know, he doesn't swim, I remember thinking.. . . "I'm conflicted." I remember thinking "I'm conflicted," because what do we do now? And that has been a real question that I still have. Could I have done something else, should we have done something else? (interview July 31, 2018)

At the workshop Brynja shared that, when Erik slipped under the water, appalling though it might be to remember, she thought it fitting that Nerthus should have a sacrifice, and they had failed to provide one apart from themselves. Later she recalled,

that first year, I remember sitting on the bench. I was still shaking and Auz looked at me, . . . and he said "so do you wish he died?" And the question caught me off guard, but the answer inside my head terrified me, because I [thought] . . . "well, yeah." He didn't, and now I'm conflicted because that's the way it was, and the way it should be if . . . we were to reconstruct that how it was, and recounted, what the Hel[4] do I do now, you know? And it made me face a very dark part of myself. (interview July 31, 2018)

In the current procession of Nerthus at Raven's Knoll as part of Well and Tree Gathering, in the mid-afternoon Brynja (see Figure 3.2) leads the procession through the campground and into the vé dedicated to Nerthus, with the cart pulled by Erik and another man, serving as oxen. Nicole assists Brynja in gythia duties, along with two junior gythias and two child "gythias in training" who range in age from five to fifteen years. Jade serves as herald, announcing the procession and leading numerous hails to Nerthus. As we parade through the campground we sing this song, written by Kate Lumsden, who used to take part in the procession as a gythia, but has since moved outside the region:

> Mother Nerthus, rides through the countryside
> Mother Nerthus, hear our call.
> Mother Nerthus, glorious and powerful
> Mother Nerthus, bring us joy.
> Mother Nerthus, regal and triumphant
> Mother Nerthus, hear our call.
> Mother Nerthus, primal mother goddess
> Mother Nerthus, bring us joy!

Figure 3.2 Gythia Brynja Clark.
Photo by author.

Figure 3.3 Offerings to Nerthus.
Photo by author.

We arrive back at the Nerthus vé, and the junior gythias offer us water from the Sacred Well to cleanse ourselves before entering the vé. Brynja and Nicole welcome us into the presence of Nerthus and invite us to make our offerings to her (see Figure 3.3). One by one we do so, most of us sharing our words with one another in addressing her. Some ask for help with specific things, and others express gratitude for gifts already received. A number of people prostrate themselves before her. Erik recounts in his Nerthus booklet,

I know that in the early years the Holy Mother was far more tumultuous (still is to some today). Some of the worshippers in fervency ate the dirt of Her bounds to quicken the womb (a few children having been born from Her blessings).[5] I know of others who have been taken by Her possession, to some unknown purpose (subsiding without issue, but freaky nonetheless). At one time She also demanded fresh meat, such as raw beef, to quell Her appetite for sacrifice (now Dude [Breadman] suffices, or as I am told). For all these reasons and more . . . her cultus has become more than a "frivolity," but a religious compulsion towards pleasing She-Who-Gives and can easily *take* so suddenly away. (emphasis in original, Lacharity 2018)

When we are finished making our offerings and exit the vé, some people relax around the fire, and others play games or prepare dinner. Later we gather for a "Bardic" event hosted by Jaimcos, sharing stories and songs around the campfire in a sprinkling of rain. Jaimcos, who refers to himself as an "atheist scientific spiritualist" (or "ASS" for short, he is quick to point out) regards the Bardic as a ritual. He explains,

for me, bardic is actually part of my spiritual path. Leading the bardic, for me the idea of encouraging people to come up and share with the community, stories, is an act of energy exchange between the presenter and the audience. If you're doing it right it's not a one-way event. It's a chance to share yourself with the audience, and the audience to share back, and that energy feeds and helps everyone become part and enjoy. . . . And for me, giving out tokens is also part of that. People give the gift of their performance, and I give them a gift of a token in return for appreciation, and for coming up. (interview June 20, 2018)

The next day begins with pit cooking, a method called *seyeir* in the Old Norse sagas. Auz orchestrates this at the large firepit in a big open sandy area near the permanent Vé to the Æsir. A shallow pit is dug in the sand. This time of year the water table is high, and digging too deep results in a water-filled pit. Sometimes rocks are used to line the pit to keep the fire above the water line. The fire is kindled with old god posts from the Æsir Vé,[6] as well as charcoal from the Wicker Man burned at KornuKopia Gathering (a Pagan fall feast event) in this same firepit. Stones are then heated in the fire. Foil-wrapped potatoes of multiple varieties are layered in wire cages, with beef roasts wrapped in foil placed in the top layer. Auz explains the cooking method, which he is filming for his YouTube channel "Heathen Hearth."[7] The stones are spread across the pit, and Auz gives leeks and ale over them as an offering to Nerthus (see Figure 3.4). The pit, he says, represents the womb, and the leeks and ale "quicken" it. At this same fire pit, at the large Pagan festival called Kaleidoscope Gathering each year, people offer ashes and tokens of their loved ones in remembrance since the womb of the mother represents life and return at its conclusion. Fresh-cut birch or alder branches are layered into the pit, and the food placed on top, followed by more fresh-cut branches

Figure 3.4 Auz, pit cooking for Nerthus.
Photo by author.

and sheets of wet fabric, followed by a tarp, and then covered with the sand that was dug out, to make the pit, to hold the heat in.[8]

Some hours later we sit down to eat together back at the tables around the Keyhole firepit or, if there is a lot rain, in the Rookery (an old camp building that is open to the air through a large hangar-like door). Auz has made switchel (made from honey and cider vinegar) for us to drink and prepared a variety of herbed butters, and there is fresh horseradish, as well as baked leeks and turnips seasoned with juniper, red cabbage, and crispy fried onions, along with the baked potatoes and roast beef. Brynja recalls,

[i]t's hearth, it's all about the community . . . no matter what tradition you have, feasting together, eating together, you know, pass the salt, pass the butter, and you're chit-chatting and you're talking. . . . It's also really fun to see Auz have such a passion to provide for the community through food and cooking, and using that scholarly wisdom of traditional cooking . . . . It is so fun to watch him doing that, and taking such pride in it, and then seeing everybody so happy, and "oh my gods this is so good," and "you should try

this with this" and it is truly exemplary. I will sit there at various points and I just look. I just watch. I love watching it. It is fantastic to watch. I—this is going to sound so ridiculously corny, [sniff] because I kill a man every year. I love watching the smiles . . . to see a real smile or a real belly laugh, or real tears, real emotion shared, it really is amazing. I'm really thankful that's become a tradition. (interview July 31, 2018)

The man she's referring to killing is the Breadman, "Bob." This is what the procession leads up to, the moment when Nerthus returns to the Well with the offerings and intentions of the community and the ultimate sacrifice of the Breadman standing in for a human being. On the last morning of the gathering, Brynja and Nicole, together with their daughters and the "mini-gythias" who are Erik's daughters, lead the procession back to the Sacred Well (see Figure 3.5). Brynja alone carries the offerings to the Well beyond the trees, while the people wait. No one sees what she does there. She washes Nerthus and places the offerings of the community in the sacred water. Finally, she takes the Breadman. She recalls,

it terrifies me to think what it must sound like, but Nerthus is not "love and light," "thoughts and prayers." It's not like that. This is real sacrifice, on so many levels. . . . It's haunting, and it takes a piece of me. . . . The way bread is, it's porous, so [long pause] I yell out because it hurts me to do it. But I cry, I sob because when you have a little dude Breadman, shaped like a little brown belly and stumpy legs and whatever . . . when you put him in the water—I say thank you and that—but when you put him in the water, and you push him under the water, because we make a face on him, air bubbles will come out of his mouth. And it's really haunting to look at, when you're looking at him, because you know at some point those bubbles will stop. (interview July 31, 2018)

A Watershed Moment

The first procession of Nerthus at Raven's Knoll was a watershed moment in the community, experienced as a hierophany in the manifestation of Nerthus's power over life and death in Erik's near drowning, through which participants learned at a visceral level that offerings are required when she is evoked.[9] Participants in the initial procession of Nerthus at Raven's Knoll

Figure 3.5 Gythia Brynja with "oxen" pulling Nerthus's cart.
Photo by author.

describe their first attempt at reconstructing the ritual without providing an offering as an "oversight," "blunder," and more colorful expressions of having made a mistake that resulted in not only a near-drowning but also in serious long-term health problems for the ritual leaders.[10] However, the first procession was a formative learning experience for the community. Through continued practice of sacrifice and making offerings, the effects of the procession continue to ripple through the community.

Ritual and the Creation of Moral Order

When I participated in the procession of Nerthus, it seemed to me that ecological conscience was a consequence of participation in this ritual, but describing how that happens was not so straightforward as it initially appeared. Émile Durkheim (1912) indicated that ritual generates moral force in society, but he did not provide a transparent explanation of how it does this. Early scholars of religion such as Mircea Eliade tended to interpret ritual as though it mapped out a religion's worldview, giving a straightforward model of how the world should be.[11] He argued (1959 [1957], 29) that an ideal of cosmic order is maintained by the repeated creation of sacred space in ritual, indicating that it recapitulates cosmogony (creation of the world by the gods). This creation of sacred space *"founds the world* in the sense that it fixes the limits and establishes the order of the world" (Eliade 1959 [1957], 30, emphasis in original). We can interpret some components of the procession in Eliadian terms. Practitioners associate the tree in Nerthus's vé with Yggdrasil, the tree referenced by the name Well and Tree Gathering that the procession is part of. Yggdrasil is the world tree in Norse mythology and easily fits Eliade's understanding of *axis mundi*, a pole that orients the world, but what is being modeled in the procession of Nerthus? What organization of the world is recapitulated? In this ritual, we find an irruption of Nethus's power, but it is not linked to a cosmogony so much as renewal in the Sacred Well.

Eliade also discusses another sort of ritual that he associates with cosmogony and that fits the procession more closely, in those that entail sacrifice. He says sacrifice is "often a symbolic imitation, of primordial sacrifice that gave birth to the world" (Eliade 1959 [1957], 55). We could interpret the sacrifice of the Breadman in this way, as a recapitulation of how the gods killed Ymir and made the world from his body, as described in Norse mythology,[12] but that story is not referenced in the procession, nor does it tell us much about what values are operant in the ritual or what sort of ethical orientation participants might gain from it. This sort of interpretation of ritual takes a static view of tradition, assuming that ritual supports the status quo, but this does not adequately describe how this ritual functions in contemporary Heathenry. Participants are reconstructing a ritual from another time and place yet find new meaning in it. They do not aim for an uncritical reconstruction of the past. They have no desire to enslave people or conduct human sacrifice as described in Tacitus's account, but they do find the story of Erik's near drowning, the sacrifice of the Breadman, and giving offerings to Nerthus meaningful.

Sacrifice as Establishment of Moral Order

Eliade (1959 [1957], 48) speaks of how establishing order requires vanquishing chaos, often symbolized by some sort of killing of a monster. French historian and theorist René Girard interpreted such stories as distorted memories of violence and scapegoating preceding the establishment of social order. Girard (1977, 1986, 1987) argued that scapegoating is the origin of human culture and religion. He described it as a practice that developed to cope with what he saw as a basic human propensity for violence and predisposition toward mimetic rivalry. Based on analysis of novels and religious myths, Girard suggested that we get our desires from competition with others, wanting what they want. He said the sacrifice of the scapegoat or a surrogate victim is the foundational way to mediate the basic rivalry of conflicting desires for the same objects. He avowed (1977, 8) that "there is a common denominator that determines the efficacy of all sacrifices. . . [namely] internal violence—all the dissensions, rivalries, jealousies, and quarrels within the community that the sacrifices are designed to suppress. The purpose of the sacrifice is to restore harmony to the community, to reinforce the social fabric." The scapegoat is blamed for the conflict and violence of rivalry and then held to be sacred once their death is dedicated to the gods. In this way, Girardian theory indicates that the sacrifice of the scapegoat through sanctified ritual violence is the hidden foundation of human society that secures peace.

If the Breadman could be said to stand in for the ills of the community, it might make sense to interpret it as a scapegoat, but this is not how participants understand the sacrifice. The sacrifice of the Breadman to Nerthus has some elements that are open to a Girardian interpretation. The noise of the procession and games played prior to offering the Breadman, for example, might be interpreted as conflicts within the group that need to be symbolically cast upon a surrogate victim to be apotheosized, as Girard (1977, 123) interprets such events, but there is no sense of conflict apparent in the event. Girard (1986, 66–75) analyzed the Norse story of the death of Balder (*Völuspá* 32–34, 56–60; in Larrington 2014, 8, 11–12) as an instance of collective murder of a scapegoat, although it is usually described as an accidental fratricide.[13] He assumed the story of Balder is an imperfect recollection of a ritual murder, though it may have more to do with the agricultural cycle, as Ellis Davidson (1964, 109) suggests and remembrance of the fact that we literally have to kill to eat, whether that is grain in the field or animals on the hoof. The flexibility of Girard's theory allows it to claim universality, but to interpret the offering of the Breadman as a scapegoat obscures other things this ritual does and ignores its current cultural context. Others (Smith 1987; Traube 1979) have criticized Girard for this tendency to ignore context. Girard's analysis of myth and ritual makes sense of them, but not necessarily the same sense they make to practitioners.

As Graham Harvey has said, Girardian theory presents one way of understanding the necessary violence of consumption and mediating rebounding violence, but ritual can also sustain a different dynamic: "the processes of mutuality and dialogue can take place, make place, establish spaces in which people can stand, make guests out of strangers, share breath and food, and go on to seek further ways of relating" (Harvey 2013, 111). This would seem to be a better fit for Heathen rituals such as the procession of Nerthus. Brynja sees the Breadman as a willing sacrifice for the good of the community and the land, which fits with Girardian theory, but the context of this ritual is that of offerings given in relational ontology. In my view, sacrifice is how offerings are understood within the dominant individualized ontology of modern society. In Heathen relational ontology, which is shaped by gifting relations, the Breadman is an offering, not something oneself is depriving oneself of, but a gift offered in generosity. There is, of course, much more that could be said about sacrifice in Heathen tradition, but here I focus on what ethics emerge from the procession of Nerthus at Raven's Knoll.[14]

The moral order that participation in the procession and making offerings to Nerthus negotiates and affirms is that of gifting relations. The values that are brought to mind in the procession of Nerthus and depositing the sacrifice and other offerings into the Sacred Well include generosity, sharing, frith, and inclusion. Gratitude, frith, and inclusion are made explicit in the ritual. Gratitude is mentioned explicitly by Brynja when participants are invited to place seeds into the Breadman. Participants must agree to uphold the value of inclusion to participate in Well and Tree Gathering and sign a form affirming this as part of their registration for the event. Those who enter Nerthus's vé must take an oath to enter in frith, setting aside weapons and any intent to use them. The values of sharing, generosity, and giving thanks are implicit in the practice of giving offerings. But how does participation in the ritual generate ethical sensibility, the desire to abide by the moral order negotiated and upheld as an ideal in ritual practice?

Sacrifice as a Death Prime That Operationalizes Values

The story of Erik's near drowning and the offering of the Breadman provide powerful death primes in the annual ritual of the procession of Nerthus.[15] These reminders of mortality occur in conjunction with practices of making offerings to Nerthus, asking for blessings, giving thanks for gifts already received, and bringing to mind the values of reconnection, community, and generosity. Participants in this event say that it inspires gratitude and the desire to give in turn. It reconnects people in the community that includes the more-than-human world, inspiring a gift ethic. Some practitioners identify Nerthus with the Ottawa Valley, the region in which this event takes place, and her procession has precipitated an outpouring of giving offerings in the Heathen community of Raven's Knoll and beyond.

As with Vindisir's Dísablót, applying terror management theory to the procession of Nerthus suggests that making mortality salient operationalizes the values made salient at the same time as long as those values are part of the participants' worldview. This theory provides an explanation backed by empirical evidence for how rituals activate the values present in them. Rappaport (1979, 196–197; 1999, 121–123) argued that ritual operationalizes values made salient to participants. Applying terror management theory suggests that death primes in ritual make people want to act in defense of their worldview, understood as their value system. The story of a near-drowning and the Breadman standing in for a human sacrifice as part of the procession of Nerthus are accompanied by the values of frith (peace and maintaining good relations), generosity, reconnection, and inclusion made salient with the giving of offerings and expressions of thanks. These values are part of the worldview of Heathens in this community. The death primes of the story of the near-drowning and the sacrifice of the Breadman remind participants of their mortality while also bringing to mind the values of inclusion, frith, and generosity in giving offerings. Reconnection is also brought to mind as the stated purpose of the event. Applying terror management theory suggests that the values brought to mind in the procession should be actualized in the community, but rituals do not always accomplish in practice what we might expect from theory.

Learning Ethics through Ritual Experience

Like Rappaport, Grimes applies speech act theory to ritual. They both draw attention to ritual's performative aspect, interpreting ritual as performative action not just in the theatrical sense but also in the sense of accomplishing something. Grimes, however, builds on philosopher of language J. L. Austin's (1975) recognition that speech acts can be infelicitous and fail to perform what participants intend them to do. Sincerity is not always enough to ensure ritual efficacy, and sometimes people speak without sincerity. Ritual failure, infelicitous ritual, and mistakes made in ritual describe an emergent area of interest in ritual studies. Grimes initiated this line of inquiry by developing a typology of infelicitous ritual (Grimes 1988) and applying what he calls "ritual criticism" in several case studies (Grimes 1990). Others (Hüsken 2007a) have further developed his initial forays into investigating how "mistakes" in ritual are part of the dynamics of change in religious communities. The ways in which rituals "fail" can also be instructive for a deeper understanding of how ethics are learned and co-constructed through ritual.

Grimes indicates that rituals combine multiple sorts of actions and succeed and fail variously in those actions. He identifies a few different, sometimes opposing vectors of ritual action, such as succeeding in providing psychological comfort while failing to protect participants from harm (Grimes 1990). Rituals can succeed socially while failing empirically, be effective politically while failing ethically, succeed in providing meaning while failing ethically or politically, and/or be efficacious in confirming agreements while failing to be festive (Grimes 1988, 105).

An implied purpose of the procession of Nerthus is to ensure the fertility of the land and the prosperity of the people. If we think about this in terms of the health of the community, the procession appears to be successful in that the community is flourishing, with stable numbers of participants, little conflict, and general satisfaction with how the event proceeds. The "mistake" in the first procession at Raven's Knoll had mixed consequences, some of which were negative for individual health, but it was a learning experience that has benefited the community as a whole. The first procession of Nerthus at Raven's Knoll was a "blunder" in the words of participants because they evoked Nerthus without providing her with a gift. In Grimes's (1988) terms it was a "hitch" because the rite was incomplete without providing a sacrifice. Through the experience of failing to provide an offering, participants learned what the important parts of the rite are. When historical practices are revived, participants choose what parts are dispensable and what parts are required in contemporary practice. Obviously they did not want to sacrifice a human being, but they found that sacrifice was not altogether dispensable. In retrospect, participants see not giving an offering as a significant error of omission.

However, the ritual did not fail in the sense that participants still experienced the presence and power of Nerthus, felt as a hierophany. Erik used this term (coined by Eliade 1959 [1957], 11) himself in discussing the ritual—contemporary Heathens tend to read a lot of academic writing on religion and anthropology, including Eliade. That the statue did not sink when no offering was provided could be seen as part of what religion scholar Ute Hüsken describes as "The tendency of some ritual systems to 'incorporate' deviations in ritual by attributing them to superhuman agency and thus considering them as part of the ritual process" (Hüsken 2007a, 23). If the statue was an offering from a practitioner point of view, it was rejected and Nerthus made it known that she expected more through Erik's near-drowning. If the first procession was an offence against Nerthus, which I think is a fair characterization of Brynja and Erik's perception, the fact that the idol floated instead of sinking might be seen as an omen signifying her displeasure. From a participant point of view it makes sense to say that their error created an opportunity for Nerthus to make herself known and manifest her power. Ultimately, this "blunder" may have been a gift, in teaching the importance of making offerings. In the longer term, it may even make sense to see it as a "calculated catastrophe" to use religion scholar Christoph Emmrich's (2007, 134) phrase, presenting an opportunity for restoration in that it "enables the performance of a breakdown, restoration to a pristine state, forgiveness and wellbeing" (Emmrich 2007, 134). This is not how practitioners currently describe it, but it may yet come to be seen that way if participants begin to see new iterations of the event as restorative rather than an ongoing act of atonement.

In current practice, telling the story of what happened in the first procession at Raven's Knoll teaches participants the importance of making offerings. This illustrates Hüsken's conclusion that "'Failed ritual' directs our attention to 'what really matters' to the performers and participants and others in one way or another involved in a ritual" (Hüsken 2007b, 337). As she says,

> in many cases participants and spectators alike learn more about the "correct" performance of a ritual by deviating from, rather than by adhering to the rules. . . . One might even say that solely the definitions and examples of "ritual failure" and "error"—and how they are coped with—prove the existence of decisive norms for ritual actions, even when the former are imagined deviations from imagined norms. (Hüsken 2007b, 337)

To call something a mistake "draws attention to the actual purpose of the broken rule and the values it is based on" (Dücker 2007, 78). Participants' repeated description of the first procession as a taboo-breaking blunder establishes the importance of giving offerings in the community. That participants called it a "blunder" means they regard it as part of a learning process, that there is a right way to do it, and that they did not meet expectations. Calling the omission of the offering a mistake or blunder makes the values of giving, sharing, and generosity come to mind and forcefully instills the value of giving. In conjunction with the reminder of mortality, participants are moved to act on these values in defense of their worldview. Participants in the procession of Nerthus learn that sincerity and good intentions are not enough, that doing the ritual requires giving offerings. Through this learning process, participants are developing a shared sense of how people should relate through a gift ethic.

The Emergence of a Gift Ethic

The story of Erik's near-drowning recounted each year at Well and Tree Gathering, and the subsequent sacrifice of the Breadman each year at the conclusion of the procession of Nerthus, reconnect people with one another, the land, and the water in gifting relations. Giving inspires gratitude for what one has, and, as participants come to know Nerthus, they value reconnecting with each other and with the land and water in frith. As we will see, Nerthus is not exactly a "Mother Earth" figure, but more identified with the local terrain "of birch and bog," historically and in contemporary practice.[16] Participants say Nerthus is "Prima" at Raven's Knoll, the force of life and death in the Ottawa Valley. Giving offerings to Nerthus, making the values of generosity, sharing, and reconnection salient, results in a gift ethic in conjunction with Heathen relational ontology.

Reconnecting

When I asked participants about the meaning and consequences of the ritual of the procession of Nerthus, people said its purpose is to continue, that it has to happen, and that it enables people to reconnect with one another and the land. The value most explicitly mentioned in the ritual is frith. When entering the vé, each participant vows to enter in frith. Participation in the procession establishes frith, a temporary laying down of arms that operationalizes this value in the community. Frith, as Auz says and notes in the Hail and Horn program (2018), is more than just peace as the absence of strife; it is a dynamic peace. In my understanding, frith is the adaptive relationality of maintaining and extending alliances accomplished through the distributed system of indirect reciprocity: gifting in the context of relational ontology. In vowing to keep frith in Nerthus's vé and in participating in her procession through the land, the people are reconnecting into the distributed system of wyrd relations that include the land, the water, and everything in the bioregion. The procession of Nerthus around the campground echoes the cord that sets her vé as held in frith, symbolically including Raven's Knoll and the watershed in relations of frith, rippling out in concentric circles like waves from a pebble dropped in a pond.

When I asked about the consequences of the ritual of the procession and its purpose, Brynja said it is a celebration, and "it's a way for the folk after such a long and dark winter to come back together, open up camping gear, open up, you know, put their feet back on the land, reconnect, and in frith. It's about getting back together" (interview July 31, 2018). Brynja used the verb (re)connect more than twenty times in this interview alone, and it also appears often in other interviews about the event. Her words express the desire for relation and the importance of relationality, connections between people and the land, between people in the community, and with Nerthus, whom practitioners describe as a primal force associated with the Sacred Well, identified with the Well of Wyrd. One of the most important and meaningful parts of the gathering for Brynja is the time she spends alone at the Sacred Well, washing the figure in which she evokes Nerthus for the procession. She describes this as a peaceful time for her to reconnect with Nerthus and the Well and to open herself to connection with the people gathered for the procession. This event creates intimate interpersonal relations and might potentially sustain larger patterns of interrelations through gifts given to other processions. Brynja has gifted a Nerthus figure used previously at the Knoll to Nicole and Aesc "to gift a connection" between their hearths and has also expressed a desire to forge connections with other processions of Nerthus in this way (interview July 31, 2018).[17] These sort of gifts, along with offerings to Nerthus, weave interlacing patterns of connection that support the formation of something like what Aldo Leopold (1966 [1949]) called a "land ethic."

Leopold's Land Ethic

The ethic that the procession of Nerthus inspires is a gift ethic that includes the more-than-human world and may function somewhat as Leopold imagined his land ethic should, but it is grounded in a different ontology. Leopold starts from a perspective of individualized ontology, with the land ethic developing as an extension of the idea of community, whereas the gift ethic emerges from a relational ontology in which we are already embedded in relations of wyrd. Leopold framed his understanding of the land ethic as an extension beyond the human: "The land ethic simply enlarges the boundaries of the community to include soils, waters, plants, and animals, or collectively, the land" (Leopold 1966 [1949], 219). Heathens support an understanding of community that includes the more-than-human world, and they are more likely to support something like a land ethic than would the general population. In my survey findings, Heathens and other Pagans were much more likely than the random sample to agree or strongly agree with the statement "My sense of community includes plants, animals, land, and water," which I designed to test for adherence to Leopold's concept of the land ethic.[18] In the survey, 56% of Heathens and Pagans agreed strongly, compared to 28% of the random Canadian sample. Heathens were somewhat less likely to agree strongly than other Pagans, but more likely to strongly agree that ritual practice is important, which may make Heathens more likely to live an operationalized land ethic than those who do not find ritual practice important.

Leopold challenges the modern perception of land as commodity, suggesting it should be seen as community (Leopold 1966 [1949], x). From a logical perspective, he is right to link commodification with the exclusion of the nonhuman from moral consideration. But rational argument only gets us so far. The exclusion of nonhuman others from the moral community is a modern phenomenon, arguably brought on by the development of market economy relations in which "things" are sent out of the community and thus no longer perceived to be part of the network of social relations of the interspecies moral community, as observed, for example, by Danny Naveh and Nurit Bird-David (2014). The Nayaka they studied were beginning to keep some domesticated species for trade but still living as hunter-gatherers. They treated the forest as their home, shared with various nonhuman persons, while regarding domestic animals as things for use. From the perspective of individualized ontology treating nonhuman others as persons looks like a category mistake or a delusional projection of anthropomorphism. But from a perspective of relational ontology it is not so much that we need to extend our sense of ethics but instead, as Harvey indicates (2006), realize that not all people are human.[19] This difference is not amenable to rational argument but can be shifted through nonrational processes.

Part of what is compelling about Leopold's perspective is that his argument is embedded in a narrative, and that narrative arouses mortality salience in conjunction with environmental values. Leopold's "thinking like a mountain" is influential in part because of a death prime embedded in his narrative. He recalls as a young man in the 1900s coming upon a mother wolf and her cubs and shooting them, as was common practice at the time. He describes seeing "a fierce green fire dying in her eyes" (Leopold 1966 [1949], 130). This experience was transformative for him. He realized that the deer and the mountain knew something he did not, that the mountain needs wolves to maintain relations between deer and plant life or the deer overgraze, the plants die, and the soil washes away. Hearing this story arouses mortality salience in conjunction with a positive valuation on the lives of nonhuman others in mutually sustaining relations. It makes environmentalists want to maintain those relations.

Similarly, Val Plumwood's account of nearly being eaten by a crocodile in 1985, while canoeing alone in Kakadu National Park in Australia's Northern Territory, illustrates the efficacy of combining mortality salience with environmental values. Plumwood's account celebrates the value of the crocodile who tried to eat her as "a symbol of the power and integrity of this place and the incredible richness of its aquatic habitats" (Plumwood 1995). She recognized herself as prey, describing her terror at being bitten and dragged under the water, but also apologizing to the crocodile as she escaped. She felt remorse at her intrusion into the crocodile's habitat, as well as a sense of wonder at still being alive and a lasting sense of gratitude. These stories are dramatic and memorable, and they arouse mortality salience in conjunction with the value of wilderness preservation and a positive valuation of the lives of predators.

Discourses in environmental ethics and politics have assumed that what is cognized becomes part of our consciousness and that, if we rationally explain something in an intelligible way, then it automatically becomes part of our worldview. But this is not how worldviews are formed and not how conscience develops. Coming to a verbal agreement means very little when the rules go against the encultured core values and metaphors structuring our perception (Lakoff and Johnson 2003). People vote in accord with their values, even when it is against their rational self-interest (Lakoff 2014). Narratives such as Leopold's story of the wolf and Plumwood's of the crocodile are effective because they activate nonrational motivations in support of their rational arguments. Ethics are not automatically generated by premises but can be inspired by gratitude and a sense of indebtedness. Ethics do not so much require "thinking like a mountain" as coming into relation with them. If our core values are what motivate our actions and these are not consciously adopted but are part of the shared collective unconscious shaped in part by the rituals we participate in—the unconscious aspects of the "as if" negotiated through ritual—then rituals that make gifting relations with the natural world salient can nudge participants toward a more relational ontology.

Leopold, and much subsequent environmental discourse, assumes that conscience is about consciously held values, but conscious knowing and rational deliberation do not change worldviews. Following Levinas, ethics are not about reason, but felt obligation. In my application of his theory of ethical sensibility, it is gifting relations between persons that inspire ethical relations, obligations, and relational indebtedness—and some of these persons are other than human. We can use rational argument to say that land should not be regarded as a commodity, but it may be easier to recognize nonhuman others as persons in a nonpropositional way, in a relational rather than reasoned way, through practices of making offerings.

Rather than trying to think like a mountain we need to reweave ourselves into the land by participating in larger gift economies with nonhuman others. Realizing our places in the mutual upholding of social ecological systems requires ceding human primacy, decentering ourselves, and finding gratitude for all that other species do for us. This does not mean that human rights can be dispensed with in favor of an abstract sense of ecocentrism or biocentrism but that our lives are interlaced in larger distributed relational networks that include nonhuman others.

Entering into gifting relations with nonhuman others helps infuse relational ontology because to receive a gift is to feel obligated. Blain (2016, 23) discusses giving offerings as a way of building relationships with wights, including *landvaettir* and house wights, those whom others might term household "spirits." As Harvey explains, extending Marcel Mauss's (1990) analysis of gifting, "Recipients of gifts are not only obliged to enact the outworking and continuity of their relationships, they are ontologically constituted as related persons by the receipt and reciprocation of gifts" (Harvey 2006, 12). Gifting relations are part and parcel of animism. Harvey explains: "People reciprocate gifts given by other people and thereby demonstrate that they are indeed related people. By acting towards other people in particular ways, people enact personhood. . . . They are people because they give and receive gifts" (13). In the context of animist and relational ontologies, gifting relations extend beyond the human and include the whole world in relations of social obligation. In this sense, animism supports "ecological" more so than "environmental" ethics because the world is not just "our environment" for humans (179). We are surrounded by "the environment" but we are embedded in complex relations with many active agencies, called *vaettir* or wights in Heathen terms.

Giving gifts to Nerthus prompted me to think about how anything I can think of to give has been given to me by another. If I give flowers, they are given to me by the plants that grew them. If I give coffee, this action includes a transactional chain spanning half the globe. There is no gift that is enough because I have already been given so much, but giving something and sharing my words enables me to participate in relations of giving, to give in turn in whatever small ways I can. This giving inspires gratitude in place of guilt. We have done terrible things in modern society, but we can still contribute meaningfully to the life of the world if we reenter relations of respect, gift, and gratitude. Each of us in affluent society contributes to ecological damage, but feeling guilty about it solves nothing. What we need is collective action. This is one of the things ritual is good for because it does not require articulating a consensus but instead creates one in acting together through the use of metaphor and symbol (see Seligman et al. 2008). This co-constructs the collective unconscious where our values reside, not as an abstract universal collection of archetypes but as culturally specific patterns. Nerthus is an important part of this in the Heathen community of Raven's Knoll.

Mother Earth?

In his account of the procession of Nerthus among the Seubians in what is now Denmark in *Germania* 40, quoted above, Tacitus equates Nerthus with "Mother Earth." Nerthus is a name not otherwise attested in historical sources. Tacitus presumes she is a "Mother Earth" figure, but this interpretation does not seem to fit other historical evidence or contemporary practice at Raven's Knoll. There is archeological evidence of processions from the time of Tacitus's writings through to the time of Christianization (Ellis Davidson 1964, 95), but Ellis Davidson (1964, 111) indicates that there is little, if any, evidence of a Mother Earth figure in pre-Christian Scandinavia. Scholars and practitioners speculate on connections of Nerthus with Skaði's husband Njord and suggest she was perhaps mother to Freyr and Freya. Njord appears to be an Old Norse variant of Nerthus, indicating perhaps that Nerthus may have been partnered with Njord as Freyr to Freya or that Nerthus later underwent a shift in gender to become Njord (106). Ellis Davidson links Nerthus to Gefn, a name of Freya meaning "the giver," one who is open-handed with her gifts (113). Another form of this Goddess name, Gefion, is related also to Old English *geofon*, poetically linked to the sea (114).

My understanding of Nerthus is as a more primal face of Frigg, not domesticated. Frigg's abode in Norse mythology is Fensalir, meaning the hall of or home in the fen, or a bog-like marshy area that floods. Nerthus is the giver of life, but also takes it away: "She-Who-Gives and can easily *take* so suddenly away" (emphasis in original, Lacharity 2018). She is not exactly a nurturing mother figure. Similarly, nature is generous but not always benevolent. Brynja says, "I call her a beautiful nightmare, because if you look anywhere in the world . . . there is a cycle of life and death so you have these natural elements, and you're part of that element, but you have a lot of catastrophic, often tragic events that must proceed" (interview July 31, 2018).

Nerthus is Prima, foremost—first in importance, before all others, according to Erik, Brynja, and Nicole. She is a primordial force, not part of the Æsir or the jötnar. If paired with Njord, it would make sense to see her as part of the Vanir, but Nerthus is not "friendly" in the way that the Æsir and Vanir are. Nerthus is both the generous giver of all and the bringer of death. As Prima she is more powerful than the other gods, but she is not the "Earth Goddess." She is not abstract nature but the power of birch and bog in the here and now. She is place-bound, having power of life and death over the Ottawa Valley, according to the Heathens of Raven's Knoll. Revering her does not endow us with Gaian consciousness or herald the creation of a Gaian civilization, but nudges participants toward good relations within this place. Nerthus is not "the Land" but "this land" in particular. When practitioners call her "Prima" they mean the foremost power in the Ottawa Valley.[20] She is more like a powerful personification of the landvaettir than a Mother Earth figure.

When I asked if Nerthus is the "Earth Mother" Erik replied, "You could say that," but immediately clarified "Not all of the Earth, but specifically the earth of the Ottawa Valley." He likened his perspective to that of first-century residents of the watershed of the Rhine River and other parts of Europe where the cult of the *Matronai* was often associated with local hydrographic features of the land. He said that, for him, Nerthus "is specifically tied to the Ottawa Valley and the river, the Ottawa River watershed" and that she "is the personification of deity which inhabits the Well at Raven's Knoll." He explained that, for him, "she is tied to place, so more of a *genius loci*" or generative power of place, like the landvaettir. He said that he has come to know her through historical sources "but also through the gifting relationship between herself and the community has made it so that she has made herself very well known and powerful in this world." She holds power over life and death in the region, he said, "and the community specifically that interacts with her." She is "Prima," the primary power in the Ottawa Valley that is responsible, he said, for "the fecundity of the land and the prosperity of the folk" (interview November 21, 2018).

One might wonder, if Nerthus is identified with the Ottawa Valley, then why does the procession go to the Well rather than the Bonnechere River, which drains into the Ottawa River? For practitioners, the Well is a repository of offerings and of words and intentions. Brynja explains,

> sometimes people have wondered, "well, why not use the Bonnechere River. It's right there." It has a deeper mysticism when you have a standing body of water. . . . The Bonnechere is flowy . . . it doesn't make any sense even just off the surface because you're washing away, like it appears that you're just washing away intention, whereas at the Well. . . . [is] able to contain intentions. So when we sacrifice the Breadman and the offerings people have made over the course of the weekend folk resonate with either the collection of intentions down or the collection of intentions up through that grove of trees around the water. (interview July 31, 2018)

Nerthus is associated with the Sacred Well at Raven's Knoll and the watershed. She is like the landvaettir (for whom Erik used the Latin term *genius loci* above), who are not associated by Heathens with any pantheon but with natural features of the land and, similarly, are not wholly benevolent in their orientation toward humans, as discussed in the previous chapter.

Returning to Wyrd Relations

Returning to the well, participating in rituals of making offerings and giving thanks, episodically returns participants to wyrd, weaving us into relation and reconnection with one another and the land. The procession of Nerthus renews a sense of connection for practitioners as Nerthus emerges from and returns to the Well. As discussed above, the Sacred Well represents the Well of Wyrd, associated with spinning, water, fate, and webs of relations. Wyrd is the whole network of relations between living humans, ancestors, gods, and members of other species. In my interpretation, our relations in wyrd are sustained by what we are given and what we give in turn. When we give gifts not only to humans in making offerings, we include the more-than-human world in the gift ethic.

The procession of Nerthus is not exclusively Heathen, and it is not just for Heathens. Other Pagans and people who follow other traditions or do not identify as religious are welcome to participate in Well and Tree Gathering. While the rituals of the event are Heathen, participants need not be. Because of this, the event is even more inclusive than other Heathen events at Raven's Knoll. The value of inclusivity fits with the ethic of welcome expressed in the *Hávamál*. In that work, verses 2–4 and 132–136 speak of the duty to welcome the stranger, to give them food, shelter, and other gifts. I see the vé bond, the rope or cord wrapped around the posts that makes an open circle, as emblematic of this positive valuation of welcome and inclusion. I see it not as a boundary that excludes but as a hearth that is always open to those who come in frith. The vé bond establishes an area of inclusion in frith and is a symbol of maintaining good relations, but wyrd extends to all relations, recognized or not. The vé bond does set a required vow not to invite other powers into the vé. It marks a place set aside for honoring Nerthus in this case, or the Æsir and their allies in the Æsir Vé. To me, it is a symbol of welcome and generosity. Nerthus's vé, like the Æsir Vé, forms an open circle echoing the shape of the penannular arm rings. To me this represents "the debt that is always open," to use Levinas's (1990, 152) phrase. We are obliged to always welcome the other because we are always already indebted for the gifts we have already received in wyrd. The inclusivity of Heathens such as those at Raven's Knoll and Vindisir is not a totalizing desire to consume all difference into one right way. They have no desire to convert the world to one faith or to police the boundaries of who belongs. They welcome all who want to participate with the value of inclusion. They, like me, value a vision of the future that supports diversity "not under one big tent but under the stars, which each people names in their own tongues and sees in their own constellations" (Davy and Quilley 2018), in which we welcome each other in turn with frith.

Processing from Guilt to Gratitude

There is a penitential character to the procession of Nerthus at the Knoll, as the original revivors of the rite seek to make amends for what they see as blunders in their initial procession. Brynja takes on the role of gythia who calls Nerthus to be present with the folk, washes and cares for her image, and sacrifices the Breadman for the good of the folk, shielding them from any reprisal from the "Primal Mother," who's power, she says, is "raw, and real." Brynja and others walk barefoot along the stony pathways and wear no coats despite the often cold May weather. Erik does not take the role of gothi for this event, instead submitting to a role serving as one of the oxen pulling the cart. Brynja carries the heavy figure of Nerthus by hand to the well, symbolically shouldering the burden of shielding the folk from her power, so that other participants in the procession enjoy only the benefits while she takes on the risk of evoking a primordial power.

I cannot help but see a parallel in the brokenness of the original figure of Nerthus used in the first procession and the brokenness of our relationship with the Earth in the Anthropocene, the age of human impact on the Earth, as those of us in the affluent industrialized world seem to increasingly dominate the fate of the planet, breaking the ability of ecosystems to sustain themselves. The revivors of this ritual practice are not individually to blame for this brokenness, yet they assume the burden. In fact, the Earth is not broken, and, despite the ravages of climate change and other environmental damage, we cannot break her because she is much more powerful than us. Our actions break ourselves and the ability of ecosystems to sustain us. While the Anthropocene appears to be culminating in a sixth mass extinction event (Kolbert 2015), which is something we should work toward repairing, life on Earth will continue with or without us. She can swat us off like a troublesome blackfly if we do not figure out how to repair our relations with other forms of life and regenerate adaptive relations within her living systems. She will endure and is quite willing to help us heal ourselves, if we would only let her. And as Robin Wall Kimmerer (2013, 122) says, "the land loves us back," and feeling that love is transformative. Nerthus is terrible and powerful, but also the source of life and love, and she rejoices in our vitality. Despite the penitential aspects of this event, it includes entertaining elements and is greatly enjoyed for its powerful sense of community and support. It is a celebration of reconnection and inclusion.

It seems to me that some participants in the procession of Nerthus have a residual sense of guilt and feel a need for penance but that they are in the process of moving from guilt to gratitude. The procession of Nerthus is one example, in many ways unique, but it suggests that giving offerings in conjunction with mortality salience might nudge participants toward a more relational ontology and can inspire a sense of obligation toward the more-than-human world. Just doing a procession, without offerings, would not be enough to generate ecological conscience. Perhaps also though, in doing this without there being any tangible connection to resource use or broader engagement with dominant economic systems, it will have minimal impact beyond the immediate participants. In conjunction with other rituals, the procession supports tendencies toward developing gifting relations at the Knoll and in Heathen community, but this does not extend out into relations beyond the immediate community of participants.

Another component in engendering a land ethic is evident from considering how Leopold developed it: by living on the land for an extended period of time, getting to know it and come into relation with it. This is an "apprenticeship in nature" as Sharon Butala (1994, 2000) puts it. Similar methods are recommended for developing religious practice rooted in the land by Jenny Blain (2016), Paul Rezendes (1998), Gordon MacLellan (2004), and Barry Patterson (2004). Patterson and MacLellan work as environmental educators and are both Pagan practitioners in the United Kingdom. Similar methods are recommended in ecopsychology (see, e.g., Harris 2014). These practices take time, dedication, and effort. Individual apprenticeships such as these provide examples of efforts to return to frithful relations with place. Other examples might be found in eco-communities, transition towns, and various localized efforts to live sustainably in place. Such endeavors can generate pockets of good relations with place, and, if continued over generations, may help people develop adaptive relations with the land and those who live within it. Perhaps when we have become ancestors and our names have been forgotten, we will become landvaettir of people who live in a storied world, but we are a long way from being Indigenous.[21]

At this point Raven's Knoll is a place that community members visit. They have initiated gifting relations with the land but do not live wholly within those relations. Many of us do not reside in the watershed, and there is little watershed consciousness in the Ottawa Valley. Our economic lives depend on jobs in cities and buying things made elsewhere. There is relatively little food produced in the watershed. Some community members frequent the Knoll often enough to maintain gardens there, but food production is more symbolic than substantial. It is unlikely that the land could support our numbers even at a subsistence level, let alone at the levels of affluence to which we are accustomed. However, the actions of practitioners giving back a sense of connection and gratitude may spread like ripples in a pond. If these ripples become waves, they may help generate larger shifts in society.

4

How Pro-Environmental
Are These Heathens?

In this work, I set out to show how Heathen rituals support ecological conscience formation, meaning how these rituals contribute to a pro-environmental orientation or encourage a disposition toward ecological behavior, not to what degree this conscience manifests in action. Due to methodological limitations such as not tracking behavior before and after participants began involvement with Heathenry, I cannot prove what pro-environmental behaviors are caused by Heathen ritual practices rather than other factors. However, I can describe what sort of pro-environmental behaviors I saw (and did not see) at Raven's Knoll and in Vindisir and give some sense of the significance of such actions.

Activism

I saw little overt environmental activism in this community. Most practitioners are not visibly involved in direct action campaigns or protests, at least in terms of environmentalism. What I saw of this sort of political activity in the community was directed at issues of inclusivity, with a number of people participating in Black Lives Matter and LBGTQ+ political actions during my fieldwork and encouraging other group members to participate in these events. Some practitioners actively lobby governments at municipal, provincial, and federal levels on environmental issues such as protection of endangered species, habitat conservation, recycling, municipal composting, and waste management. Some advocate for better environmental practices in their workplaces, use their positions to implement more sustainable practices, and challenge other corporations to do better. However, some practitioners in the community do not identify as environmentalists at all. One person told me he did not participate in my survey on environmental values because he did not want to "skew" my results. Yet I saw little

Wyrd Ecology. Barbara Jane Davy, Oxford University Press. © Oxford Univesity Press 2025.
DOI: 10.1093/9780197804957.003.0005

evidence that he is any less pro-environmental in his day-to-day actions than I am. The Heathens in this community have not made any claims to be pro-environmental or to self-identify as environmentalists, but it may still make sense to regard this community as engaged in pro-environmental religious practice.

Environmentalism means different things to different people. It can mean producing scientific research to document harmful effects; conducting restoration projects; pursuing public education or legal actions; overseeing improvements to environmental assessments and regulations; advocating for conservation of resources or wilderness preservation; pursuing sustainable development, economic change, or environmental justice; orchestrating international agreements; or participating in Green Party politics, grassroots organizing, lobbying, direct action, and protests. All of these forms of environmentalism are important and necessary.

Personal actions may seem insignificant in comparison with collective efforts. Sarah Pike implies that activism is necessary to give evidence of significance beyond the personal. She says,

> [o]n one end of the spectrum is the entirely private pursuit of transformation in which one consults information in books and on the Internet for guidance. At the other end is involvement with public protest actions such as the Neopagan group march as a "living river" at the World Bank meeting protests in Ottawa in 2001. (Pike 2004b, 37)

Although she says self-transformation and actions aimed at societal transformation are on a continuum, evidence of participation in protests seems to be stronger evidence of greater political commitment. I agree that participating in protests indicates a high level of personal commitment to a cause, but this is not the only indicator of commitment, and such actions may be less politically effective than is sometimes supposed. Social movement research focuses on confrontational politics and often disregards other forms of political action (Colli and Adriaensen 2020).

Despite widespread consensus among social movement theorists that the nonviolent disruption caused by blockades and strikes is the best strategy, this is a theory not yet supported by data. Nobody tracks participation in environmental protest the way labor movement participation is tracked. According to the *Global Atlas of Environmental Justice*, participation in fossil fuel and hydroelectric project resistance is almost as likely to result in arrest or death (12%) as it is to be successful (15%). Resistance movements are more likely to be successful in preventing new developments than stopping those already in action.[1] More research with attention to what sorts of actions work better in different contexts for different issues is necessary. It is worth noting that risking arrest in direct action or protests is more serious for people of color (Bowman 2020).

I actually participated in the Ottawa demonstrations against the World Bank and G20 meetings that Pike used as an example, and that event was a turning point in my participation in environmentalism. There were thousands of us at that demonstration and at other protests that year, and it seemed to me at the time that they accomplished nothing. Maybe this was simply a "cold heaven" experience. Frances Westley, Brenda Zimmerman, and Michael Quinn Patton (2006) describe "cold heaven" as the burnout experience of social innovators when it seems that what they are doing is not working and that what they give to the cause or movement will never be enough. However, twenty years later, I continue to question the efficacy of protests as a strategy for change. Protests inconvenience people and make them angry, but that anger is often directed at the protesters rather than at the reasons for which protests are organized. While direct action campaigns of occupying places to protect them can be effective so long as protestors remain there, as seen in the UK anti-road campaigns of the 1990s (see Letcher 2000, 2004), they do not necessarily change the systems that generate the pressure to build more roads. Protests can raise awareness of problems but are not themselves solutions. It may be more effective to raise the salience of pro-environmental values in communities of practice than to raise awareness of environmental problems. Also, as Jade commented regarding their past involvement in political demonstrations and direct action campaigns, community building is important for countering the effects of burnout.

Impact of Personal Actions and Personal Norms

Protest can be an effective way to apply pressure to governments and raise awareness of issues, but this does not mean that small-scale personal choices are unimportant. Environmental sociologist Michael Maniates, in an influential essay, provocatively questions the efficacy of individual actions, saying "you can't plant a tree to save the world" (Maniates 2001, 44). He criticizes the much-loved Dr. Seuss story *The Lorax* for placing environmental responsibility on individuals. "*The Lorax*," he says, "both echoes and amplifies an increasingly dominant, largely American response to the contemporary environmental crisis" (32). The story suggests that the problem of consumption can be resolved simply through better consumer choices. This is the "individualization of responsibility," but what we need, he says, is to "think institutionally" (33).

Maniates explains how environmentalism is marginalized by relegating it to personal consumer choices instead of working for institutional and policy changes. Corporations have explicitly aimed to put the onus on consumers while themselves lobbying against putting pro-environmental institutional structures in place. Maniates gives the example of the container industry spending "tens of millions of dollars to defeat key 'bottle bill' referendums in California and Colorado, and then vigorously advanced recycling—*not reuse*—as a more practical alternative" (Maniates 2001, 43). He argues that the focus on international agreements ignores the power of states and transnational corporations to frame discussion in ways that advantage them rather than citizens and that corporations are the ones that benefit most from framing the issues in terms of consumer responsibility (44). Individuals are not always free to choose the best environmental options, like refillable containers, eating organic free-range local food (unless they are affluent), and good public transit. These require institutional structural change. Collective action is required to challenge our lack of good choices as consumers (50).

However, former chief of staff of the American Environmental Protection Agency Michael Vandenbergh points out that "individuals are now the largest remaining sources of many pollutants" (Vandenbergh 2004, 518), including climate change gases (Vandenbergh 2005, 1103). Industrial contributions have been substantially regulated, he says, but personal actions can have a substantial impact even on large-scale problems such as climate change. Changing household behaviors could reduce national carbon emissions by 7.4% in the United States (Dietz et al. 2009, 18452).

Regulations against personal behavior are hard to implement through legislation because people are very resistant to being told not to do things. Such regulations are inefficient and costly to enforce (Vandenbergh 2005, 1103), which leads Vandenberg to recommend focusing on activating personal norms as a strategy for shifting social norms to work toward sustainability.

In some cases, norm activation will change direct environmental behaviors. In many other cases, particularly where direct behavior change requires sustained or substantial effort, norm activation will generate the back-ground political support necessary for policymakers to invest in financial incentives and new infrastructure. (Vandenbergh 2005, 1106)

He suggests providing better information through public education to activate personal norms, assuming that if people are better informed about the consequences of personal actions they will act rationally and support environmental policy. We need collective action to solve large-scale environmental problems such as climate change, to secure better government regulations to reduce carbon emissions and implement infrastructural solutions such as better transit, and public education is a necessary part of securing public support for such collective actions. However, while accurate information is necessary, it is not sufficient in itself to motivate behavioral change (Davy 2021). Activating personal norms and values can make implementing effective policy solutions politically viable.

Collective action may be facilitated by activating personal norms and values through individual actions such as planting trees. Planting one tree will not "save the world," but forest restoration could substantially mitigate climate change (Bastin et al. 2019). If done as a ritual, planting a tree could inspire further pro-environmental behavior. Planting a tree can be a purely symbolic, seemingly insignificant action but involving people in tree planting as a ritual could inspire care for the tree and the desire to do more to care for the environment. We could design tree planting to be effective secular rituals to promote pro-environmental behavior by shaping ecological conscience through priming effects and value salience. This is likely to be more effective in preexisting communities of practice than in civic society more generally. Governance specialist Nives Dolšak's (2017) research in Slovenia suggests that there is increased uptake of environmental campaigns within preexisting voluntary associations that entail frequent face-to-face interaction. Religious communities are a ready source of potential groups that can be engaged in this way, but other groups, such as the hunter's groups Dolšak studied, may be similarly mobilized.

Heathen gifting practices support pro-environmental values that can influence behavior and may help shift social norms. Heathens and other practitioners of new religious movements are not just individualists in a marketplace of spiritual ideas, but instead are "engaged in causes that in some way are reflective of their spirituality" (Berger 2019, 155). Berger notes that what has been called "religious individualism" results in greater political commitment (154–155). Heathens and other Pagans are part of larger trends toward decentralized religion. Berger (2019) discusses this in terms of tendencies toward disorganization and fragmentation: "The groups are often unstable, falling apart. . . . They may be re-created with some of the same people and some new ones" (157). However, she argues (162) that the social networks underlying these groups have enduring effects. I would suggest that, rather than characterizing such groups in terms of religious individualism, it may make more sense to look at how they are developing engaged relational ontologies that are not "disorganized" or "unstable" so much as distributed, flexible, and adaptive incipient emergences of ecological conscience.

Ecology as Way of Life

If Heathen ritual practices nudge participants toward the activation of pro-environmental values, this suggests that such practices can support the development of an ecological way of life. A shared lifeway emerges from the community of practice, shaping and co-constructing participants' sense of what counts as important, what actions become second nature, and what becomes unthinkable. A pro-environmental orientation emerges from Heathen practice in this community in nonexplicit and nondiscursive ways. It is not just about conscious choices, but grounds a more basic orientation that influences decision-making, including who has agency and with whom we are in relation that deserve moral consideration. Relational ontology shapes the range of dispositions that structure our relations with others. Evidence of such an orientation can be found in the lifestyle of participants because ritual influences participants' way of life. "Lifestyle" refers to people's habitual way of living, of conducting oneself, or of relating with others. While participation in Heathen ritual does not necessarily produce conscious adherence to environmentalism or participation in political activism, there is some evidence that it supports ecology as a way of life. Lifestyle is where we should expect to find evidence of this.

It is hard to identify unconscious pro-environmental effects that demonstrate an ecological conscience because it emerges organically through tacit learning in practice, rather than the more conscious expressions of a political point of view. As someone who is embedded in the way of life as a Heathen practitioner, I found some of these things hard to notice. I needed to think about what, at Raven's Knoll and Vindisir events, differs from how events might be run in other contexts. It was particularly difficult to notice what is not there and what has become unthinkable yet continues in other contexts. Pro-environmental behavior is also not always apparent to me as environmental behavior because it is just "how things are done" in my social circles. Recycling is perhaps like this for most people my age in modern affluent society. In my social circles, composting, which I grew up with, has also become second nature. Similarly, up-cycling (repurposing previously used items), reuse, thrifting, clothing swaps (hand-me-downs), foraging, local sourcing, ethical consumption (prioritizing environmental, humane, local production and worker protections), and rejection of disposables (including cutlery and dishes, but also replacing paper towels with reusables, reusable menstrual products, and cloth diapers) are all common practices in my social circles that are not necessarily widely shared in affluent society. Such practices are less noticeable to me because I am immersed in them but may also present a hazard for me in assuming that my pro-environmental behaviors are shared with other practitioners in my community. I noticed a general tendency toward anti-capitalist sentiment in the community but did not explicitly inquire about people's political orientations. I also did not ask about day-to-day environmental actions or political involvement in interviews because I had no expectation that Heathens would be any more pro-environmental than other Pagans. Practitioners' environmental concerns were most evident in their expressed preferences for local, homegrown, sustainably foraged, and humanely sourced offerings, which are things I did ask about.

Heathen Consumerism

Lifestyle has been turned into a marketing tool to identify population sectors that have particular value profiles (and corresponding consumption habits), which has led to lifestyle being denigrated as being simply about consumer choices. Marketers have perhaps been better at recognizing the influence of value orientations on behavior than have those seeking political change. Marketing creates or identifies new lifestyles to sell more products.[2] Consumer society teaches us to buy things to express our identity and to think that we can buy happiness by emulating an image of what is advertised to us. (How many times have I bought athletic clothing for camping that I more often wear sitting around the house than outdoors?) Lifestyle marketing has coopted environmental lifestyle as a marketing tool—known as "greenwashing"—to encourage the consumption of specific products for consumers to signal their green identity, thus enabling companies to sell additional versions of similar products (Maniates 2001, 34).

Heathens are not immune to lifestyle marketing, and there is some evidence of consumerism linked to producing Heathen identity. This includes the Heathens of Raven's Knoll, as documented by Joshua Harmsworth (2015, 165–167). When I began to identify as Heathen, I bought a mjolnir (a pendant in the shape of Thor's hammer) and began wearing it to signify that identity. Other markers of Heathen identity evident at Raven's Knoll and in Vindisir are drinking horns, ritual garb, amber jewelry, tattoos, and Heathen music such as that produced by the Norwegian band Wardruna. There are lots of things marketed to Heathens, such as themed t-shirts, other clothing and ritual garb, mugs, and stuffed toys. This market segment is profitable enough that an American company trademarked the word "Heathen" in 2006, to secure the rights to sell clothing and other items with the word on it. In 2019, they successfully applied to extend that trademark to apply to stickers and other items. The Swedish company Grimfrost secured the rights to the word in the European Union after being threatened with legal action by the American company. Their intention was to prevent the same situation developing in Europe as in the United States and to allow free use of the term. Since they were unable to determine any means of legally keeping the term in the public domain, they sought to launch a nonprofit foundation to protect the use of the word (Grimfrost 2020; Wild Hunt 2020).

Reuse and Thrifting

Choice architecture promotes pro-environmental behavior through the absence of disposables at Raven's Knoll and Vindisir events. Communal meals are a regular feature at these events, but there is no use of disposable dishes and cutlery. Organizers at Raven's Knoll have set things up so that the default choice favors pro-environmental behavior in that no disposables are provided, and they ask people to bring their own dishes and cutlery. At Hail and Horn they provide some reusable options, including cloth napkins for everyone, as well as bins of wooden dishes, cutlery, and serving dishes (largely sourced from thrift stores) for people to use for communal meals. This preference for thrifted items carries over into things such as the repurposed fabric used for pit cooking at Well and Tree Gathering, as well as gifts within the community, such as drinking horns, animal skulls, and furs.

Reusable beverage containers are the norm in this community. The organizers of Hail and Horn Gathering provide drinking water during blót rituals in the Vé at Raven's Knoll because the weather is often very hot and the Vé can be very sunny. They do not buy bottled water for this, but instead volunteers fill dozens of used two-liter soft drink bottles with tap water. At other times, people typically bring their own reusable water bottles and other beverage containers. Home-brewed mead and other alcoholic drinks are also typically presented in reusable bottles such as reused wine bottles or flip-top bottles. This form of home-brew consequently has a small carbon footprint. Other reusables evident in the community include some use of cloth diapers and menstrual products such as the Diva cup, although I did not collect data to give a sense of the prevalence of the use of these less-visible reusable items. Everyone in Vindisir that I interviewed who has children used cloth diapers.

Relations with Animals

Pets are welcome at Raven's Knoll so long as they can handle being there without harm to themselves or others. Dogs are the only pets I have seen there, and these have been well-treated. Any tendency not to treat animals well is condemned. On one occasion, for example, I heard someone express concern that another had not given a new rescue animal sufficient attention when bringing them to an event at Raven's Knoll. First aid at events includes volunteer veterinary care. Practitioners show a decided preference for rescue animals, although some pets come from reputable breeders. Sumbel gifts referenced donations to shelters, and toasts recognized extensive volunteer work with animal shelters.

In some cases, relations with wild animals may seem to be based more on mythic associations and imagination than empirical knowledge, but actual relations with animals living in the wild is not easy to observe because people have little contact with them. All the animal parts used in rituals that I was able to obtain information on are ethically sourced, if not strictly legal. Regarding the bird bones she has, Jessica noted that "It is technically illegal to pick up a crow" since the government wants to track the spread of West

Nile virus, but she "did report that it was there." She identifies as a crow, and "crows take care of their own" so she felt that picking up the uncollected crow was a matter a of taking care of their own: "so my crow was taking care of their crow." She said that "the flock just yelled at me but I left offerings and thanked them and told them what was going to happen. They quieted right down, that was all the permission I needed." She has acquired a lot of bones but does not purchase them. She said, "as for the rest of my bones they've all come to me in various ways. Found, gifted, rehomed. All ethically. When you start working with the dead they all find their way to you" (personal communication, December 7, 2020).

Many of the Heathens in this community like fur and show a preference for real fur rather than fake fur, which is made from plastic and is not good for the environment. Rather than buying new fur items, they mostly use handed down fur, thrifted fur, and up-cycled items. Some of it is sourced from roadkill. One hide of significance to Vindisir is from a fawn that had been struck by a car and that kindred members found on their way back home from Hail and Horn Gathering. They found him dying and did what they could to ease his passing. They named him Skuldwif and shared his flesh for a Powwow event in exchange for help with processing the hide. They salvaged his skull and other bones for ritual items. Those involved explained that they see Skuldwif as a gift to Vindisir from Skaði, a sign of thanks that the kindred was successful in advocating that Skaði be the next deity honored with a pole in the Vé at Raven's Knoll. The name "Skuldwif" means "return gift to the women."

Some people are more concerned about ethical sourcing of ritual items than others, and the desire to "look the part" can overtake people's sense of obligation to source things ethically. I am not aware of anyone unethically sourcing animal parts, but I did hear one person express concern that the desire for such items might be fulfilled inappropriately. When it comes to buying things, I more often have heard concerns about not supporting racist suppliers than concern over other aspects of ethical sourcing. A lack of financial resources can make people less picky, but choice architecture comes into play with who sells things at Kaleidoscope Gathering, which is a major source for such items. There is no market at Hail and Horn or Well and Tree because these events are too small to make it worthwhile for venders, but Kaleidoscope Gathering is bigger, and venders at that event are vetted for ethical sourcing.

Relations with Food

A small number of practitioners raise some of their own food animals due to ethical concerns both for environmental issues and animal welfare. These include chickens (for eggs and meat), rabbits (for meat and fur), and goats (for meat and ritual items). Some keep bees for honey. Some are vegetarian or vegan to reduce their impact on the environment and/or because they feel it is unethical to consume animal products. Some source most of the animal products they consume from ethical sources, and others would prefer to but cannot afford to do so. Some ingredients for the húsel feast at Hail and Horn Gathering come from Costco because it is cheap enough to provide the large quantities needed affordably. Meat served at Well and Tree Gathering comes from Costco for this reason. Ethically raised local and organic food is preferred but is often prohibitively expensive. This is an area in which systemic change through government regulation imposing more humane and pro-environmental standards could help bring costs down, whereas leaving it to consumer choice may simply diversify market segmentation. Some people feel it is pointless to choose organic options when the same companies that own the cheaper regular foods sell organic versions of them at premium prices, while others choose organic options because they think they are healthier or better for the environment.

Some ingredients for húsel at Hail and Horn are ethically sourced, in particular those that are shared as offerings in blót. Since some practitioners are vegan, there are always vegan dishes provided as part of the feast. One of these is prepared as a sacred dish, and includes plants sustainably foraged at Raven's Knoll, such as goosefoot (leaves of a kind of amaranth, also known as lamb's quarters or pigweed), linden leaves, sweet fern, wood sorrel, and mushrooms, which were cooked together to into "Nine Worlds Stew" for the 2018 húsel at Hail and Horn. For that same event Auz had prepared switchel, a drink made from honey and cider vinegar, with added sweet fern from the Algonquin Tea Company, which is a local wildcrafted (foraged) source. Other wildcrafted items in that húsel included juniper that Auz used to make an elk pate, as well as bog myrtle harvested from the Bonnechere River, and local wild blueberries (Auz, interview July 23, 2018).

Ethical sourcing is always a prime concern for meat offered in blót at Hail and Horn Gathering. For the past three years goats have been served. These are humanely raised by community members in the local area, and parts of them are offered in blót. They are not slaughtered as part of the blót, but they are blessed and given names in a separate ritual on the farm where they are raised. This blessing, as when god poles are raised in blót, parallels a Heathen baby-naming rite. When I asked Auz why the god poles are asperged he said it was "to wake them" and explained that

> [t]he Norwegians and Icelanders would sprinkle water over a baby and give it a name. And after they gave it a name it became part of society, it became part of the social structure. Before that a baby was a being that was tied to the parents, but they didn't have a social rank. . . . Only after you had a name were you a social being. (interview July 23, 2018)

Naming and asperging recognize the goats as relational beings, as persons embedded in wyrd, just as, in Norse mythology, when the gods asperged the driftwood to make Ask and Embla persons in relation, who have orlog and are entwined in wyrd.

Animal sacrifice is rare in contemporary Heathenry (Calico 2018, 440; Snook 2015, 63; Strmiska 2005b, 40, 2007), and Winterfinding is the only Vindisir blót that includes it. For this ritual rabbits or chickens are humanely raised by one of the kindred members. They are humanely killed in ritual and offered to the goddesses favored by the kindred, then cooked and shared in the húsel feast. Vindisir's animal sacrifice exemplifies what Calico calls "farm to altar to table" practice (Calico 2018, 440), prioritizing sustainable food production and ethical consumption. As Calico found with Heathens who practice animal sacrifice, for Vindisir participants the animal must be well treated and have a good death to make a good offering.[3]

Shrine Leavings

The appearance of nonbiodegradable items left as offerings at outdoor altars and shrines causes me some environmental discomfort, and I have some reservations about the ecological impact of using the Sacred Well at Raven's Knoll as a repository for offerings. As Jenny Blain has observed, "one person's votive offering is another's eyesore" (Blain 2000, 25). She expressed dissatisfaction with finding "a collection of ritual litter, primarily candles and wax," left at Avebury, a Neolithic henge site in England. She suggested that "whatever was foremost in the minds of those who had performed their rituals around specific stones of this great circle the night before, it was not environmental care—at least not in any way that envisaged practitioners' own actions as potentially causing problems" (Blain 2000, 25).

I see this as a matter for me to address within my community as a practitioner, and I suspect that doing so discursively is probably not the most effective approach. Shaming people is probably less effective than modeling by leaders what offerings to give and how to give offerings. Auz spoke of giving one of the provided apple pieces as a personal offering to Nerthus and, similarly, offering to Skaði a piece of the ice provided by the ritual organizers as a way of modeling that this is a totally fine way of making a personal offering and to show that participants do not need to buy something to offer (interview July 23, 2018). I chose to give Skaði an offering of poetry that I had written for similar reasons. I had hesitated to share the poem because I am not at all sure that I have any skill for composing poetry, but I wanted to model giving a nonmaterial offering that was personally significant to me. Reading the poem aloud was for me an act of bravery and thus suitable as an offering to Skaði, who is a fierce figure in Norse mythology. Giving offerings in this way, modeling how to give in a sustainable and environmentally friendly way, may be more effective than criticizing others for leaving offerings that do not decompose.

Relations with the Land

Raven's Knoll is the cleanest campground I have ever been to, and although this is anecdotal information, it is not a small sample size since I have camped extensively in Ontario, Quebec, Pennsylvania, and New York for decades. Part of this lack of litter is due to choice architecture implemented by Auz and MA and crews of volunteers at the Knoll. Because of the fire hazard that cigarette butts pose, metal cans are provided to collect this waste and visitors are reminded in event programs to use these cans exclusively. I have never seen a cigarette butt on the ground there. Garbage cans are also provided, as well as an onsite recycling depot, although visitors are requested to pack out their waste as much as possible. I am not the only person who packs out compostables and recyclables. There are also unwritten rules against littering in the community. Although I have not seen any mention of picking up after the dogs that people bring to Raven's Knoll, there is no evidence of pet waste problems there. It is possible that some people clean up after others. I have cleaned up a few stray beverage cans myself in the morning around the communal fire pit.

Volunteers help care for the land at Raven's Knoll. Anthropologist Harry Weaver, in his research on material culture at Raven's Knoll, found that "communal work weekends . . . promote a sense of stewardship in maintaining Raven's Knoll" and that "the groups at the Knoll resacralize the land they occupy, and promote an appreciation for the natural spaces" (Weaver 2018, 14).[4] Work weekends are events organized for volunteers to contribute to the upkeep, improvements, and care of Raven's Knoll. Volunteers get to camp for free when they participate in these events, so this can be seen as part of the development of an incipient gift economy in the community. I live too far away to participate in work weekends at Raven's Knoll, but I suspect they would reveal more about peoples' relationships with the land.

Some Knollians and Vindisir participants fantasize about buying land and starting a commune, and a few are experimenting with forays into raising their own food; some are experienced gardeners, but most live in cities. The Heathens of Raven's Knoll have formed attachments to the land, and some fondly refer to visiting there as going "home." The Knoll is home in an emotional sense and contributes to having a sense of fictive kinship with chosen family there and connection to the community, including the ecosystem community. The attachment they have formed to the land at Raven's Knoll is one of belonging to the land and community, rather than the land belonging to them.

Knollians may regard Raven's Knoll as home, but they do not see it as a homeland and evince little interest in developing a bioregional attachment to place, despite identifying Nerthus with the Ottawa Valley. Environmentalism is a common concern between right- and left-leaning Pagans, as Adrian Ivakhiv (2005a) has observed. Although inclusive and folkish Heathens may share a sense of attachment to place and a common identity as Heathens, how they understand and express this connection is not the same. Speaking against the "Mexican" presence in California, Stephen McNallen wrote, "We must sink down roots in the soil, and insist on our right to be here. . . . Our forebears fought and died to carve out this place in the world, and we will not give it up" (McNallen 1998). This was in an essay originally distributed in *The Runestone*, a newsletter distributed by the Asatru Free Assembly, now the Asatru Folk Assembly. As Jefferson Calico notes regarding this text, "McNallen's rhetoric of soil and roots harkens to the blood and soil, 'Blut und Boden' language of völkisch Germany" (Calico 2020, 32). Despite continuing to deny such associations with Nazi ideology, the Asatru Folk Assembly recently purchased two small-town churches, one in Murdoch, Minnesota, and the other in Linden, North Carolina, to operate as "whites only" religious groups (Ball 2021).

Michael Strmiska explains that folkish Heathenry grew out of the "development of ethnic identity as a rallying point for national independence movements, and even revolutions, that would seek to carve out new nation-states organized around ethnic identity" (Strmiska 2020, 4). It developed out of the use of ethnic identity and folklore to create a sense of national identity in the nineteenth century. "This intermingled," Strmiska says, "with the romantic reevaluation of nature to create a new glorification of land and nature in connection to identity [and] ethnic history, that is to say, the 'blood and soil' idea" (Strmiska 2020, 4). Folkish Heathens thus appropriate a Nazi version of an imagined Germanic heritage and attempt to recreate it in the United States, whereas the Heathens of Raven's Knoll and Vindisir have more in common with other Pagans. Blood and land are not important to identity for inclusive Heathens. There is a clear dichotomy between folkish and inclusive Heathens, with those on each side regarding the other in mutually exclusive terms. While they may disagree on how they describe themselves versus how the other side sees them, they tend to agree on who belongs on what side.

Repugnance for blood and soil ideology may prevent the development of bioregional identity within inclusive groups such the Heathens of Raven's Knoll and Vindisir, yet they have much in common with bioregionalist approaches of promoting pro-environmental lifestyles in terms of positive framing of what people can do differently to "overgrow" the system rather than confront and oppose it through political mobilization, as Bron Taylor (2001) describes in work detailing the differences between bioregionalists and radical environmentalists.

Transit

The organizers and sometimes the participants of events organize ride-sharing via social media to get to the venues. Most seem to travel to Raven's Knoll by car, as households, perhaps due to the practical limitations of transporting camping equipment and the lack of public transit to the venue. Vindisir members who have access to cars often drive others to events. Some preference for hybrid vehicles is evident in Vindisir, and some choose to commute by motorcycle to reduce carbon emissions, but most of us walk, cycle, and use public transit to get around day to day. Members of Vindisir tend to drive less than average. Fewer than half of us are licensed to drive or own a vehicle, but this may be due to reasons other than pro-environmental concerns. Several members are Millennials, who are less inclined to drive or who obtain licenses later than other demographics (Gilboy 2020; Roberts 2019). This is partly because car use is expensive and less necessary in densely populated areas such as Toronto, where some members live.

Socioeconomic Factors and Survey Data

Sociological research on religion and environmentalism has found that individual religious commitments correlate only weakly with environmentalism and that political affiliation and socioeconomic status are better predictors of pro-environmental attitudes (Berry 2013, 458). Some practitioners would likely be content for Heathenry to be simply their religion and not concern themselves with environmental politics. Andy Letcher (2000), studying contemporary Paganism in the United Kingdom, found practitioners to be less politically active than he expected, though this may be because of his focus on strategies of direct action. However, Helen Berger, Evan Leach, and Leigh Shaffer's (2003) census found higher than average environmental activism in Pagans compared with the general population.

Regina Oboler (2004) suggests that higher levels of environmental activism among Pagans may simply correlate with higher levels of education. Like Berger, Leach, and Shaffer, Oboler found that Pagans are more likely to take environmental action than the general population. She speculated that any discrepancy between stated environmental views and greater environmental action of Pagans might be due to higher education levels because environmental concern generally rises with higher education levels. This may be the case for the Heathens of Raven's Knoll and Vindisir.

Oboler suggested that her ethnographic research indicated that Paganism's pro-environmental reputation may have attracted people to it who already were pro-environmental before becoming Pagan, which may also be true of my research community. Berger's more recent survey (2019, 153) indicates that Pagans are significantly more politically active than others and that more Pagans identify with environmentalism than with the other social movements she studied (149). Similarly to Oboler, Berger suggests this may be because environmentalism has become part of Pagan identity as practitioners of Earth-based or nature religion. While all Pagans are more likely to be politically active than average, she found that "More Canadian and British contemporary Pagans participate in alternative political groups and environmental groups than American contemporary Pagans" and "Contemporary Pagans in the United Kingdom are more active in environmental groups than those in the United States or Canada" (152).

Berger (2019, 134) suggests that while the statistics cannot prove causation, it may be that participation in group practices encourages more environmentalist activity through the reinforcement of other group members. It is noteworthy that Heathen and Pagan respondents to my survey, and Heathens to a greater degree (55% strongly agree, 30% agree that ritual practices are important) than other Pagans (48% strongly agree, 35% agree), find ritual practices to be significantly more important than the general population (8% strongly agree, 17% agree), which suggests that such practices may be important for activating environmental values.[5] Environmental protection and reciprocity are widely held values in modern society (Vandenbergh 2005, 1117–1118), and it may be that if they were brought to mind more often in ritual people would act on these values more often in their day-to-day lives.

My survey results provide some evidence that Heathens and other Pagans present a consumer profile that differs from the general public, being more likely to prioritize ethical concerns when making consumer decisions (Table 4.1). Heathen and other Pagan survey respondents strongly agreed that giving thanks is important more than did the random sample of Canadians. Heathens and other Pagans were (self-reportedly) more than twice as likely to support ethical consumption, prioritizing humane production, environmental effects, and supporting local businesses over cost and quality than the random Canadian sample. In my survey, 84% of Heathens and other Pagans said their sense of community includes plants, animals, the land, and water (an indication of espousing Leopold's "land ethic"), compared to two-thirds of random Canadians. Almost two-thirds of Heathen and other Pagans strongly agreed that environmental protection should be a high priority for government, while considerably less than half of random Canadians said so. The greatest difference between Heathen and Pagan respondents in comparison with the random sample was that ritual practice is much more important to them than to the general population. Berger's (2019, 75) most recent survey data corroborate the importance of

Table 4.1 Summary of significant differences between general population and Heathen and Pagan sample

	Heathens and Pagans	Random Canadians
Giving thanks is important strongly agree:	46%	36%
Ethical consumption most important consideration:	44%	21%
Support for "land ethic" strongly agree or agree:	84%	66%
Prioritize environmental protection strongly agree:	64%	35%
Ritual practices are important agree or strongly agree:	65%	25%

These figures are based on cross-tabulations conducted in SPSS, with chi-square and z-tests to check for statistical significance. All figures cited have p values of less than 0.05. The sample sizes for the international sample of Heathens and other Pagans ($n = 643$) and the random sample of Canadians ($n = 241$) are not large enough to give an error margin of less than 6% and, strictly speaking, are not directly comparable.

ritual for Heathens, reporting that Heathens are more likely to meet frequently for ritual practice than are other Pagans.

Conclusion

Trying to show how pro-environmental a group of people is can become a pointless posturing of "we are better than you." It seems like a sort of competitive status-seeking that is more likely to generate shaming, scapegoating, and backfire or boomerang effects than to produce pro-environmental behavior. When people believe they are doing more for the environment than others, they tend to stop trying to improve (Schultz et al. 2007) and can even be prompted to higher consumption levels when they are convinced their actions in one area are morally offset by other green choices (McFarland Taylor 2019, 74). There are lots of specific groups in various religious communities that are pro-environmental—quite probably some more so than the Heathens of Raven's Knoll and Vindisir. Although I find some evidence of the development of an ecological way of life in the lifestyle of these Heathens, their ritual practices are not directly linked to resource use and do not function to self-regulate social ecological systems because practitioners remain embedded in modern society. But personal actions do have environmental impacts, and there is potential in shifting personal and societal norms to change the contours of what collective actions become politically viable. To paraphrase zero-waste chef Anne-Marie Bonneau (2021), it is possible that we do not need a savior who is perfectly virtuous so much as we need billions of us imperfectly practicing environmentalism. Maybe we do not need more environmental crusaders so much as we need more community builders with ecological conscience, such as can be found among the Heathens of Raven's Knoll and Vindisir.

5

From Here to There and Back Again

I set out to understand how Heathen ritual practices of making offerings and giving gifts are related to ecological conscience formation and how they contribute to the development of ecological habitus among practitioners. What I found is that gifting rituals in this community embody tacit knowledge of how to relate through practice and support an inclusive sense of imagined community that extends into the more-than-human world. Participation in sumbel at Hail and Horn and other ritual gifting practices inspires gratitude and a desire to give in turn. Making offerings, giving gifts to ancestors and landvaettir, supports an inclusive sense of imagined community such that practitioners' sense of moral community includes the more-than-human world. Terror management theory and other studies of priming effects offer an explanation of how moral order is enacted through ritual, but examination of "mistakes" in ritual, such as the initial procession of Nerthus at Raven's Knoll, shows how our sense of how we should relate with the more-than-human world is negotiated through ritual practice. Ritual does not just tell us, or even just show or teach us, how we should relate, but it can be a means of negotiating how we should relate. Through ritual practice practitioners can co-construct a shared sense of how we should relate with the more-than-human world.

Experiential knowledge shaped through ritual can inspire ethical sensibility and motivate pro-environmental action. Conscience can be shaped by learning how to relate in rituals of giving gifts and expressing gratitude. Participation in Heathen gifting rituals can inspire ethical sensibility and prompt the desire to give in turn. It can promote pro-environmental behavior through the development of a gift ethic. While not fully formed or perfectly expressed, this ethic is emerging through Heathen ritual practices as practitioners co-construct it in the community of practice.

In conducting this research, I took the cognitive risk of seriously asking "What if doing ritual matters?" Prior to this work, I was not ritually inclined and had only rarely made offerings, and usually only at the prompting of others in group practice. For this research I participated in ritual even

Wyrd Ecology. Barbara Jane Davy, Oxford University Press. © Oxford Univesity Press 2025.
DOI: 10.1093/9780197804957.003.0006

though I had no particular belief in deities or experience of the presence of ancestors. I was fairly sure of the presence of landvaettir as powers of the land (understood in terms of naturalistic animism) at the outset, but I was not a theistic Pagan. I approached participation with curiosity about what would happen if I did ritual and acted as if the gods are real. My perspective has changed somewhat through practice, but not entirely. I started out with the attitude that belief in deities was not necessarily important to religious practice. I still think that it does not necessarily matter if the gods are real or not; ritual practices have real effects, and participation in ritual does not require explicit belief or articulated agreement with the beliefs of other participants. In practice, belief does not matter, but, to misquote Carl Jung, life tastes better with gods in it. This is not a delusion, but a choice to inhabit a meaningful world, a multidimensional more-than-human world, and to be grateful for the gifts I have received, wherever they come from.

The foregoing chapters develop an idealized interpretation of what inclusive Heathenry offers for the pursuit of environmental sustainability. I describe how Heathen gifting rituals can support the development of ecological conscience, but one might ask "so what?" Any religion, ideally practiced, will generate ethical behaviors, albeit some more pro-environmental than others. I hope some readers will find a positive resonance with the metaphors of wyrd embedded in English and other Indo-European languages that will help facilitate an understanding of relational ontology in this tradition. Heathen understandings of wyrd and gifting practices can draw on the substantive rationality built into the English language—metaphors of "turning into," "strands of" this, "threads of" that, "patterns woven into" as structural metaphors of relationality that remain despite a few centuries of dominance by economic metaphors that lead us to speak of environmental "costs" or of getting "purchase" on or "buy in" to ideas.

I hope to have initiated a process of interpretive drift in skeptical readers, to interrupt the business-as-usual attitudes of individualized ontology and make sense of Heathen ritual practices. I want readers to get to a point where they can shift perspective and experience the tug of ecological conscience without feeling cognitive dissonance about the possibility that giving offerings creates the awareness of the obligations that sustain our social ecological systems. Following Tim Ingold's (2000) suggestion that all knowledge arises from following a particular path, I tried to structure this work to lead people down a path in which it makes sense to think that we should make offerings to nonhuman others in order to include them in our moral communities. The path becomes much clearer in practice. Making offerings, giving gifts to nonhuman others, includes them in our imagined community. It is a practical means of enacting Leopold's land ethic, recognizing ourselves as members of our ecological communities.

Inviting Wyrd Relations

When we make offerings to nonhuman others we invite them into relation with us. This is not just make-believe, pretending we see other-than-human persons until they appear. It is a process of interpretive drift, but it is also a matter of learning to be more open to possibility—what Tim Ingold (2000, 219) discusses in terms of cognitive attunement. This involves a certain looseness of interpretation of what is going on, what is real, and what is imaginary.

There is such a thing as being so open-minded that one's head becomes full of nonsense or too much "woo." Practitioners are often quite circumspect about sharing accounts of encounters with other-than-human persons for fear of being dismissed as "flaky." When Heathens share such experiences they often identify them as "UPG," meaning "unverified personal gnosis,"[1] but, in discussion, some of these experiences are transformed into a shared imaginary. When they become part of the shared "as if" of ritual, they can become collective learning. The Heathens of Raven's Knoll and Vindisir are engaged in a negotiation of what counts as real and who can be persons in the development of a new relational ontology. This remains a matter of interpretation, but, in Heathen practice, it need not be an either/or in terms of what is "really" happening.

By way of example, I offered my dad some peach on the hearg in my backyard several months after he died. His father used to grow peaches in this region, and, thinking of how much my dad enjoyed having a fresh-picked peach ripe enough that just rocking it slightly by cradling it in the hand brings it off the tree, I wanted to share. I heard a squirrel chattering in a nearby tree and thought they will likely eat it. This led me to recall Ahmad Ibn Fadlan's writings on the Rus, which I learned of first from Auz in discussion of how offerings left in the Vé at Raven's Knoll are eaten by wild animals. Food offerings there are left out only for a short time to avoid attracting bears, but birds and small animals eating offerings are welcome signs that the offerings have been accepted. Auz recounted that when Ibn Fadlan questioned the

Rus about the appropriateness of dogs eating their offerings and suggested that the offerings were not getting to the ancestors or gods, they laughed saying that the fact the animals ate it means the offering was accepted (see Ibn Fadlan 2017, 33–34). This example shows a nonliteral understanding of what "really" happens in making offerings, rather than getting stuck in cognitive dissonance of who "literally" gets the offering. It is both eaten by wildlife and accepted by the ancestors—in the case of the peach, my dad. Only a "literate" interpretation insists on one or the other rather than a more poetic, and more meaningful, interpretation.

For some, playful engagement may be a necessary first step, a "way in" as Grimes says, to taking ritual more seriously.

> Too full of bilgewater and balderdash? Well, okay, for the likes of us who've made it to the next millennium, it may be that ritual is possible only in a ludic-ironic-metaphoric, clowny-subjunctive-disjunctive fiddledeedee mode. But embraced-to-the-point-of-embodiment, metaphoric-ironic-ritualizing, however perverse and silly, is a way in. (Grimes 2002, 158)

Or perhaps we get more out of ritual by not taking it too seriously. It may be that we do not all need to get the same affect out of participating in a ritual for it to be effective.

Refusing to give offerings to see how it changes perception and one's sense of obligations can be likened to Galileo's critics, who refused to look through his telescope (Deming 2012, 165) to see the moons of Jupiter and the phases of Venus that proved the planets circle the sun because they were afraid to let their view of the world be questioned. Ontology and epistemology are entangled, not separate. How we are or understand ourselves to be in relation to others governs how we know, what we know, how we perceive, and what we perceive. This is the basic insight of phenomenology underlying Levinas's (1989, 75–87) insistence that ethics must precede ontology and epistemology. As I have argued previously (Davy 2007), who we can meet as a person depends on how we approach them and whether or not we invite them into relation.

Levinas identifies openness to being put in question by the views of another with ethical relations. Not to take the views of the other seriously, to refuse to allow one's own views to be put in question, what he calls "being at home with itself," is precisely that for which Levinas criticizes modern Western ontology. Sociologist of religion Marcus Davidsen (2012) criticizes

Norwegian theologian Jone Salomonsen for allowing her understanding of the world to be put in question by Pagans. But taking the cognitive risk of immersing herself in Pagan practice—not just behaviorally in conducting participant observation, or even just emotionally in empathy with participants—allowed her to take belief seriously in terms of emotion and cognition. Investigating ontological otherness and alternatives requires this sort of risk and helps us understand other ways of relating. Ritual practices, in periodically interrupting the business-as-usual attitudes of modern individualized ontology, can allow different attitudes to come to mind and influence behavior toward a more sustainable way of life.

Motivating Action through Affect

Ritual practice can generate attachments that motivate behavior and can provide a means for coming to agreement (negotiating) about meaning and how we should relate (ethical praxis). As Seligman et al. (2008) say, ritual helps us negotiate a shared "as if." Levinas argues that in face-to-face relations, the other puts one's view of the world in question, and this creates ethics. The other's challenge to one's view of the world "puts in common a world hitherto mine" (Levinas 1969, 174). Ritual practice in community can do this collectively, beyond Levinas's dyadic description of face-to-face relations. Ritual can negotiate or co-construct a shared sense of what is real, how the world should be, and how we should relate with one another. Faith in scientific objectivity undermines this process when ritual is presented as pointless superstition. It makes way for economics and the pursuit of profit without ethical obligations in desocialized transactions.

If we want to change peoples' behavior, science is not enough. Science provides a way for people of diverse cultures to come to consensus about empirical reality, but over-reaches with claims that empirical reality is all that "counts" as real. The problem is not that science does not tell us real or true things—it does. The problem is the frequently accompanying belief that it tells us everything that is important or that nothing else matters, that values, power, and politics do not matter. Science provides us with a method for objective progression of verifiable understanding of what is happening, but does not explain the *significance* of what is happening.

As I have argued (Davy 2021), there is a gap between detached knowledge and action. This gap can be bridged through involvement and attachment.

We have lots of detached knowledge about climate change, but this in itself does not motivate a shift to more pro-environmental behavior because we are not entirely rational. Our actions are not just the result of rational decision-making but are also based on felt obligations or stimulated by unconscious forces such as mortality salience and consumerism. Knowing this does not make the unconscious motivations go away. To get from "is" to "ought" requires tacit learning of ethical sensibility through involved knowledge that becomes embodied in our actions. Cultural factors shape how we see the facts and what we regard as important and real. Cognitive frame shifts can be initiated by ritual practices and change our affect to motivate behavioral change.

Rational deliberation may generate consensus or assent to common principles, but science and reason do not determine human behavior. Science does not necessarily yield a worldview capable of protecting the natural world, but religious activities might (Rappaport 1979, 98–101). Local stories about scary encounters may regulate our behavior better than data in a graph, and giving offerings may help us to regenerate and preserve adaptive relations in social ecological systems better than scaring people with climate data. Stories about scary monsters are effective in keeping people away from dangerous areas when we cannot measure or control the danger. Science may provide ways to measure when it might be safe to return to a spot, but does not in itself motivate us to change our behavior to stop producing the dangers of environmental harms. Scientific understanding of climate change, for example, has not succeeded in motivating behavior to remedy the situation. People's involved knowledge is in conflict with their detached knowledge and is all too often a stronger motivator of human behavior.

Religious imagination, facilitated through story and ritual, can produce emotional attachment and felt obligations. Science can help us understand behavior, but cannot itself motivate behavior. Ritual practices can motivate behavior, generate ethical sensibility, and negotiate a shared sense of how to relate with others. Connecting my research on Heathen ritual to Margaret Wetherell's (2012, 2015) application of social psychology to affect theory seems a good direction for future inquiry, looking at ritual as "affective practice." Wetherell argues that practice generates affect. If "affect" can include ethical sensibility, I have contributed to affect theory in developing an understanding of how ethical sensibility is inspired by ritual practices.

The View from Here

I have tried to give an accurate description of the rituals I participated in and articulate the ethics of the ways of relating implicated in these rituals, but my account is inevitably positioned and partial. Each position affords different views. But even from within a community of practice, describing what is done constructs a narrative that inevitably leaves things out. Some Heathens are much more god-focused than I am and would likely present their traditions somewhat differently. Giving offerings may be less important in other Heathen communities, or may be more focused on deities who are imagined to be other-worldly or transcendent of nature.

Geertz's often-quoted phrase about how anthropology makes "small facts speak to large issues" concludes with the less often quoted "because they are made to" (Geertz 1973, 23). The ethnographer makes data speak through their description and interpretation. What I have given is my interpretation of the Heathens of Raven's Knoll and Vindisir, not a total description. I am preoccupied with ecological relations; not all Heathens are. In this work, I describe how I see ritual contributing to ecological conscience formation in inclusive Heathen practice. Obviously, Heathenry does not make practitioners into perfectly virtuous people (any more than any other religion does so). What I found is that Heathenry contributes to pro-environmental behavior in nonobvious ways. Investigating ritual practices may have revealed more pro-environmental aspects to Heathenry than just asking about people's values or ethical outlook would have.

Bias

As a practitioner I appreciate the best in the traditions I participate in, but I also have an obligation to recognize the limitations of Heathenry and the shortcomings of my perspective on it. Ultimately, it is up to other researchers to say whether I am unduly biased, but I can reflect on how my interpretation is partial, what my agenda is, and in what ways my account is self-serving.

I have a duty to hold my community to account because I am part of it. This includes looking more closely at inclusive Heathenry and the "othering" of "folkish" Heathens as racist. Labeling them as racist enables inclusive Heathens to feel less culpable for racism because we are not overtly racist, without necessarily examining how we benefit from systemic racism. Much as how Canadians use Americans as a foil that makes us feel better about ourselves, criticizing "folkish" Heathens allows inclusive Heathens to feel smugly superior. As in contemporary Paganism more generally, Heathenry can be an identity that enables affluent white people to identify as victims, as part of a marginalized religious community. It is uncomfortable to realize that we have privilege, and one way to make it easier is to adopt an identity that is not privileged. But the marginalization of Heathens in Canada is generally quite minor compared to racial discrimination. Some inclusive Heathens are well aware of these dynamics and self-critical about it. I learned more about this from inclusive Heathens (particularly Auz and Jade) than I knew before beginning this study. Most Heathen groups are predominantly white, and even when we say we are inclusive this does not entirely translate into everyone feeling welcome. There is still work to be done in making Heathenry more inclusive, even within Vindisir and the Raven's Knoll community. Hail and Horn Gathering has had to deal with death threats against trans folk at Raven's Knoll as recently as 2017. How to deal with this, and ongoing issues of racism in the wider community, is somewhat under negotiation. Some practitioners pursue education to combat prejudice when possible, but others prefer to exclude or eject those who do not respect inclusive values to keep practitioners within the group safe.

Davidsen's criticism of what he calls "loyalism" in Pagan studies presents another concern. I hope that readers will not dismiss my work for being biased simply because I am part of the community I study. Loyalty to my religious community might lead to confirmation bias, "cherry-picking" evidence to present only that which supports my interpretation. Regarding relational ontology, I find this present in Heathenry, but it would be an overstatement to say this is dominant in contemporary Heathens. Heathens live in modern society and are subject to the influence of dominant tendencies, including modern individualized ontology. But relational ontology is evident, too, and supported by contemporary interpretation of historical sources and contemporary ritual practices in the groups I studied. The more of us who are influenced by this view, the stronger its effects will become in society.

I studied only inclusive Heathens, so I do not have a comprehensive picture of contemporary Heathenry—but no ethnography can be completely comprehensive. And I highlight a previously understudied part of Heathenry in studying inclusive Heathens, which my survey suggests are actually dominant in terms of numbers of practitioners. Although my purposive snowball sampling method may have biased my survey results toward progressive practitioners because I have more personal connections in progressive segments of the Heathen and Pagan communities, I did attempt to address this by reaching out to groups I knew included "folkish" practitioners. My findings on the political orientations of Heathens are corroborated by Berger's (2019) most recent survey. In this respect, my research on inclusive Heathens is corrective in the sense that it serves as a counter to the "anchoring" bias of many early studies of Heathenry (with the exception of Blain [2002]) that presented it as dominated by racist attitudes. *Anchoring bias* refers to the tendency of an initial assessment to set an expectation of further assessments to fall within a nearby range.

Blain's (2002) study focused on *seiðr*, a form of esoteric ritual that is practiced in Vindisir and the Heathens of Raven's Knoll. Such practices in Canada have developed independently of how they are done in the Troth, as described by Blain, although recent increased contact between Jade Pichette and Troth members will likely influence how these rites proceed within Vindisir and at Raven's Knoll. My decision not to include esoteric rituals in my study gives an incomplete picture of Heathen ritual practices that may function to "normalize" Heathen practice to non-Heathen readers. *Sumbel* is an accessible ritual. So, too, is the procession of Nerthus, but these rituals are a good place to start for people who are not familiar with Heathenry. Esoteric rites such as seiðr do not appeal to everyone, and they tend to include more unverified personal gnosis than other rituals. They are also often more theatrical and more likely to result in what Emile Durkheim (1912) called "collective effervescence" or what Victor Turner (1969) called "communitas." My decision to defer discussion of *blóts* other than Dísablót to future work may also make the work more accessible and avoid possible controversy with discussion of animal sacrifice. However, it also removes what I see as some of the best evidence for the positive influence of ritual practices directly on consumption habits.[2]

Another form of bias I may be guilty of is *attribution bias*. Attributing the development of ecological habitus to Heathen ritual is somewhat self-serving, but perhaps no more so than any other positive research findings. I found that Heathen gifting rituals can support ecological conscience formation and that, for at least some Heathens, gifting relations extend beyond human social relations to include other species, but this research cannot demonstrate causality. Lisa Sideris's criticisms of proponents of what she calls the "new cosmologists" (who support the "epic of evolution" or "the Universe Story") may apply also to my work. She argues (Sideris 2017,

157–158) that, rather than being caused by the story of the new cosmology, pro-environmental attitudes preceded proponents' involvement with it. Heathens' pro-environmental tendencies may precede their involvement with Heathenry. As Helen Berger (2019, 149) suggested, practitioners may gravitate toward Pagan traditions because these traditions have become known as pro-environmental. Personal pro-environmental orientations may come from childhood experiences that form attachments to nature, as Sideris (2017, 197) suggests of proponents of the new cosmology.

Attribution bias may be at play also if I am guilty of setting up a "Humpty Dumpty" problem in making "ritual" mean what I want it to. The positive reception of this work by my research community would indicate that I have not distorted Heathen practice to fit my theory of ritual, but selection bias is a factor in my choice of religious community. The theory I developed fits because it was developed for this study.

Finding What I Want to See

Selection bias was a factor in that I chose to study a community that fit with my values. Vindisir invited me to join them because we already had a lot in common. Similarly, people in the Raven's Knoll community welcomed me, and I felt comfortable there because these are my kind of people. I had no interest in studying racist Heathens, and they are excluded from these groups. As I said in the Introduction, I picked Heathenry because I was interested in it and I thought it fit the description of an "enchanted" view of nature. I expected to focus on the immanence of divinity in nature and *genius loci*, but this is not what I found to be of most importance in community practice. I describe some of the ritual practices important to practitioners in the groups I studied, I asked them to reflect on the consequences of those ritual practices, and I made observations about the consequences apparent to me.

My understanding of the connection between gift economies and relational ontologies was formed prior to beginning participant observation research (see Davy and Quilley 2018). I was pleasantly surprised to find aspects of both in Heathenry. Gifting is important to Heathens from their understanding of the lore, and this accounts for why I received similar understandings of gifting from multiple practitioners. Shared practice is also a factor, particularly given the overlaps between participation in Vindisir and at Raven's Knoll.

It may seem too convenient to have found relational ontology in Heathenry, that I found what I wanted to see, but I found these practitioners appealing because of preexisting resonances in views, attitudes, and dispositions we shared. Participating in Heathen ritual practices brought much of this into greater clarity for me and provides ethnographic evidence supporting the argument (Davy and Quilley 2018) that gifting economies are mutually self-sustaining with relational ontologies. To presume that Heathens cannot be so "other" from the dominant norms of modernity and exhibit a relational ontology brings to mind the "sometimes we can still hear their voices" phenomenon that accompanies erasure and silencing. This quote, perhaps familiar from a popular Internet meme, comes from the character Mabel in Disney's film *Brother Bear* (Williams et al. 2003) who tells everyone her husband Edgar is dead. Edgar then speaks from off camera, saying "Quit telling everyone I'm dead!" which prompts her to say wistfully, "Sometimes, I can still hear his voice." To insist that Heathens cannot exhibit relational ontologies because individualized ontology has replaced relational ontologies functions to support the dominant individualized ontology I call into question.

Regarding concerns that my account lacks critical distance, I am not simply repeating what practitioners tell me to say. As I said at the outset, this work is a co-labor. It is the product of my relationship with my research community. Sarah Pike (2004a, 101), in discussion of her study of Pagan festivals, similarly speaks of her ethnographic work in terms of intersubjective meaning construction between researcher and community. As Chaudhry (2018) says of such work, the knowledge is co-constructed. My interpretation of these rituals emerged in the relations between myself and my research community. Much of it comes from them, but I also shaped and directed our encounters through who I pursued relations with and the questions I asked them. I also selected, arranged, and interpreted the quoted material in dialogue with academic literatures.

Just as my research community influenced how I came to interpret ritual practices, my integration into the community is influencing how it develops. This is an observer-expectancy effect, or what some might call "polluting the data" by influencing the group. The Heathens of Vindisir and Raven's Knoll may be more likely to become more pro-environmental over time through my participation, not just because it is important to me but because when people know it is important to my work, this may influence them to include or emphasize things in ritual that will further my work. An example of this might be including Jörð, a *jötunn* associated with earth and the ground, and talking about climate change in Vindisir's 2019 Winterfinding ritual. I have a pro-environmental agenda, and if I am advancing this within my religious community I do not see it as a bad thing. This might be a problem if I was trying to measure or quantify how environmentalist Heathens are rather than see how they are environmentalist (the process of how their rituals can foster ecological habitus). My participation may have made pro-environmentalist tendencies more evident, but it also suggests some possibilities for how to encourage such tendencies.

Wider Significance of Findings

It is helpful to try to make unconscious biases conscious through reflection, but also good to realize that this process is never complete. The unconscious is "turtles all the way down," so to speak. Reflection does not require complete detachment, but it does require some pulling away from immersion in practice to consider how others may react to it and looking at the wider significance of my findings. One way to look at significance is to consider the effects of Heathen ritual practice on Heathens and the potential spread of the religious tradition. A more important way to look at significance is in terms of what this research suggests for understanding unconscious motivations of pro-environmental behavior and how ecological conscience is formed (or fails to form) in other communities of practice.

Heathen Transformations

Heathenry has been around since the late 1960s in North America, and has longer roots in Western esotericism in Europe. The groups I studied were ten years old or less, though some participants have been Heathen since the late 1980s. It is possible that these groups may not persist beyond the involvement of the current generation, but there are efforts to involve children and pass on traditions. The junior *gythias* at Well and Tree Gathering seem quite interested in participation and leadership within Heathenry, but not all children of practitioners are. Heathens include children in ritual practices such as blót, giving offerings, the procession of Nerthus, and feasts at Heathen gatherings, although they are not necessarily encouraged to participate in sumbel until they are older teens. Those who have been involved longer, such as Auz, Erik, Brynja, and Jade, implement what Auz said about ceding enough control of traditions to let what is being built be felt to belong to new generations and new participants by encouraging active participation in ritual and in sharing leadership roles. This bodes well for the continuation of this Heathen tradition. Of course, much of this depends on current leaders within the Heathen communities I have studied and may change over time. Raven's Knoll is privately owned, and the community may change significantly with the passing of Auz and MA. However, Auz and MA did not originate the community that continues at Raven's Knoll, but "inherited" the care of it from others in the Pagan community who had been responsible for continuing long-running events such as the annual pan-Pagan event Kaleidoscope.

Some Heathens are actively working to transform society, particularly in terms of equity and inclusivity. The shared "as if" negotiated in ritual can be a good way to try out new possibilities, and this could be a way toward a more sustainable path. Ritual plays out the core values of how we should relate. Ritual practices and the social imaginary it negotiates and co-constructs provides a venue for exploring variations on how we should relate with the world. In his dissertation on Heathen groups related to the Raven's Knoll community, Harmsworth (2015, 219) discusses Luhrman's discussion of "playful," "let's pretend," qualities of magical practices. He (2015, 228, 231) found that practice can create belief, suggesting that playing make-believe helps people believe—or at least act as though they do. Doing this in groups can be effective, particularly if you do not know if you are the only one just playing along. People copy each other and often do not want to be the odd one out. But practitioners may be more likely to think of this in terms of establishing relationships with other-than-human persons, not as coming to believe in them but inviting them into relation through making offerings or attuning ourselves to them in coming into gifting relations with them.

Play, and deep play in ritual, allows collaborative exploration of ways of relating. Harmsworth discusses play in terms of psychologist D. W. Winnicott's "transitional space" in relation to Heathenry at Raven's Knoll and in Runatyr Kindred (Harmsworth 2015, 214–217). Winnicott's "potential space" can be seen as an "adjacent possible" to explore in play. The adjacent possible is what biologist Stuart Kauffman (2008) calls the state space of possibilities or field of various possible interactions afforded by the context of a complex system. Similarly to Winnicott's potential space of the self, ritual and re-enchantment can be an adjacent possible in which to explore ways of relating. Ritual allows play in this "potential space" to explore subjunctive possibilities.

Luhrmann discusses the "as if" character of ritual (magic in her terms) in relation to historian Johan Huizinga's (1955 [1950]) and Roger Caillois's (1962) theories of play. Playing "as if" in ritual sets the rules that apply outside it.[3] People know what they are doing is set apart in ritual, not regular action, but it is serious.

> While playing, the imaginative fabric provides the "as-if" context which is the play-context, different from the real, bounded and all-encompassing and at times, intensely serious. If it is a serious play, the nature of that bounded context and its rules becomes opaque: the play is not "only" play, but somehow also a real commitment to a particular understanding of the world. (Luhrmann 1989, 332)

Through ritual practice we can negotiate and co-construct a shared sense of what is real, what is important, and how we should relate with others.

More recently, Roberte Hamayon (2016, 64) has referred to the "negative flaw" in play as "source of its internal dynamic." The internal dynamic of play is the comparison between what is and what could be, between current existence and the adjacent possible. In ritual, the play between what is and what participants are negotiating should be—the is and the ought—and the framing of the action as "not reality" or "extraordinary" creates a frame of what reality is, what we agree that it is. A story about the gods or ancestors can teach about reality by including fantastical elements and teach right actions through depicting the consequences of wrong actions or exploring possible unforeseen consequences, as in the cautionary tales of the sagas that describe the negative consequences of forcing unwanted marriages and pursuing vengeance. Like stories in myth and saga, ritual allows the imaginative playing out of possibilities. We play, tell stories, and do ritual as practice for life, trying out different options as part of our adaptive process. Play and ritual are part of what enable us to be not *Homo economicus* but *Homo accomodare*, meaning "the ones who adapt." Play, and the play of meaning in ritual, allows us to try out different options as part of our adaptive process.

Ancestor veneration, the veneration of "spirits" of place, along with seasonal celebrations, can prompt people toward resilient relations with ecological systems, but a religious solution is not enough in itself in the context of modernity because it is the disembedded economy that is causing ecological damage. Economic change is also necessary, but this may be facilitated through ritual practices, re-embedding economic transactions into social relations that generate a gift ethic that includes the more-than-human world. The episodic interruption of business as usual for practitioners can encourage interpretive drift toward more sustainable social ecological relations.

For some practitioners, Heathenry is just a religion. They may be happy to live compartmentalized lives gifting with Heathens and perceiving deities as transcendent while otherwise engaging in transactional exchanges. In addition, following the findings of sociological studies (see Taylor et al. 2016, 328), the appeal of religions such as Heathenry are likely to be limited in the context of culturally dominant traditions that oppose "paganism" and "idolatry." For those who hear "Heathen" as "unbeliever" or "heretic," Heathenry will either be either desirable for being perceived as transgressive by those who want to rebel or unappealing to those who find this threatening. This limits the broader influence of Heathen ritual as a useful conduit to sustainability.

But what matters about this study of Heathen ritual is not the potential spread of Heathenry and its effects. Rather, it suggests we should take a closer look at what ritual does in other contexts and what unconscious motivations are in play in other communities of practice. What values are made salient, and what priming effects are evident? What sort of relations do rituals in other traditions enact, and how can we use unconscious factors that influence our behavior to nudge us toward more pro-environmental choices in secular society? Some people are likely to feel uncomfortable about using ritual practices to motivate pro-environmental behavior, but environmentalists do not benefit from trying to claim a supposed moral high ground in appealing only to reason. Even when we become conscious of how priming effects influence behavior, they continue to have an impact on us. We can consciously structure rituals, using specific imagery to produce particular results, and encourage pro-environmental behavior by nudging participants toward less consumptive behavior.

Social Change

Relational ontologies and gift economies go hand in hand (Davy and Quilley 2018), but the effects of gift economies are limited to participants. If everyone were to re-enter gifting relations with the nonhuman world this might help restore right relations by re-embedding the economy in social ecological systems and allow relational ontologies to re-emerge more widely. Economic change is crucial for environmental sustainability. Changing cognized worldviews is not enough, and lifeways may not change on a fundamental level without also changing economic relations. The economy needs to fit within the biophysical limits of the planet, and living within local ecological resources would seem to be a reasonable way to do that. Heathen gift economies are a step in the right direction, but currently minimal in their effects in wider systems of overconsumption. The benefits of developing informal economies are limited in the current dominant economic system of globalized industrial capitalism. Wider change is necessary but unlikely to develop without shocks that destabilize the global economic system. Arguably these shocks have begun, evident in the effects of climate change and the COVID-19 pandemic, which may give informal gifting economies a chance to redevelop.

Of more significant concern in my view are the social consequences of economic change. Market economies developed out of gift economies. What is to prevent that happening again, if we did redevelop gift economies? If the global economy collapses and there is a resurgence of informal economies and gifting practices, will society devolve into chiefly societies and a new feudalism, or can we imagine a better future? Arguments about the nature of historical societies and the accuracy of sociologist Norbert Elias's (1978) theory of how ontology, society, and the material bases of society are linked would take me well beyond the scope of my current project describing how environmental values emerge out of Heathen ritual practices. It is possible that a de-growth future will entail a resurgence of socially conservative values, as Stephen Quilley (2013) argues, but it may be that it matters quite a lot what values we make salient in civic and other rituals to shape future trajectories in ways that fit our desired outcomes.

So long as modern economic systems remain dominant, larger social transformation will be limited. I see potential for Heathenry to build community resilience through the development of informal economies within the existing system and interrupt the dominance of individualized ontology through participation in rituals that support relational ontology. Gifting relations are currently minor in terms of economics but very significant in terms of social relations, both for interpersonal relations (emotional support, recognition of relational worth) and for inter-group relations through alliances. The Heathen community is not my survival unit but my "thriving" unit. It provides the emotional resilience that sustains me. Heathenry's strengths are in community building, community resilience, and alliance building. Like other religions in the modern context, it is a voluntary association. Members can step away at any time, but this would mean ripping ourselves out of relations that sustain us. To be "disfellowshipped" (declared *nið* or *nithing* in Heathen terms) from my kindred or banned from the Knoll would be devastating. I could survive, but I would be much diminished—not that the community would do such a thing simply for someone leaving a kindred. There is a process for doing that amicably, for example, in Vindisir Kindred. Declaring someone nið is for those who commit reprehensible acts.

Where Do We Go from Here?

Given the tendency toward worldview defense when presented with alternative views or challenges to one's own view, how can change be fostered? It may be helpful to bolster people's sense of relational worth first and then challenge their existing views to avoid triggering unconscious defense of the dominant operationalized worldview of consumerism. This might be accomplished through participation in rituals of giving thanks and expressing gratitude, such as sumbel, and extended into a wider gift ethic through making offerings.

Rituals such as the procession of Nerthus at Well and Tree Gathering may be a useful model for what ritual can do for us in complex cosmopolitan society. Applying anthropologist Victoria Strang's (2004) findings suggests that such rituals can facilitate civic engagement, and, if paired with relocalization of control of resources, the revival of festivals celebrating bodies of water or watersheds could build a resilient sense of participation in the regional community to foster a greater commitment to sustainable relations in larger social ecological systems and prompt pro-environmental behavior. These do not have to be framed as Pagan or Heathen. They could thrive as community-based festivals.

It might be supposed that a potential problem for the idea of using civic ritual to remediate environmental problems is the fact that climate change is frequently raised as an issue in civic events by, for example, the prime minister and the king of Norway in speeches on New Year's Day (Norgaard 2011, loc 634), with little social impact. Sociologist Kari Norgaard suggests that this does not work because it is too abstract. However, in these instances, the problem was made salient. It is not the problem that needs to be made salient, but pro-environmental values that need to be made salient to operationalize them. We need to make pro-environmental values come to mind more often to shift our operationalized view from consumerism to adaptive regeneration.

Strang's findings suggest that, to be effective in resource conservation, rituals would need to be directly linked to resource use. If those who preside over such rituals have the authority to turn on and off harvesting or the use of resources, ritual could effectively regulate social ecological relations. It may be that seasonal rituals have the capacity to shift group behavior in a way similar to how rites of passage prompt changes in behavior and patterns of relations. Ritual participation can accomplish resource conservation when those who conduct rituals governing resource use are also involved in monitoring and maintaining relations with relevant species. In Indigenous societies, the performance of songs used in ritual is often restricted to those who have the responsibility of maintaining the relevant relationships. I suspect this is a determinant reason why it is unacceptable to take Indigenous ritual practices out of context without permission. Historical, ethnographic, and empirical studies in this direction may be fruitful areas for future research.

The First Salmon Ceremony in the Pacific Northwest provides an example of a ritual practice that can help adaptively regulate human behavior. Robin Wall Kimmerer (2013, 248–249) describes how this ceremony, which includes expression of gratitude to the fish "actually aided the upstream passage of the fish by releasing them from predation for a critical time. Laying salmon bones back in the streams returned nutrients to the system." Kimmerer concludes that "These are ceremonies of practical reverence" (Kimmerer 2013, 248–249). The traditional ecological knowledge embedded in this sort of ritual does not need to be consciously understood to be effective in ensuring sustainability, but perhaps it would be more effective in resisting modernization if it was.

Allowing ritual involvement in control of resources requires a high degree of trust in individuals who decide when and how rituals happen. This is not democratic, unless decisions are made by some sort of local governing council, and can entail accountability problems about who gets a say and who counts as a stakeholder. There are problems in how this has been defined in First Nations groups in Canada, for example, with band councils and chiefs accepted as authorities by the state, ignoring cultural traditions of land management by family groups and of water management by women.

Integrating citizen science initiatives and civic ritual could also be effective. In this way, science and enchantment can be integrated in what Kimmerer calls "two-eyed seeing." As Kimmerer says, "Educational events like wildflower weekends and Christmas bird counts are all steps in the right direction, but they lack an active, reciprocal relationship with the more-than-human world" (Kimmerer 2013, 251). We also need practical, pragmatic adaptive rituals for city living to restore human relations with the more-than-human world. Creating random rituals celebrating nature will not create sustainability. They need to actually serve the ecosystem and support actual relations of reciprocity. Neither science nor ritual is dispensable, but together they could improve social ecological relations.

As much as we like to think we rationally decide how to act, unconscious motivations continue to influence us. Not to take this into account allows business interests that use these unconscious factors to influence our behavior and effectively direct society to their own ends. While we argue about what to do about climate change, mortality salience prompts us to continue to overconsume. But we may not need to come to universal agreement to solve environmental issues. Rational discourse is not the only way we come to agreement and perhaps not the best way to come to agreement when it comes to values. Ritual may negotiate this more effectively than rational discourse.

Survey Questions

1. I am aware that my submitted answers from the survey will be digitally recorded and analyzed with statistical analysis software, and the data will be retained for a minimum of seven years on a password-protected computer and secure servers of the University of Waterloo, and I give permission for the use of anonymous quotations in any thesis or publication that comes from this research, and I agree of my own free will to participate in the study, and that I am 18 years or older.
   - o Yes, I agree.
   - o No thanks, or no I'm not 18 years or older.

Demographics

2. What is your age?
   - o 18–29 years old
   - o 30–49 years old
   - o 50–64 years old
   - o 65 years and over

3. What is the highest level of education you have completed?
   - o Grade 8 or less
   - o Some high school
   - o High school diploma or equivalent
   - o Registered apprenticeship or other trades certificate or diploma
   - o College, CEGEP, or other non-university certificate or diploma
   - o University certificate or diploma below bachelor's level
   - o Bachelor's degree
   - o Postgraduate degree above bachelor's level
   - o Prefer not to answer

4. Which of the following categories best describes your current employment status? (You may check all that apply.)
   - o Working full-time, that is, 35 or more hours per week
   - o Working part-time, that is, less than 35 hours per week
   - o Self-employed
   - o Unemployed, but looking for work
   - o Homemaker
   - o A student attending school full-time
   - o Retired
   - o Not in the workforce
   - o Prefer not to answer

5. Which of the following categories best describes your total household income? That is, the total income of all persons in your household combined, before taxes?
   o Under $20,000
   o $20,000 to just under $40,000
   o $40,000 to just under $60,000
   o $60,000 to just under $80,000
   o $80,000 to just under $100,000
   o $100,000 to just under $150,000
   o $150,000 to just under $200 000
   o $200 000 and above
   o Prefer not to answer

6. What is your occupation?

7. What is your gender?
   o Male
   o Female
   o Nonbinary
   o Prefer not to answer
   o Prefer to self-describe

8. How many people live in your town or city?
   o Less than 5,000
   o 5,000–15,000
   o 15,000–50,000
   o 50,000–100,000
   o 100,000–500,000
   o 500,000–1 million
   o More than 1 million

9. How would you describe your political views?
   o Very conservative
   o Conservative
   o Moderate
   o Liberal
   o Very liberal
   o Alt right
   o Progressive
   o Other (please specify):

10. What country do you live in?

Community

11. When I do a favor for someone, I expect them to reciprocate in kind.
    o Strongly agree
    o Agree

o Neither agree nor disagree
o Disagree
o Strongly disagree

12. Friends and neighbors should do things for one another regardless of whether or not they get paid back directly.
    o Strongly agree
    o Agree
    o Neither agree nor disagree
    o Disagree
    o Strongly disagree

13. It is important to me that other people think they can count on my help in times of need.
    o Strongly agree
    o Agree
    o Neither agree nor disagree
    o Disagree
    o Strongly disagree

14. Individual freedom is more important to me than community.
    o Strongly agree
    o Agree
    o Neither agree nor disagree
    o Disagree
    o Strongly disagree

15. My sense of community includes plants, animals, the land, and water.
    o Strongly agree
    o Agree
    o Neither agree nor disagree
    o Disagree
    o Strongly disagree

16. Trees, stones, and/or bodies of water can have feelings.
    o Strongly agree
    o Agree
    o Neither agree nor disagree
    o Disagree
    o Strongly disagree

17. How often do you do things for extended family, neighbors, or community members without expecting direct recompense or compensation?
    o Every day
    o Every week
    o Every month
    o Rarely
    o Never

18. How often do you trade goods and services without monetary exchanges?
    o Every day
    o Every week
    o Every month
    o Rarely
    o Never

Economy

19. Everyone should have food and shelter, regardless of whether or not they earn money.
    o Strongly agree
    o Agree
    o Neither agree nor disagree
    o Disagree
    o Strongly disagree

20. I enjoy growing, harvesting, or making things for my family to use.
    o Strongly agree
    o Agree
    o Neither agree nor disagree
    o Disagree
    o Strongly disagree

21. I like to give to charitable and/or political organizations.
    o Strongly agree
    o Agree
    o Neither agree nor disagree
    o Disagree
    o Strongly disagree

22. I prefer to do less paid work, even if it means earning less money.
    o Strongly agree
    o Agree
    o Neither agree nor disagree
    o Disagree
    o Strongly disagree

23. How much of your own food do you produce (through hunting, fishing, trapping, gardening, farming, etc.)?
    o None
    o Hardly any
    o Some
    o Lots

24. Thinking of unpaid activities you do, how much time each week do you devote to
    (Please indicate the number of time in hours, rounding to the nearest whole number.)
    _____ Preparing food
    _____ Caring for children

_____ Caring for elders
_____ Caring for animals
_____ Caring for plants
_____ Volunteering (including volunteer activity that may include ariums or minimal pay, such as volunteer firefighting or search and rescue services)
_____ Political activities (including with NGOs, local and/or party politics)

25 When you buy food and other products, what is the most important thing to consider?
[list rotated randomly in presentation to survey participants]
o Cost
o Convenience
o Quality
o Humane production
o Supporting local business
o Environmental effects

Environment

26. I like to spend time outside whenever I can.
o Strongly agree
o Agree
o Neither agree nor disagree
o Disagree
o Strongly disagree

27. Environmental problems can be solved with better technology.
o Strongly agree
o Agree
o Neither agree nor disagree
o Disagree
o Strongly disagree

28. This world is the only one we have, so we better look after it.
o Strongly agree
o Agree
o Neither agree nor disagree
o Disagree
o Strongly disagree

29. Human lives matter more than other species.
o Strongly agree
o Agree
o Neither agree nor disagree
o Disagree
o Strongly disagree

30. My community includes members of other species.
    o Strongly agree
    o Agree
    o Neither agree nor disagree
    o Disagree
    o Strongly disagree

31. How much time per week did you spend outdoors as a child?

32. How much time per week do you spend outdoors currently?

33. Environmental protection should be a high priority for government.
    o Strongly agree
    o Agree
    o Neither agree nor disagree
    o Disagree
    o Strongly disagree

34. Do you consider yourself sympathetic to the environmental movement?
    o Yes
    o Somewhat
    o No
    o No opinion

35. Do you personally consider yourself an environmental activist?
    o Yes
    o Somewhat
    o No

36. Do you think of yourself as an active participant in the environmental movement, sympathetic toward the movement but not active, neutral, or unsympathetic toward the environmental movement?
    o Active
    o Sympathetic
    o Neutral
    o Unsympathetic
    o No opinion

37. Do you belong to any large national or international environmentalist organizations such as Sierra Club or Greenpeace?
    o Yes
    o No

38. Do you belong to any environmental groups or organizations in your local community, region, or state?
    o Yes
    o No

39. How likely, do you think, is it that the Earth will be destroyed by an environmental disaster within the next century?
    o Very likely
    o Somewhat likely
    o Somewhat unlikely
    o Very unlikely
    o Not Earth but humans
    o No opinion

40. Which of these, if any, have you done in the past year?
    (Please check all that you have done in the past year.)
    o Avoided using certain products that harm the environment.
    o Been active in a group or organization that works to protect the environment.
    o Voted/worked for candidates because of positions on environmental issues.
    o Contributed money to an environmental, conservation, or wildlife preservation group.
    o Contacted a public official about an environmental issue.
    o Contacted a business to complain about its products or policies because they harm the environment.
    o Signed a petition supporting an environmental group or some environmental protection effort.
    o Attended a meeting concerning the environment.
    o Tried to use less water in your household.
    o Bought some product specifically because you thought it was better for the environment than other competing products.
    o Voluntarily recycled newspapers, glass, aluminum, motor oil, or other items.
    o Reduced your household's use of energy.
    o Bought or sold stocks based on the environmental record of companies.

Religion/Spirituality

41. Ritual practices are important to my religious or spiritual practice.
    o Strongly agree
    o Agree
    o Neither agree nor disagree
    o Disagree
    o Strongly disagree

42. The divine, sacred, or holy is not present in nature.
    o Strongly agree
    o Agree
    o Neither agree nor disagree
    o Disagree
    o Strongly disagree

43. Some places are more sacred than others.
    o Strongly agree
    o Agree

o Neither agree nor disagree
o Disagree
o Strongly disagree

44. Giving thanks for the good things in my life is important.
    o Strongly agree
    o Agree
    o Neither agree nor disagree
    o Disagree
    o Strongly disagree

45. Scientific progress outweighs damage done to society and/or the environment.
    o Strongly agree
    o Agree
    o Neither agree nor disagree
    o Disagree
    o Strongly disagree

46. The earth gives freely, like a parent's unconditional love.
    o Strongly agree
    o Agree
    o Neither agree nor disagree
    o Disagree
    o Strongly disagree

47. The ability of natural systems to sustain us depends on how we treat the earth.
    o Strongly agree
    o Agree
    o Neither agree nor disagree
    o Disagree
    o Strongly disagree

48. How often do you attend or participate in religious activities?
    o Every day
    o Every week
    o Every month
    o Rarely
    o Never

49. What is your religious preference or identification?

50. What is your connection to nature, what would you like it to be, and how does it
    matter to you?

Survey Data Results

36 Heathen respondents in Canada, 50 other Pagans in Canada. Some respondents in survey of Pagans and Heathens preferred to identify their religious preference as atheist (1), spiritual (1), or none (1).

Table A2.1 Education

Highest education level completed	Heathens	Pagans	Heathens and Pagans	Random Canadians
Some high school	2%	0%	1%	3%
High school diploma or equivalent	14%	12%	13%	21%
Registered apprenticeship or other trades certificate or diploma	6%	6%	6%	4%
University certificate or diploma below the bachelor's level	14%	10%	10%	4%
College, CECEP, or other non-university certificate or diploma	15%	12%	13%	23%
Bachelor's degree	28%	26%	23%	28%
Postgraduate degree above bachelor's level	20%	33%	28%	10%

Table A2.2 Income

Household income	Heathens	Pagans	Heathens and Pagans	Random Canadian Sample
$20,000 to $40,000	18%	19%	18%	16%
$40,000 to $60,000	20%	15%	16%	23%
$60,000 to $80,000	11%	14%	13%	11%
$80,000 to $100,000	11%	10%	9%	9%
$100,000 to $150,000	16%	8%	9%	20%
$150,000 to $200,000	4%	6%	4%	4%
$200,000 +	6%	2%	3%	1%

Table A2.3 Gender

Gender	Heathens	Pagans	Heathens and Pagans	Random Canadian Sample
Female	33%	61%	52%	54%
Male	59%	32%	37%	39%
Nonbinary	6%	4%	4%	0%

Table A2.4 Land ethic

My sense of community includes plants, animals, land, and water	Heathens	Pagans	Heathens and Pagans	Random Canadians
Strongly disagree	2%	1%	1%	1%
Disagree	5%	2%	3%	4%
Neither agree nor disagree	9%	4%	4%	18%
Agree	37%	28%	28%	38%
Strongly agree	46%	65%	56%	28%

Table A2.5 Immanence

The divine, sacred, or holy is not present in nature	Heathens	Pagans	Heathens and Pagans	Random Canadians
Strongly agree	2%	3%	2%	10%
Agree	2%	0%	0%	10%
Neither agree nor disagree	3%	2%	3%	31%
Disagree	16%	10%	9%	19%
Strongly disagree	77%	84%	65%	18%

Table A2.6 Ritual

Highest education level completed	Heathens	Pagans	Heathens and Pagans	Random Canadians
Strongly agree	55%	48%	39%	8%
Agree	30%	35%	26%	17%
Neither agree nor disagree	10%	13%	10%	27%
Disagree	4%	4%	3%	16%
Strongly disagree	1%	0%	0%	19%
Strongly agree	55%	48%	39%	8%

Table A2.7 Consumption values

Most important thing to consider when buying things?	Heathens	Pagans	Heathens and Pagans	Random Canadians
Convenience	2%	2%	2%	3%
Cost	26%	17%	19%	32%
Environmental effects	12%	20%	16%	7%
Humane production	11%	17%	14%	5%
Quality	3%	25%	23%	32%
Supporting local business	15%	17%	14%	9%
Ethical concerns	38%	55%	44%	48%

Table A2.8 Political orientation

How would you describe your political views?	Heathens	Pagans	Heathens and Pagans	Random Canadians
Alt-right	2%	2%	2%	2%
Conservative	6%	3%	3%	16%
Liberal	20%	19%	20%	28%
Moderate	14%	13%	12%	30%
Other	3%	18%	20%	5%
Progressive	30%	25%	21%	2%
Very conservative	14%	0%	1%	5%
Very liberal	2%	19%	16%	5%

Table A2.9 Cumulative percentages used to calculate median household incomes

Household income	Heathens	Pagans	Heathens and Pagans	Random Canadian Sample
Under $20,000	14%	27%	27%	16%
$20,000 to $40,000	32%	46%	46%	32%
$40,000 to $60,000	52%	61%	61%	56%
$60,000 to $80,000	63%	75%	74%	66%
$80,000 to $100,000	74%	85%	84%	75%
$100,000 to $150,000	90%	93%	93%	95%
$150,000 to $200,000	94%	98%	97%	99%
$200,000+	100%	100%	100%	100%
Estimate fraction of $40,000–$60,000 to get 50%	90.00%	27.78%	27.94%	75.89%
Estimate income at 50%	$58,000	$45,556	$45,588	$55,179

Table A2.9 shows calculated cumulative percentages up to the top of each income range. All of the groups hit 50% in the $40,000–$60,000 band. Assuming that the distribution of incomes is uniform in the $40,000–$60,000 band (probably not true, but the data do not allow being more specific), the second to last row shows the calculation determining at what point through the $40,000–$60,000 band each group hits 50% to reach the median. Last row shows taking that % of ($60,000–$40,000) and adding it to $40,000 to get the estimated median income. My thanks to Jon Davy (an actuary) for providing me with these calculations.

Notes

Introduction

1. I first heard Grimes pose this question at "Between Nature," a conference in Lancaster, in 1999. His paper "Performance is currency in the deep world's gift economy: an incantatory riff for a global medicine show," was first published in 2002, in *Interdisciplinary Studies in Literature and Environment* and has subsequently been included in various anthologies. See Grimes, as quoted in Harvey (2014, 503).
2. "Early Medieval English" is a term that some scholars and Heathen practitioners following their work prefer to "Anglo-Saxon." The International Society of Anglo-Saxonists, for example, recently changed its name to the International Society for the Study of Early Medieval England (see http://www.isasweb.net/AB091919.html).
3. The term "Ásatrú" comes from Iceland. Despite being less theistically inclined than practitioners in North America, Heathens in Iceland felt pressured to adopt a name indicating dedication to a group of gods (Ásatrúarfélagið) in order to obtain government recognition as an official religion. Originally, Icelandic practitioners proposed the name "Vor Sithur," meaning "Our Custom" (Strmiska 2000), which parallels the meaning of similar terms in Denmark, Sweden, and Norway. The use of these terms in is flux. Racist use of "Forn Siðr" has led some to prefer variations of "Ásatrú" in Scandinavia, but use of "Ásatrú" in North America may be rejected for similar reasons. In Eastern Europe, Heathens sometimes identify themselves by variants of terms meaning "Native Faith/Tradition" and may see themselves as reviving Indigenous traditions (see Aitamurto and Simpson 2014; Ivakhiv 2005b; Strmiska 2005a). However, in North America, Heathenry is not Indigenous, though some practitioners are part Indigenous. Contemporary Heathenry is inspired in part by Norse mythology, much of which is based on sources beginning from around the fifth century CE in northwestern Europe that have been preserved in the Eddas, two collections of stories and poems recorded in the thirteenth century, *The Prose Edda* and *The Poetic Edda*. Contemporary Heathens regard the Hávamál and other parts of the Eddas as important sources of what they call "the Lore" informing contemporary practice, but some Heathens, including those in this study, take them more as a jumping off point than something to measure historical accuracy against. The most familiar influence on contemporary Heathenry to a general audience is the Viking era, the eighth- to eleventh-century migrations of northern Europeans south into Europe and the British Isles. For some practitioners this is the idealized era of what they are trying to revive and reconstruct, but the Heathens of this study are also interested in how people lived prior to the differentiation of Celtic and Germanic peoples (circa 1200 BCE) and even earlier in the European Bronze Age (2500–500 BCE). Sources of inspiration include archaeological studies and speculation; early written texts, including not only the Eddas but also Icelandic poetry and saga literature; and other sources, such as the early English text *Beowulf*, Tacitus's *Germania*, and Ahmad Ibn Fadlan's *Mission to the Volga*. Heathens in this community are not strict reconstructionists. Although they value academic knowledge about pre-Christian religious and cultural practices they explicitly recognize that there are aspects of ancient tradition (such as human sacrifice and slavery) that they do not want to emulate. Inspired but not overly constrained by the past, they reimagine tradition to create something self-consciously new. For these Heathens there is just enough historical information to provide a foundation to build on, but not so much written material as to constrain contemporary elaboration, although there are disagreements about interpretation and gaps in evidence. Practitioners follow academic discourse and they debate what is historically accurate and how to circumscribe the geographical and chronological limits of the origins of Heathen traditions, as well as what aspects of tradition are worth emulating. There is no published history of Heathenry in Canada, and no text dedicated to the emergence of Heathenry more generally,

which is complicated by different timelines and trajectories in different countries. A comprehensive account would need to be transnational and include multilingual research beyond the scope of this work. See von Schnurbein (2016) for an overview. The Heathen Confederation of Canada, a nonprofit organization representing inclusive Heathens in Canada to government, law enforcement, the media, and other groups, emphasizes that contemporary Heathenry is a new religious movement that began emerging in the nineteenth century. Since incorporation as a nonprofit requires a clear identification of membership they have developed a description of what they call "modern Germanic Heathens" as "anyone participating in and identifying with religious behaviours, values and beliefs which are modeled upon and associated with those of ancient Germanic Heathens and that these same behaviours, values and beliefs form their primary religious identity" (Heathen Confederation of Canada FAQ explaining bylaws; provided by Erik Lacharity, who is their National Council Chair and official spokesperson). Members can be of any ethnicity or cultural background but share a common identity through their religion. They acknowledge that ancient Heathen traditions inspire modern practices but want to avoid what they see as a problematic identification of Heathenry as an Indigenous tradition with any significant continuity with pre-Christian traditions. Some contemporary Heathens in Europe are less troubled by identifying Heathenry with Indigenous traditions (see Aitamurto and Simpson 2014; Harvey 2020; Rountree 2018 for a range of positions). I prefer "Heathenry" to terms such as "Germanic Neo-Paganism" because the latter too easily suggests an ethnic identity when the relevant descriptor for the whole of contemporary Heathenry is the language group and the cultures of those who spoke these languages across Europe prior to the development of modern nation states. Aspects of these cultures were romanticized in early nationalist movements of Iceland in the 1300s, Scandinavia in the 1700s, Germany in the 1800s, later nationalist movements in Germany in the 1900s (Nazism in particular), and other racist or ethnicity-based nationalisms in Europe in 1900s and into the twenty-first century. Some branches of contemporary Heathenry that developed in the United States in the 1970s took inspiration from racist nationalist movements, but liberal and more progressive versions of Heathenry emerged in Iceland with Ásatrúarfélagið in 1973 and in the United States with the development of the Troth and other groups in the 1980s. Heathenry entered Canada in the 1980s through individuals such as Austin Lawrence, who belonged to American groups or were in contact with American Heathens, and it spread more rapidly with the development of the Internet in the 1990s. Heathen communities on the East Coast of Canada and in British Columbia in particular may have had different origins. For a more extensive history of the emergence of contemporary Heathenry in the United States, see Calico (2018).
4. I was unable to attend the inaugural Stave and Spindle, an event focused on Heathen sorcery, due to the passing of a family member. Some, but not all, Heathens in this community use the term "sorcery," rather than "magic."
5. As religion scholar Talal Asad has observed (1983), even focusing on religion in terms of outlook or worldview rather than lifeway and the actions that people engage in is a result of a post-Protestant focus on religion as "expressive."
6. My understanding of how ritual "operationalizes" values is indebted to Grimes's and Rappaport's applications of speech act theory to ritual, but also influenced by Seligman and his colleagues' (2008) sense of the negotiative capacities of ritual. According to speech act theory "performative" speech does something rather than just says something. Speech acts have real effects, such as declarations of ceremonial openings. J. L. Austin (1975) introduced modern speech act theory with his idea of "performative utterance," further developed by John Searle (see Grimes 1988, 106). Building on Searle's *Speech Acts* (1969), Rappaport (1979, 196; 1999, 121–123) argued that the origin of morality is in acceptance of obligation through public participation in ritual. He suggested that participation in a ritual functions like a speech act to enact the moral order contained within it. Rappaport observed that participation in ritual indicates public acceptance of what the rules of society should be and acceptance of the personal obligation to abide by them. This does not necessarily prevent people from breaking rules, he argued, but shows agreement about what rules and obligations there should be. Thus Rappaport argued that ritual establishes moral order: "Although usage may not be faithful to it, that which is represented in liturgy is not a fiction, and the performance does more than *remind* individuals of an underlying order. It *establishes* that order" (Rappaport 1979, 197).
7. See Calico (2018) and Strmiska (2007). Blót and other terms that may be unfamiliar are defined in the glossary at the end of this work. Blót practices are diverse, and fully analyzing them would require referencing large bodies of research in Norse literature and the anthropologies of

feasting and sacrifice. I collected substantial ethnographic data on blót practices both at Raven's Knoll and with Vindisir. Adequately dealing with this material as a whole would require a book-length treatment on its own. For discussion of Vindisir's Winterfinding blót and animal sacrifice, see Davy (2023).

8. *Bragafull* (ed. Pearce, Lacharity, Layoun and Lawrence [2020]) includes several descriptions of esoteric rites at Raven's Knoll.

9. By "dominant modern way of life" I mean modern society as German-British sociologist Norbert Elias (2001) describes in terms of proceeding toward a "society of individuals." German sociologist Ferdinand Tönnies (2001 [1887]) discusses this in terms of a movement from *gemeinschaft* (small-scale traditional community-based life) to *gesellschaft* (large-scale economic-based cosmopolitan society). Rather than using Tönnies's German terms in this work I use the more familiar terms "modern" and "traditional." Like Tönnies, I use these terms as ideal types to contrast poles on a continuum.

10. The idea of relational ontology initially emerged out of studies in what came to be known as the "New Melanesian ethnography," with roots in work by anthropologists Roy Wagner and Marilyn Strathern, in comparison with other contexts (Holbraad and Pedersen 2017, 200). Peruvian anthropologist Marisol de la Cadena (2015) and others studying Indigenous traditions in South America started using the term "relational ontology" in what has come to be known as "the ontological turn" in anthropology. Ramos (2012) and Chandler and Reid (2020) criticize writings on relational ontology and Eduardo Viveiros de Castro's characterization of perspectivism as essentialist and reductionist for presenting a homogenized view of Indigenous ontologies.

11. In some parts of Europe, especially Eastern and Central Europe, people reviving pre-Christian traditions often do regard their traditions as "indigenous" or "indigenizing" (see Aitamurto and Simpson 2014; Harvey 2020).

12. I developed an interpretation of the relational ontology of gift economies in contrast to the individualized ontology of market economies in dialogue with Stephen Quilley (see Davy and Quilley 2018) following sociologist Norbert Elias's (2000 [1939]) analysis of changes in ontology over time, from feudal violence to courtly knights, to the modern society of individuals (Elias 2001), in conjunction with anthropologist Bronislaw Malinowski's (2015 [1922]) writings about the Kula Ring and Karl Polanyi's (2001 [1944]) understanding of the transition from gift economies to market economies.

13. Harvey uses the term "relational ontology" only once in *Animism: Respecting the Living World*, so far as I noticed (Harvey 2006, 168), showing a preference to speak of animism and, on occasion, "animist ontologies" (Harvey 2006, 203). Heathen scholar of religion Rune Hjarnø Rasmussen describes what he calls "Nordic animism" as a form of the new animism in dialogue with Harvey's work. For Rasmussen, Nordic animism is a broader category than Heathenry, extending into the development of Christian traditions (Rasmussen 2020, 19). Others developing the new animism include Bird-David (1999), Green (2013, Hornborg (2006), Naveh and Bird-David (2014), and Wilson (2008). The phrase "the more-than-human world" originates with Abram (1996).

14. A. Irving Hallowell (1969) introduced the phrase "other-than-human persons" in his description of Ojibwe (Anishinaabe) ontology to make sense of how stones could be grammatically animate beings and classed as persons, or potentially people. Hallowell's essay has been significantly influential in the new animism and anthropology describing relational ontologies.

15. Literature on gift economies begins with Malinowski's study of the Kula ring (2015 [1922]), debated and extended by Marcel Mauss (1990 [1950]), Marshall Sahlins (1972), Karl Polanyi (2001 [1944]), Rappaport (1979), and others, with more recent contributions by Nurit Bird-David and her colleagues (1990, 1999; Bird-David and Darr 2009; Naveh and Bird-David 2014), among others. Gift economies are not always or automatically pro-environmental. For those who are familiar with gift economies primarily from studies of potlatch in the Pacific Northwest, the idea that gift economies might be good for the environment may not be credible. However, Mauss's (1990 [1950], 37) discussion of potlatch is atypical of gift economies, describing the development of a "delayed return" economy (accumulating a surplus for later redistribution) in a hunter-gatherer society disrupted by colonization and that may have been developing state-like institutions prior to colonial contact. The destruction of material goods in displays of prestige as part of potlatch does not fit the pattern of gift economies as originally described by Malinowski (2015 [1922]) or later by Bird-David (1990). Bird-David and Asaf Darr (2009) refer to such destructive developments as "economies of excess," indicating that they are not typical of what Bird-David (1990) prefers to call "gifting economies." See also Hamayon (2016, 94).

16. For a more extensive treatment of interrelations between ontology, ritual, and economy, see Davy and Quilley (2018).

17. Levinas is little known outside of postmodern theory and Jewish philosophy, but it was his work that inspired what is known as "the ethical turn" in Continental thought, serving as the direct inspiration of Jacques Derrida's widely known essays "Violence and metaphysics" and "At this very moment in this work here I am" (Bernasconi and Critchley 1991, xii). My interpretation of Levinasian ethics is a critical reconstruction. For Levinas, ethical relations happen between humans and cannot include other animals. Levinas would be troubled by my extension of his work beyond the interhuman (see Davy 2003, 2007), as well as my application of it in the context of Heathenry (see Davy 2005).

18. Social psychologists Jeff Greenberg, Tom Pyszczynski, and Sheldon Solomon (1986) developed terror management theory to test cultural anthropologist Ernest Becker's ideas in *The Denial of Death* (1973) and *The Birth and Death of Meaning* (1962).

19. This may be as much as one-eighth of the Heathens in Canada. Based on the distribution in the United States of Heathens comprising about 3% of the Pagan population (see Berger et al. 2003; Calico 2018, 14–16; Lewis 2012), among the approximately 25,495 people who identified themselves as Pagan in the last Canadian census there should around 800 Heathens in Canada. This is consistent with Karl E. H. Seigfried's (2014) informal Heathen census, which had 805 self-identified Heathen respondents in Canada, 7,878 in the United States, and 16,700 worldwide. He found more Heathens in the United States than anywhere else, but found that Heathens comprised a higher percentage of the total population in Iceland, Denmark, Norway, Sweden, and Australia, with the United States and Canada having similar percentages to Australia (at 0.0025, 0.0023, and 0.0025 percent of the total population, respectively).

20. The Troth, a Heathen organization in the United States, also identifies itself as inclusive. *The Troth* (https://www.thetroth.org, 2020). From what I know of Troth members in the United States and internationally from my participation in their online event Frith Forge 2020, they support similar political views to Heathens I have studied in Canada. Other anti-racist Heathen organizations identified by Michael Strmiska (2020, 12) include Heathens Against Hate, Heathens United Against Racism, and the Alliance for Inclusive Heathenry.

21. Pedagogical and management literature show a similar shift in focus from increasing diversity to inclusion as a necessary practice to achieve that goal. See, e.g., Shore et al. (2011).

22. *Canadian Pagan Declaration on Intolerance* (http://pagandeclaration.com, accessed May 3, 2018). Jade Pichette, one of the gythias of Vindisir Kindred, spearheaded this declaration, released on December 10, International Human Rights Day, in 2016 (Jade Pichette, personal communication May 21, 2020). This broadened the anti-racist "Declaration 127" by *Huginn's Heathen Hof*, an international Heathen website, developed in response to racist attitudes publicly supported by the Asatru Free Assembly in the United States. "Declaration 127" cites verse 127 of the *Hávamál*, part of the Old Norse text *Poetic Edda* that many Heathens regard as an important source of inspiration, which reads: "When you see misdeeds, speak out against them, and give your enemies no frið." To give "no frið" (frith) means to give them no peace and to exclude them from the community.

23. See Asprem (2008), Bjørgo (1997), Emore and Leader (2020), Kaplan (1996, 1997), Kaplan and Bjørgo (1998), Kaplan and Weinberg (1998), Gardell (2003), Goodrick-Clarke (2002), Ivakhiv (2005a), Rood (2020), Snook (2013), Strmiska (2018), von Schnurbein (2016).

24. My survey had 123 Heathen respondents and 362 other Pagan respondents, which I compared with an overall sample of 643 Heathen and Pagan respondents (some of whom categorized their religion as "spiritual" or "atheist," leading to a discrepancy between counting Heathens and Pagans separately and together), as well as a random sample of Canadians of 241 respondents. Lest readers suspect that some of these respondents misunderstood "Pagan and Heathen" in the popular sense of meaning nonbelievers or non-Christians, there is a segment of contemporary Paganism that self-identifies as atheist or non-theist (see Halstead 2016).

25. Jefferson Calico (2020, 22–46), documents Stephen McNallen's ongoing recruitment activities for white separatism. Sociologist Helen Berger found that Heathens are, like other Pagans, more likely to be progressive than the general public and less likely to identify with the far right than the general public in her most recent survey of contemporary Pagans. Berger (2019, 38, 144) indicates that while most Heathens are not racist, a small minority (1.1%) identify as far right. These are mostly to be found within the youngest people she surveyed. She (Berger 2019, 145) indicates that Heathens (77.2%) are more likely than other Pagans (75.5%) to have

"extremely negative attitudes toward Neo-Nazis" and the "vast majority, feel the need to protect themselves and their religion against Neo-Nazis who self-identify as Heathen."

26. This is for the safety of group members. Kindreds typically meet in practitioners' homes, so they do not want to invite people to such events unless they are sure those people will be inclusive. Some kindreds have designated members who are willing to do outreach with those who may not be ready to join an inclusive kindred but are open to talking about inclusion.

27. No one identified themself to me as Indigenous, but other practitioners identified two participants as Indigenous people. Asking people what their ethnicity is is rarely socially acceptable and would be poorly received in this inclusive community.

28. As printed in the program for Hail and Horn Gathering, 2019. A similar statement appears in the 2017 and 2018 programs.

29. See Jade Pichette, "#HavamalWitches: We Are the Witches the Havamal Warns You About" *Spiral Nature* (https://www.spiralnature.com/spirituality/witches-the-havamal-warns-about/, August 2, 2017).

30. While the numbers of respondents were not always large enough for statistical significance, I offer a brief summary to give a general sense of how Heathens and Pagans differ from one another and others to suggest how the Heathens of my case fit into the broader landscape. These survey results suggest that in many ways Heathens and Pagans differ similarly from the general population, but Heathens are different from other Pagans in that men outnumber women in Heathenry by about 2 to 1, while in other Pagan traditions the reverse is true. Helen Berger's (2019, 21) most recent survey finds that there are still more women (71.6%) than men in contemporary Paganism, but Heathens have become more gender-balanced than in her previous survey (Berger et al. 2003), now also having more women than men, changing from 65% male and 35% female, to 50.8% female and 47.8% male in her most recent survey. The difference in the gender split between Berger and my survey may be due to me reaching a broader political spread of Heathens if there are more men in more socially conservative Heathen groups, which anecdotal evidence suggests may be the case. See Appendix 2 for some tables summarizing my survey findings.

31. A *dís* is a divine female figure of some kind, sometimes a goddess, sometimes an ancestor, or some other sort of female figure. Skaði is a *jötunn* (giant) who married into the Æsir group of deities, so some practitioners regard her as a goddess. The term "dís" is useful to preserve the emic categorization of figures like Skaði.

32. When anthropologist Marie-Françoise Guédon was first conducting field study in Alaska she heard quite different stories from previous researchers in the same community. When she asked why, the people said they were telling her the stories she needed to hear as a young unmarried woman, whereas they told previous researchers stories relevant to their stages of life and relations with others (Guédon 1988).

33. Scholar practitioners in Pagan studies have reflected fairly extensively on their positionality in their work (see, e.g., Blain et al. 2004). Most of them engage in some form of what ethnographers variously term "self-reflexive ethnography," "auto-ethnography," or "experiential ethnography." Experiential ethnography takes the researcher's own experience as data (Young and Goulet 1994). This is not a good description of my methodology because while I am part of the group under study, the research is not about me. While my experience as a practitioner informs my understanding of what is happening in a ritual and affords some insight into what the consequences of participating in the rituals are, my interpretation comes not only from my experience but also from other participants in my research and from the academic literature I draw on. The term "auto-ethnography" might be assumed to signify the same thing as "experiential anthropology" but generally refers to Marilyn Strathern's sense of "anthropology carried out in the social context which produced it" (quoted by Wallis 2004, 196) and Anthony Jackson's (1987) "anthropology at home," indicating that the researcher is part of the group studied. In general, the use of the terms "auto-," "self-experiential," "reflexive," and "self-reflective" anthropology/ethnography take the researcher's standpoint as resource rather than liability, following Alison Wylie (Wallis 2004, 196). While double-insider research can offer insights not necessarily apparent to etic "objective" research, it can also be biased and self-serving. Marcus Davidsen (2012) finds Pagan studies scholars guilty of this. He notes that the problems he identifies in Pagan studies are indicative of wider problems in the study of religion—specifically of "believer" perspectives on the religion studied. He argues for keeping the study of religion scientifically objective in the positivist sense, which is the preference of a minority of scholars in the field. Most, he says, take a more

phenomenological or hermeneutic approach, leaving aside the reality of what practitioners believe.

34. The descriptive and interpretive focus of most studies in religion eschews evaluation or anything that might be seen as prescriptive. This is largely because religious studies as a discipline emerged out of the academic study of theology, and religion scholars fear being accused of supporting believer perspectives if they engage in evaluation. Grimes (1990, 215) suggests that this fear has led religion scholars to leave fieldwork to anthropologists and evaluation to theologians, which he says has impoverished the study of ritual. Even description of ritual practices is tacitly critical, Grimes (1990, 216) says, because it is always description from a particular point of view.

35. For an accessible article for a lay audience, see Karns (2018). Studies show that the experience of gratitude makes people more altruistic (Karns et al. 2017), more pro-social (Tsang and Martin 2019), and more supportive (Moieni et al. 2019) and improves interpersonal relations (Algoe et al. 2013). Tsang et al. (2019) gives a good overview of previous research on gratitude and pro-social behavior.

Chapter 1

1. This account is based on my participant observation at Hail and Horn Gathering in 2018 and 2019, harmonized into a single narrative.

2. In keeping with the adage "If I am more fortunate than others I need to build a longer table, not a taller fence" (attributed to Tamlyn Tomita), if more people register for this event, volunteers add more picnic tables and tenting as necessary.

3. Such items often originate as gifts from others at this event and usually start out as found items or are reclaimed from accidental deaths, or were previously received as gifts that are passed on. The wolf pelt and large wolf skull in Figure 1.3, for example, were given to Jade as gifts by others in the Heathen community.

4. Ewan is nonbinary and uses the pronouns fae/faer, which function much as the somewhat more common nonbinary pronouns they/them.

5. Philologist Rudolph Simek (1993 [1984], 355) defines "vé" as "shrine," but for the Heathens of Raven's Knoll and Vindisir a vé usually has poles set upright in the ground, mostly encircled with a rope, leaving an opening (forming a penannular or C shape). Each year at Raven's Knoll Heathens erect a god pole to welcome a deity into the Vé. Participants choose the deity to be honored through a vote.

6. The COVID-19 pandemic precluded having in-person gatherings for 2020 and 2021, so the blót to Bragi was rescheduled for the summer of 2022. Tyr was welcomed into the Vé in 2023.

7. Heathens in Vindisir and at Raven's Knoll use the term "húsel" for communal meals in Heathen ritual. This usage comes from Austin Lawrence and Erik Lacharity, who have popularized their understanding of this at Hail and Horn Gathering and at Well and Tree Gathering. It comes from an Old English word *husl*, used to refer to the Christian eucharist that originally referred to food offerings to the gods (Pollington 2010 [2003], 46, n3). While the term is not current beyond Canada, the practice of including a shared meal as part of blót is evident in contemporary Heathen practice elsewhere (see Calico 2018, 307–333; Strmiska 2007) and in historical sources such as the Hákonar Saga Góða in *Heimskringla* (Sturluson 2016, 98), which often refer to these feasts as "banquets" (see also Simek 1993 [1984]).

8. Simek (1993 [1984], 374) indicates that the translation of "wyrd" as "fate" was a Medieval interpretation based on Christian concepts rather one than true to earlier concepts.

9. Bauschatz's *The Well and the Tree* (1982) is out of print, and the edition of it I had access to was digitized using character recognition so pagination may not be consistent with the original publication.

10. The Heathens of Raven's Knoll and Vindisir do not make reference to "chieftains" but are led by gythias and gothis. Historically some community leaders were women. Thirteen of the original landholders in Iceland were women. Carol Clover (1993, 368) notes that "Only a man could be a *goði* [gothi], but it was technically possible for women to *own* the office."

11. "The folk" here means "the people" and refers to the inclusive Heathen community, in contrast to the way some Heathens use "the folk" to refer to white people or people of a limited set of European ethnic backgrounds.

12. I suspect it would make sense to understand this as a middle-voiced process, which is hard to describe in language that has lost this way of speaking but that would fit with relational ontology. The *middle voice* describes expression that is neither in the first person ("I do something"), the second person ("you do something"), nor the third person ("they do something"), but something that emerges in between. Greek and Sanskrit, as well as Indo-European used to have this grammatic possibility (see Bauschatz 1982, 108–109; Llewelyn 1991, vix). For further discussion of the middle voice in relation to ethics, see Llewelyn (1991). Bauschatz suggests the development of preterite verbs in German devolves from something like this: these verbs as a group refer to actions the occurrences of which clearly entail other concomitant actions. They are all representative of states or nonactive, situational conditions that provide contingent restrictions governing other, related activities. The states of knowing, availing, being able, owing, daring, and needing all exist in relation to powerful contextual control that structures any consequent activity. Thus, their presence in any context would suggest the presence in it also of factors beyond those of any immediate possibility for action by any immediate actor alone (Bauschatz 1982, 107). This would seem to entail a relational ontology, which might be more easily expressed in the middle voice. Bauschatz (1982, 110) refers to the middle-voice as "medio-passive" and indicates that preterite verbs eventually developed into the passive voice ("something was done"). It is perhaps significant in this respect that in Proto-Indo-European, the word for "guest" is the same as the word "host" (*ghos-ti*), and the root for "give" and "take" (*dō-*) appears to have also been the same (Anthony 2007, 31, 238).

13. Barber (1994, 234) indicates that lab testing shows early Scandinavian fabric was more likely made from nettle than flax fibers. "Linen" has been used to apply to fabric woven from both. Nettles similarly grow in moist ground and benefit from retting in water. It seems possible that that "cloutie" practices in Celtic traditions of hanging or tying bits of cloth or ribbons on tress around wells may recall the practice of retting plants in bogs and hanging the fibers harvested on trees to dry. The Sacred Well at Raven's Knoll often has clouties tied on trees around it, as can be seen in Figure 3.1.

14. For links between seiðr (magical or divinatory) practices and spinning, see Heide (2006) and Mencej (2011). Based on her familiarity with hand spinning, British American Heathen Cat Heath (2021, 205–228) describes how it can be done as a form of "pulling" magic through which practitioners can draw things toward them and spin them into wyrd.

15. I learned this from Peter Schuler, an Ojibwe (Anishinaabe) elder of the Mississaugas of the Credit River Nation, and Kimmerer (2013).

16. Marisol de la Cadena quotes a Quechua understanding of relationality that sounds remarkably similar to Heathen understandings of wyrd: "Allyu is like a weaving . . . and all the beings in the world, people, animals, mountains, plants, etc. are like the threads, we are part of the design. The beings in the world are not alone, just like a thread by itself cannot be weaving, the thread is only when it is woven, only if it is allyu" (de la Cadena 2013, 59). There are certain commonalities across traditions that are expressive of relational ontologies in using the imagery of threads and weaving to describe our relations. Tim Ingold's thinking about "lines" in his developments of relational ontology also seems apt in relation to Auz's description of himself as connected with others along various threads. Ingold asks, "What if the living being is the line of its own movement? Then it cannot be imagined as a bounded totality, surrounded by its environment. We have to rather think of it as a line of growth of concrescence—or, more realistically, as a bundle of such lines—and of the environment as a zone in which these lines become comprehensively entangled with one another" (Ingold 2010, 300–301, quoted in Green 2013, 79). Heathen relational ontology is certainly not identical with those of Indigenous peoples such as de la Cadena and others discuss in terms of relational ontologies, but I think it is fair to say they are "partially connected" in de la Cadena's sense of that phrase, borrowed from Marilyn Strathern (see de la Cadena 2015, xxv). De la Cadena's description of relational ontology in terms of partial connections between persons shares some sense of the strands of connection between persons that constitute each as a person, which again sounds somewhat like wyrd: "The notion of partial connections offers . . . the possibility of conceptualizing entities (or collectives) with relations integrally implied, thus disrupting them as units; emerging from the relation, entities are intra-related (cf. Barad 2007) instead of being inter-related, as in the case of the units composing

mestizaje. Instead of plurality (a feature premised on units), the mathematical image congenial to partial connections is that of fractals: they offer the possibility of describing irregular bodies that escape Euclidean geometrical measurements because their borders also allow other bodies in—without, however, touching each other everywhere" (de la Cadena 2015, 32).

17. Such descriptions of how ethics come to pass may be experienced by readers as a provocation to ethics. Levinas's philosophy has been received in this way (Bernasconi and Wood 1988). Because I support the ethics I am describing, I see this as a good thing, but prescriptive writings in religious studies are often criticized because they appear to slide into what is seen as theology. Writing from the perspective of an ontology that runs counter to the dominant individualized ontology taken as the norm will inevitably seem to slide into a religious or "faith-based" perspective. Ironically, this characterization of such writing is itself a relic of Protestant views on religion that emphasize belief and sincerity and regard ritual primarily as a form of communication rather than as actions with consequences (see Asad 1983; Seligman et al. 2008).

18. These are the consequences that participants described to me in interviews and my experience as a participant. Of course, it is possible for people not to be meaningfully engaged in ritual practice or to participate insincerely. During this research I did not encounter anyone who participated in sumbel who did not find it to be a meaningful practice. I discuss possibilities of "infelicitous" ritual in Chapter 3.

19. Ritual practices of other Pagans, particularly those involving making offerings, may well also sustain relational ontologies, but my current data on this are limited to Heathen practices.

20. "They/them/their" are Jade's preferred pronouns as a nonbinary femme-identified person.

21. Anderson's "imagined community" is not just characteristic of modern nation states, but, he says, perhaps characteristic of any community larger than a village in which every face is familiar: "Javanese villagers have always known that they are connected to people they have never seen, but these ties were once imagined particularistically—as indefinitely stretchable nets of kinship and clientship" (Anderson 2016 [1983], 6). The difference in modern nation states is that the sense of nation circumscribes a limit to the imagined moral community (Anderson 2016 [1983], 7).

22. Pre-modern ontologies were different from contemporary Heathen relationality, but it is worth noting that anthropological descriptions of the relational ontologies of Indigenous peoples are of contemporary people rather than traditions of the past. I am not convinced that relational ontologies arise only in small-scale traditional societies or that it makes sense to distinguish between what Barfield (1988 [1957]) calls "original participation" before the scientific revolution and the "final participation" that he suggests becomes possible only after a necessary detour through interiorization. This distinction makes sense within Barfield's Christian eschatology but not for those who reject the characterization of the evolution of consciousness as a linear trajectory. In this work, I describe how ritual practices influence the enacting of ontology in the subculture of Heathenry in this community of practice. I do not think ontology is completely dependent on the economic system, but rather that it might be a means of shifting economic relations through changing how people relate.

23. This insight comes from terror management theory.

24. See Cialdini et al. (1990), Cialdini (2003), Cialdini and Goldstein (2004); Kallgren et al. (2000).

25. Interpretive frameworks function as what Rappaport (1979) terms an "operationalized worldview." These frameworks are modifiable through what Luhrmann (1989) calls "interpretive drift."

Chapter 2

1. This description blends details from Vindisir's Dísablóts of 2018 and 2019 into one narrative. A significantly different earlier incarnation of this chapter reporting on the 2018 event was published as Davy (2020).

2. Aloysius comes from a man who donated his body to science. Jessica receives many such oddities as gifts from people who do not otherwise know what to do with them. She has a fairly extensive animal skull "collection," all of which is ethically sourced. For Heathens such as those in Vindisir, these are not just objects, but are cared for as honored dead.

3. "Dísir" is the plural form of "dís," an Old Norse term meaning honored female or woman, somewhat as the term "lady" functions in English, reflecting historical variations in the concept. "Dísir" is variously interpreted as "supernatural female guardian" (Ellis 1968 [1943], 134–138, 184), "goddess" (see, e.g., Ellis Davidson 1998, 47, 146, 177, 185), or "woman" in modern Icelandic (see Gunnell 2000, 130). In the North American contemporary Heathen context, "dísir" often refers to female ancestors but can also refer to other female personages. The name "Vindisir," meaning "friends of the dísir," for example, references the connection group members feel with Freya, Skaði, and Frigg.

4. Vindisir Kindred includes animal sacrifice at our Winterfinding blót, sharing ethically raised chickens or rabbits. These animals are raised by a member of the kindred and humanely killed and eaten. As Calico (2018, 317) observed, with American Heathens who engage in such practices, it is very important to members of Vindisir that the animals be well treated, have a good life, and a good death to make a good offering. For a deeper discussion of Vindisir's offerings of animals at Winterfinding see Davy (2023).

5. This need to scale back was partly a result of leading a large public blót at Hail and Horn Gathering the previous season and ongoing leadership of events in southwestern Ontario.

6. Heath (2021, 18) refers to such ritual narrations as "narrative charms" and indicates that there are many examples of these in Old English medical/magical manuscripts. Variations of the story Jade narrated can be found in *Völuspá* 31–33 in *The Poetic Edda*, and in *Gylfaginning* 17–21 in *The Prose Edda*.

7. These bones are from a crow and a blue jay. Jessica found one of the birds on the side of the road, and the other was a gift from a friend who had accidentally killed it when playing golf.

8. To assign a calendar date to Dísablót or any other historically attested practice is to impose a coherence not present in the past. These events were not set by "the calendar" because the groups in question did not initially use a standardized calendar. The rites were "guide-marks" rather than "divisions," in Bourdieu's terms (see Bourdieu 1977, 105). For discussion of the development of Nordic calendars, see Rasmussen (2020).

9. For further discussion of the timing of Disting, see Rasmussen (2020).

10. The Heathens of Raven's Knoll often prefer to use the Old Norse term "landvaettir" to "land wights," especially in public, because they do not want to be me misheard as talking about honoring "whites."

11. Similarly, Michael Strmiska suggests that Icelanders understand huldufólk more as "*ultra*natural" than "*super*natural." They are not beyond nature or material existence but deeply natural. He says "They are part of the natural landscape, and their primary concern is to preserve the land in which they dwell alongside humans" (Strmiska 2000, 126).

12. Heathens in this community do not refer to this as "smudging" because they do not want to misappropriate that term from First Nations traditions. Smoke cleansing with censers and incense has long been a practice in European traditions as well, but "smudging" has become a term largely reserved for Indigenous use.

13. This was a comment made during a Vindisir Winterfinding event, when we were preparing for a late-night esoteric rite in a wooded area at an old farm. The wind had picked up, and it was pitch dark. Some people expressed feelings of trepidation about it not feeling safe outside, and the host indicated that there are parts of the land that never feel safe at night. Jade related to us that the first time the group did ritual there, the landvaettir were quite hostile, and they told us it was because they were angry about colonization.

14. "Pudding" here refers to dessert in general, as is common in England.

15. While some Heathens want to clearly distinguish their practices from other Pagans (see Calico 2018, 231–236; Snook 2015, 38–43), the Heathens of Vindisir and Raven's Knoll are less concerned with keeping their practices separate, partly because there are many mixed households in which part of the family identifies as Heathen and part as some other sort of Pagan, and also because the Raven's Knoll community explicitly fosters positive interactions between traditions, hosting pan-Pagan as well as tradition-specific events. Some in this community identify as Heathen witches.

16. See Arndt et al. (2004); Cozzolino et al. (2004); Gailliot et al. (2008); Hirschberger et al. (2008); Jonas et al. (2002).

17. Die-ins may function as death primes and thus induce the effects of mortality salience.

18. See also McKay and Whitehouse (2015) and van Elk et al. (2016).

19. See Baillon et al. (2013); Bateson et al. (2006); Ernest-Jones et al. (2011); Haley and Fessler (2005); Rigdon et al. (2009).

20. This publication is a book rather than an academic journal and contains a mix of inclusive and folkish content. The interview can be accessed at http://www.brontaylor.com/pdf/Roberg-Toll-Bron_Taylor_intv_J_Heathen_Studies(2011).pdf.

Chapter 3

1. This account reflects Well and Tree Gathering events of 2018 and 2019 combined into one narrative.
2. Brynja prefers to call this a "grove" rather than a "vé" because the term has a different resonance for her. To my mind, a grove grows in place, whereas a vé is set up. This situation has aspects of both, with the tree growing in place with multiple saplings springing up nearby and logs set up to create a vé.
3. The seeds are an intentional echo of archaeological findings of the stomach contents of "bog bodies" deposited in the early Iron Age in Europe, such as Grauballe Man (see McLean 2008).
4. For Bynja, in common with other contemporary Heathens, Hel is the goddess of the underworld as well as the name of the underworld. How Heathens imagine the afterlife is diverse, as are descriptions of it in the lore (see Ellis 1968 [1943]).
5. This means that some practitioners attribute the conceiving of their children to having asked for Nerthus's help in this, and they consumed dirt from the consecrated ground of her vé in the passion of their appeals to her. I did not see this, but witnessed tearful thanks given to her for infants brought to the event. Cat Heath (2021, 32) notes that the much later Germanic goddess Holle or Holda was "believed to hold the spirits of the children yet to be born in a local spring."
6. Some of the god posts in the Vé have had to be replaced due to insect damage, providing this source of sacred fuel.
7. The URL is https://www.youtube.com/channel/UCsKBD8H4gupJhYccMIDkqKA, but it is easier to find by just googling "Heathen Hearth."
8. In traditional seyeir, turf would have been used to cover the pit, but sand works well. This firepit is the safest place to conduct pit cooking at Raven's Knoll, with little danger of fire spreading and igniting the surrounding forest.
9. I do not include a separate section on historical and comparative context in this chapter because discussion of the historical context is included in the ethnographic vignette, and I did not find published accounts of contemporary processions of Nerthus. Practitioners I spoke with indicated that they had heard about processions in Texas with Nerthus in the back of a pickup truck and that Nerthus is venerated in a somewhat different form in the Netherlands as Nehalennia. For connections between Nerthus and Nehalennia, see Ellis Davidson (1998, 134).
10. Each of the ritual leaders attributes chronic health problems that they subsequently developed to their participation in the first procession of Nerthus at Raven's Knoll.
11. Rituals and myths can also teach what *not* to do, such as the Plough Masquerade Lia Zola describes (2011), in which men dress up as oxen being made to plow the snow while trying to escape off to the pub. Their actions give a comical parody of plowing and could be interpreted as a ritual inversion in Victor Turner's terms (1969). Similarly, some stories from the myths and sagas may be seen as cautionary tales of what not to do (e.g., feuds that destroy families).
12. See *Gylfaginning* 8 in Sturluson (2005, 16–17) and *Grímnismál* 40 in Larrington (2014, 54).
13. This story dates from the tenth century, which is rather distant from the first-century inspiration of the procession of Nerthus from Tacitus's *Germania*. Although both sources inspire the reconstruction of tradition in contemporary Heathenry, like the story of Ymir's sacrifice, the story of the sacrifice of Balder is not referenced in the procession of Nerthus at Raven's Knoll.
14. For discussion of animal sacrifice in Heathen blót rituals, see Davy (2023) and Strmiska (2007). Recent treatments of sacrifice more broadly suggest that it does not necessarily make sense to try to interpret all sacrifice as a singular phenomenon that has universal features or meaning. For relatively recent discussions covering diverse interpretations of sacrifice, see Rasmussen (2002), Olson (2002), McClymond (2004), Palmer et al. (2006), Janowitz (2011). Older influential treatments of sacrifice include Hubert and Mauss (1968), Firth (1972), Girard (1977, 1986, 1987), Burkert (1983), Valeri (1985), Hamerton-Kelly (1987). There is also more to Well and

Tree Gathering than what I have included here. The procession ritual is also about welcoming spring, the returning fertility of the land, regeneration, and the irrepressible upwelling of life. There were workshops, other details not noted here, and inevitably things I did not notice. Other interpretative frames might usefully be applied focusing on different themes, such as pilgrimage.

15. Camping may induce mortality salience as a matter of course for practitioners at Raven's Knoll because it puts people in contact with "wild" nature. Sander Koole and Agnes Van den Berg (2005) found that "wild" nature is more likely to induce mortality salience than "tame" nature. They found that "wild" nature can prime terror and awe and make mortality salient, but, alternatively, may make a sense of life and freedom arise (Koole and Van den Berg 2005, 1014–1015). Ara Norenzaya, Ian Hansen, and Jasmine Cady speculate that animists may be less likely to see the "wilderness" as a threat (Norenzaya et al. 2008, 191).

16. Brynja recommends Nicanthiel Hrafnhild, *Boar, Birch and Bog: Prayers to Nerthus* (2009) as a useful source for practitioners.

17. These sort of gifting relations between groups were evident at the 2016 protests against the proposed Dakota Access Pipeline (DAPL) at Standing Rock where, Siv Ellen Kraft (2019) reports, Sámi from Norway came to the site and met with the leader of the Hunkpapa Lakota, who were aiming to protect their water from the dangers of oil spills. They held ceremony together and gave gifts. Increasingly, Indigenous groups around the world are supporting one another in this way and developing a common identity as Indigenous, which I would argue is negotiated through such gifting ceremonies (see also Kraft 2018).

18. Findings for related questions about who is part of community and what sort of entities have feelings were less distinct from one sample to another. Phrasing seems to matter in whether or not the category of "person" includes nonhuman others.

19. Contra Quilley (2013), as Sahlins indicates (2011a, 2011b), the anthropological record shows that the restriction of the moral community to the human is a modern phenomenon. If the historical record under consideration starts with Homer and is restricted to Western philosophy, it may look like an expanding horizon of moral considerability develops, but, when compared with relational ontologies cross-culturally, it becomes apparent that this Western trajectory is unusual rather than part of a universal evolution.

20. Technically the Ottawa Valley includes the entire watershed of the Ottawa River, most of which is in Quebec, and can be said to form a bioregion. However, the Heathens of Raven's Knoll, in common with residents of the surrounding area, understand it to refer primarily to the rural areas of the watershed in Ontario.

21. J. Edward Chamberlain (2003, 1) recounts how a Gitskan elder asked government officials who were advancing a land claim for Canada, "If this is your land, where are your stories?" and proceeded to tell a story in the language of his people.

Chapter 4

1. See Temper and Martinez-Alier (2016, 33, 43, 51) for data on protest efficacy.

2. Historically, business shifted from mass marketing to market segmentation, then targeted marketing and eventually "lifestyle" marketing to increase demand for specialized products (Cohen 2003, 295, 299).

3. There is a great deal more to be said about blót practices and animal sacrifice. I investigate Vindisir's practice of animal sacrifice in Davy (2023).

4. Weaver does not mention shrine waste, garbage, or waste disposal, nor does he discuss sourcing of animal products such as skulls used in shrines. Environmental issues were not a focus of his research.

5. Ritual practice is, of course, important in other religious traditions also, but my survey results suggest that it is significantly more important to Heathens and other Pagans compared to the general populace.

Chapter 5

1. "UPG" as a concept originated on "The Asatru List," an Internet discussion board, in conversations about reconstructing Heathen traditions (Jenny Blain, private communication, March 16, 2021). Blain indicates that it originally referred to "unusual personal gnosis" and later came to mean "unverified personal gnosis." I am grateful to Rich Blackett for helping me track down the origin of the phrase.
2. For an investigation of Vindisir's Winterfinding blót and how animal sacrifice can contribute to ethical consumption, see Davy (2023).
3. The deep play of ritual may even help us learn better than discursive instruction, as play does for children. Developmental psychologist Karyn Purvis said it takes 400 repetitions to create a new synapse, but doing it through play takes only 10–20. (There is a consensus that Purvis said this but no one can track down the source of the statistic, and she's passed away). We can tell people hundreds of times not to waste energy, or we can perhaps enact such values in play or ritual in a fraction of that time.

Glossary

Æsir   A group of deities in Norse mythology who are allied with Odin, typically said to include Frigg, Tyr, Idunn, Thor, and others. According to some practitioners, may include various jötnar who have married into the group, such as Skaði.

Álfar   A term used to refer to entities such as elves and dwarves, sometimes used to refer to male ancestors, particularly in contemporary Heathen practice (though some practitioners dispute this usage).

Blót   A ritual of giving offerings, usually honoring a deity or deities, but sometimes to ancestors or other entities. Historically, this would have been an offering from a sacrificed animal and include a shared meal from this between participants.

Dísablót   A blót to the dísir.

Dís   Female honorific, divine female figure, female ancestor, Goddess, or woman.

Dísir   Honored female powers, including ancestors and/or divine entities. Historical usage of this term varies in meaning, sometimes including valkyries and fylgja, understood as female guardian spirits of ancestral lines and sometimes negatively as those who decide when one's time is up.

Eddas   Two collections of Old Norse literature written down in the 1200s. *The Poetic Edda* is a collection of poems with mythological content, some of which probably originate in oral tradition. *The Prose Edda* was written by Snorri Sturluson to retain fading cultural memory in Iceland after Christianization (which happened in 1000 CE).

Fylgja (plural fylgur)   A personal or familial protective wight, often imaged as female and sometimes in animal form.

Freya   A goddess associated with magic, female sexuality, and war.

Freyr   A god associated with male sexuality and agricultural fertility.

Frigg   A goddess associated with foresight, wisdom, household management, spinning, and birth. Wife of Odin.

Frith   The keeping of good relations and maintenance of allies through dynamic peace.

Gythia   Female or femme-identified ritual leader in Heathenry.

Gothi   Male or masculine-identified ritual leader in Heathenry.

Hearg   Old English word for an altar made of piled stones. (Old Norse *hörgr*.)

Hel   The land of the dead and/or the personification of death presented as Loki's daughter in the lore, and, for some contemporary Heathens, a revered goddess.

Húsel   A shared meal following blót, usually understood to be part of the blót; includes consuming the food and drink shared with those honored in blót. While this practice is evident in historical sources, the use of the term "húsel" is a contemporary reinterpretation.

Jötunn (plural jötnar)   Variously termed "giants" or "etins," these are powers or forces of the land, some of whom are friendly with the Æsir and some of whom are hostile in the lore.

Kindred   A close-knit group of Heathens in contemporary practice; historically, this would have referred to an extended household or small community.

Landvaettir   Land wights. Landvaettir is a historical name for the regenerative powers of the land, somewhat like the Latin term *genius loci*, often translated as land "spirits" or "spirits of place" but may be understood as corporeal beings, such as bodies of water.

Lore, the   Historical sources that Heathens draw on, including the sagas, *The Poetic Edda*, *The Prose Edda*, and other early literature from northern Europe, such as *Beowulf*.

Memory Ale   A sumbel-like series of toasts to someone who has passed on. It is like a wake in some respects but may be held apart from funeral rites.

Nerthus   A dís or goddess associated with the regenerative power of nature.

Njord   A god associated with the sea and fishing.

Norn   A female entity governing wyrd, said to sit at the well at the roots of Yggdrasil, the World Tree, and spin our destinies.

Odin   A god associated with war, wisdom, magic, and divination. Regarded by some as chief of the Norse gods and by others as a late addition. Husband of Frigg.

Ragnarok   The ending of the Æsir in a final battle, the "twilight of the gods" that ushers in a new era with those who survive hidden in the Tree of Life.

Sagas   Stories of the Viking era written in Old Norse.

Seiðr   A historically attested practice of divination, usually by women.

Skaði   A goddess or jötunn associated with the north, snow, hunting, and standing up for oneself. Known as the ski or snowshoe dís.

Sumbel   A historically attested ritual of drinking (usually alcohol) from a shared cup in public recognition of worthy actions by making toasts and sometimes giving gifts.

Troth, the   An inclusive Heathenry organization based in the United States.

Vaettir   See *Wight*.

Vanir   A group of deities that became allied with the Æsir, typically said to include Freyr, Freya, and Njord, among others.

Vé   A place set aside for honoring a deity or deities, usually outside and marked by posts sunk in the ground and a cord or rope around them, forming a circle with an opening.

Viking era   Time of migrations of Old Norse populations, from about the late 700s to early 1000s CE.

Wights   Other-than-human persons or nonhuman entities such as landvaettir, ancestors, and house "spirits," which may be understood as corporeal beings and/or disembodied forces resident in particular places.

Wyrd   The interrelations between all that has been and is given, is coming into being, turning into something or someone, and coming to pass. This is also the name of one of the Norns in Old English.

References

Abram, David. 1996. *The Spell of the Sensuous: Perception and Language in a More-Than-Human World*. New York: Vintage.

Aitamurto, Kaarina, and Scott Simpson, eds. 2014 [2013]. *Modern Pagan and Native Faith Movements in Central and Eastern Europe*. London: Routledge.

Algoe, Sara B., Barbara L. Frederickson, and Shelly L. Gable. 2013. "The Social Functions of the Emotion of Gratitude via Expression." *Emotion* 13 (4): 605–609. doi: 10.1037/a0032701.

Anderson, Benedict. 2016 [1983]. *Imagined Communities: Reflections on the Origin and Spread of Nationalism*, revised edition. London: Verso.

Anthony, David W. 2007. *The Horse, the Wheel, and Language: How Bronze-Age Riders from the Eurasian Steppes Shaped the Modern World*. Princeton: Princeton University Press.

Aðalsteinsson, Jón Hnefill. 1998. *A Piece of Horse Liver: Myth, Ritual and Folklore in Old Icelandic Sources*. Translated by Terry Gunnell and Joan Turville-Petre. Rejkjavík: Háskólaútgáfan.

Arndt, Jamie, Sheldon Solomon, Tim Kasser, and Kennon M. Sheldon. 2004. "The Urge to Splurge: A Terror Management Account of Materialism and Consumer Behavior." *Journal of Consumer Psychology* 14 (3): 198–212.

Asad, Talal. 1983. "Anthropological of Conceptions of Religion: Reflections on Geertz." *Man* 18 (2): 237–259.

Asprem, Egil. 2008. "Heathens Up North: Politics, Polemic, and Contemporary Norse Paganism in Norway." *The Pomegranate: The International Journal of Pagan Studies* 10 (1): 41–69. doi:10.1558/pome.v10i1.41.

Austin, J. L. 1975. *How to Do Things with Words: The William James Lectures Delivered at Harvard University in 1955*. Oxford: Oxford University Press. https://doi.org/10.1093/acprof:oso/9780198245537.001.0001.

Baillon, Aurélien, Asli Selim, and Dennie van Dolder. 2013. "On the Social Nature of Eyes: The Effect of Social Cues in Interaction and Individual Choice Tasks." *Evolution and Human Behavior* 34 (2): 146–154. https://doi.org/10.1016/j.evolhumbehav.2012.1.

Ball, Billy. 2021. "A Small-Town Congregation Sold Its Church. A Whites-Only Group Moved In." *Washington Post*. March 6, 2021. https://www.washingtonpost.com/national/a-small-town-congregation-sold-its-church-a-whites-only-group-moved-in/2021/03/06/ac5b6 5de-7e02-11eb-85cd-9b7fa90c8873_story.html.

Barber, Elizabeth Wayland. 1994. *Women's Work: The First 20,000 Years*. New York: W. W. Norton.

Barfield, Owen. 1988 [1957]. *Saving the Appearances: A Study in Idolatry*. 2nd edition. Middleton, Connecticut: Wesleyan University Press.

Barfield, Owen. 2010 [1923]. *Poetic Diction: A Study in Meaning*. Oxford: Barfield Press.

Barfield, Owen. 2012 [1979]. *History, Guilt & Habit*. 2nd, augmented edition. Oxford, UK: Barfield Press.

Barrett, Justin L. 2000. "Exploring the Natural Foundations of Religion." *Trends in Cognitive Sciences* 4 (1): 29–34. https://doi.org/10.1016/S1364-6613(99)01419-9.

Barrett, Justin L. 2011. "Cognitive Science of Religion: Looking Back, Looking Forward." *Journal for the Scientific Study of Religion* 50 (2): 229–239. https://doi.org/10.1111/j.1468-5906.2011.01564.x.

Bastin, Jean-Francois, Yelena Finegold, Claude Garcia, Danilo Mollicone, Marcelo Rezende, Devin Routh, Constantin M Zohner, and Thomas W. Crowther. 2019. "The Global Tree

Restoration Potential." *Science (American Association for the Advancement of Science)* 365 (6448): 76–79. https://doi.org/10.1126/science.aax0848.

Bateson, Melissa, Daniel Nettle, and Gilbert Roberts. 2006. "Cues of Being Watched Enhance Cooperation in a Real-World Setting." *Biology Letters (2005)* 2 (3): 412–414. https://doi.org/10.1098/rsbl.2006.0509.

Bauschatz, Paul. 1982. *The Well and the Tree: World and Time in Early Germanic Culture.* Amherst: University of Massachusetts Press.

Becker, Ernest. 1962. *The Birth and Death of Meaning: An Interdisciplinary Perspective on the Problem of Man.* New York: Free Press.

Becker, Ernest. 1973. *The Denial of Death.* New York: Free Press.

Bell, Catherine. 2009 [1992]. *Ritual Theory, Ritual Practice.* Oxford: Oxford University Press.

Berger, Helen A. 2019. *Solitary Pagans: Contemporary Witches, Wiccans, and Others Who Practice Alone.* Columbia: University of South Carolina Press.

Berger, Helen A., Evan A. Leach, and Leigh S. Shaffer. 2003. *Voices from the Pagan Census: A National Survey of Witches and Neo-Pagans in the United States.* Columbia: University of South Carolina Press.

Berkes, Fikret. 2012 [1999]. *Sacred Ecology.* 3rd edition. New York: Routledge.

Bernasconi, Robert, and Simon Critchley, eds. 1991. *Re-Reading Levinas.* Bloomington: Indiana University Press.

Bernasconi, Robert, and David Wood, eds. 1988. *The Provocation of Levinas: Rethinking the Other.* London: Routledge.

Berry, Evan. 2013. "Religious Environmentalism and Environmental Religion in America." *Religion Compass* 7 (10): 454–466.

Bird-David, Nurit. 1990. "The Giving Environment: Another Perspective on the Economic System of Gatherer-Hunters." *Current Anthropology* 31 (2): 189–196.

Bird-David, Nurit. 1999. "'Animism' Revisited: Personhood, Environment, and Relational Epistemology." *Current Anthropology* 40: S67–S91.

Bird-David, Nurit, and Asaf Darr. 2009. "Commodity, Gift and Mass-Gift: On Gift-Commodity Hybrids in Advanced Mass Consumption Cultures." *Economy and Society* 38 (2): 304–325. https://doi.org/10.1080/03085140902786777.

Bjørgo, Tore. 1997. *Racist and Right-Wing Violence in Scandinavia.* Oslo: Tano Aschehougs Fontenescherie.

Blain, Jenny. 2000. "Contested Meanings: Earth Religion Practitioners and the Everyday." *The Pomegranate: A New Journal of Neopagan Thought* 12: 15–25.

Blain, Jenny. 2002. *Nine Worlds of Seid-Magic: Ecstasy and Neo-shamanism in North European Paganism.* London: Routledge.

Blain, Jenny. 2016. *Wights and Ancestors: Heathenry in a Living Landscape.* Cheshire, UK: Prydein Press.

Blain, Jenny, Douglas Ezzy, and Graham Harvey. 2004. *Researching Paganisms.* Walnut Creek, CA: AltaMira.

Bonneau, Anne-Marie. 2021. *The Zero-Waste Chef.* New York: Penguin Random House.

Bonsu, Samuel K., and Russell W. Belk. 2003. "Do Not Go Cheaply into That Good Night: Death-Ritual Consumption in Asante, Ghana." *Journal of Consumer Research* 30 (1): 41–55. https://doi.org/10.1086/374699.

Bourdieu, Pierre. 1977. *Outline of a Theory of Practice.* Trans. Richard Nice. Cambridge: Cambridge University Press.

Bowman, Benjamin. 2020. "'They Don't Quite Understand the Importance of What We're Doing Today': People's Climate Strikes as Subaltern Activism." *Sustainable Earth* 3: 16.

Burkert, Walter. 1983. *Homo Necans: Interpretations of Ancient Greek Sacrificial Ritual and Myth.* Berkeley: University of California Press.

Butala, Sharon. 1994. *The Perfection of the Morning: An Apprenticeship in Nature.* Toronto: HarperCollins.

Butala, Sharon. 2000. *Wild Stone Heart: An Apprentice in the Fields.* Toronto: HarperCollins.

Caillois, Roger. 1962. *Man, Play, and Games.* Translated by M. Barash. London: Thames and Hudson.

Calico, Jefferson F. 2018. *Being Viking: Heathenism in Contemporary America.* Sheffield, UK: Equinox.

Calico, Jefferson F. 2020. "Performing 'American Völkisch.'" In *Paganism and Its Discontents.* Edited by Holli S. Emore and Jonathan M. Leader, 22–46. Newcastle: Cambridge Scholars Press.

Chamberlain, J. Edward. 2003. *If This is Your Land, Where Are Your Stories? Reimaging Home and Sacred Space.* Cleveland: Pilgrim Press.

Chandler, David, and Julian Reid. 2020. "Becoming Indigenous: The 'Speculative Turn' in Anthropology and the (Re)colonisation of Indigeneity." *Postcolonial Studies* 23 (4): 485–504. https://doi.org/10.1080/13688790.2020.1745993.

Chaudhry, Vandana. 2018. "Knowing through Tripping: A Performative Praxis for Co-Constructing Knowledge as a Disabled Halfie." *Qualitative Inquiry* 24 (1): 70–82. doi:10.1177/1077800417728961.

Cialdini, Robert B. 2003. "Crafting Normative Messages to Protect the Environment." *Current Directions in Psychological Science: A Journal of the American Psychological Society* 12 (4): 105–109.

Cialdini, Robert B., and Noah J. Goldstein. 2004. "Social Influence: Compliance and Conformity." *Annual Review of Psychology* 55 (1): 591–621. https://doi.org/10.1146/annurev.psych.55.090902.142015.

Cialdini, Robert B., Raymond R. Reno, and Carl A. Kallgren. 1990. "A Focus Theory of Normative Conduct: Recycling the Concept of Norms to Reduce Littering in Public Places." *Journal of Personality and Social Psychology* 58 (6): 1015–1026. https://doi.org/10.1037/0022-3514.58.6.1015.

Clover, Carol J. 1993. "Regardless of Sex: Men, Women, and Power in Early Northern Europe." *Speculum* 68 (2): 363–387.

Cohen, Lizabeth. 2003. *A Consumer's Republic: The Politics of Mass Consumption in Postwar America.* New York: Knopf.

Colli, Francesca, and J. Adriaensen. 2020. "Lobbying the State or the Market? A Framework to Study Civil Society Organizations' Strategic Behavior." *Regulation & Governance* 14 (3): 501–513. https://doi.org/10.1111/rego.12227.

Cozzolino, Philip J., Angela Dawn Staples, Lawrence S. Meyers, and Jamie Samboceti. 2004. "Greed, Death, and Values: From Terror Management to Transcendence Management Theory." *Personality & Social Psychology Bulletin* 30 (3): 278–292. https://doi.org/10.1177/0146167203260716.

Davidsen, Markus Altena. 2012. "What Is Wrong with Pagan Studies?" *Method & Theory in the Study of Religion* 24 (2): 183–199. https://doi.org/10.1163/157006812X634881.

Davy, Barbara Jane. 2003. "The Ethics of Being With/in." PhD diss., Concordia University, Montreal.

Davy, Barbara Jane. 2005. "Being at Home in Nature: A Levinasian Approach to Pagan Environmental Ethics" *The Pomegranate: The International Journal of Pagan Studies* 7 (2): 157–172.

Davy, Barbara Jane. 2006. *Introduction to Pagan Studies.* Lanham, MD: AltaMira Press.

Davy, Barbara Jane. 2007. "An Other Face of Ethics in Levinas." *Ethics and the Environment* 12 (1): 39–65.

Davy, Barbara Jane. 2009. *Paganism: Critical Concepts in Religious Studies,* volume 2 *Ecology.* Routledge: London.

Davy, Barbara Jane. 2020. "To Become Ancestors of a Living Future." In *Health in the Anthropocene.* Edited by Katharine Zywert and Stephen Quilley, 419–431. Toronto: University of Toronto Press.

Davy, Barbara Jane. 2021. "A Rationale for the Study of Unconscious Motivations Of Climate Change, and How Ritual Practices Can Promote Pro-Environmental Behaviour."

Worldviews: Global Religions, Culture, and Ecology 25 (2): 113–129. doi:10.1163/15685357-20211001.

Davy, Barbara Jane. 2023. "Negotiating Ecological Relations Amongst Inclusive Heathens" *Journal for the Study of Religion, Nature, and Culture* 17 (3–4): 458–480. https://doi.org/10.1558/jsrnc.24148.

Davy, Barbara Jane, and Stephen S. Quilley. 2018. "Ritual Matters: Changing Ontologies, Values, and Ecological Conscience Formation." *Journal for the Study of Religion, Nature, and Culture* 12 (4): 384–418. https://doi.org/10.1558/jsrnc.36834.

de la Cadena, Marisol. 2013. "About 'Mariano's Archive': Ecologies of Stories." In *Contested Ecologies: Dialogues in the South in Nature and Knowledge.* Edited by Lesley Green, 55–68. Cape Town, South Africa: HSRC Press.

de la Cadena, Marisol. 2015. *Earth Beings: Ecologies of Practice Across Andean Worlds.* Durham, NC: Duke University Press.

Deming, David. 2012. *Science and Technology in World History*, vol. 3: *The Black Death, the Renaissance, the Reformation and the Scientific Revolution.* Jefferson, USA: McFarland.

Dietz, Thomas, Gerald T. Gardner, Jonathan Gilligan, Paul C. Stern, and Michael P. Vandenbergh. 2009. "Household Actions Can Provide a Behavioral Wedge to Rapidly Reduce US Carbon Emissions." *Proceedings of the National Academy of Sciences* 106 (44): 18452–18456. https://doi.org/10.1073/pnas.0908738106.

Dolšak, Nives. 2017. "Bowling Together: Mobilization of Collective Action by Environmental NGOs." *Nonprofit Policy Forum* 8 (1): 25–44. https://doi.org/10.1515/npf-2016-0025.

Dücker, Burckhard. 2007. "Failure Impossible? Handling of Rules, Mistakes and Failure in Public Rituals of Modern Western Societies." In *When Rituals Go Wrong: Mistakes, Failure, and the Dynamics of Ritual.* Edited by Ute Hüsken, 73–98. Leiden: Brill.

Durkheim, Émile. 1912. *The Elementary Forms of Religious Life.* Translated by Joseph Ward Swain. London: George Allen & Unwin. Accessed April 21, 2016. http://crasseux.com/books/Emile_Durkheim_The_Elementary_Forms_of_the_Religious_Life.pdf.

Eliade, Mircea. 1959 [1957]. *The Sacred and the Profane: The Nature of Religion.* Translated by Willard R. Trask. San Diego: Harcourt Brace Jovanovich.

Elias, Norbert. 1978. "Human Interdependencies – Problems of Social Bonds." In *What Is Sociology?* Edited by Norbert Elias, Stephen Mennell, and Grace. Morrissey, 134–157. London: Hutchinson.

Elias, Norbert. 2000 [1939]. *The Civilizing Process*, revised edition, Translated by Edmund Jephcott. Malden, MA: Blackwell.

Elias, Norbert. 2001. *The Society of Individuals.* New York: Continuum.

Ellis, Hilda R. 1968 [1943]. *The Road to Hel: A Study of the Conception of the Dead in Old Norse Literature.* New York: Greenwood Press.

Ellis Davidson, H. R. 1964. *Gods and Myths of Northern Europe.* London: Penguin Books.

Ellis Davidson, H. R. 1998. *Roles of the Northern Goddess.* London: Routledge.

Emmrich, Christoph. 2007. "'All the King's Horses and All the King's Men': The 2004 Red Matsyendranātha Incident in Lalitpur." In *When Rituals Go Wrong: Mistakes, Failure, and the Dynamics of Ritual.* Edited by Ute Hüsken, 133–164. Leiden: Brill.

Emore, Holli S., and Jonathan M. Leader, eds. 2020. *Paganism and Its Discontents.* Newcastle: Cambridge Scholars Press.

Enright, Michael. 1996. *Lady with the Mead Cup: Ritual, Prophecy and Lordship in the European Warband from La Tene to the Viking Age.* Portland, OR: Four Courts Press.

Ernest-Jones, Max, Daniel Nettle, and Melissa Bateson. 2011. "Effects of Eye Images on Everyday Cooperative Behavior: A Field Experiment." *Evolution and Human Behavior* 32 (3): 172–178. https://doi.org/10.1016/j.evolhumbehav.2010.10.006.

Firth, Raymond. 1972. "Offering and Sacrifice: Problems of Organization." In *Reader in Comparative Religion: An Anthropological Approach*, 3rd edition. Edited by William Armand Lessa and Evon Z. Vogt. New York: Harper & Row.

Foor, Daniel. 2017. *Ancestral Medicine: Rituals for Personal and Family Healing.* Rochester, VT: Bear & Company.

Freud, Sigmund. 1961 [1930]. *Civilization and Its Discontents*. Translated by James Strachey. New York: W. W. Norton.

Gailliot, Matthew T., Tyler F. Stillman, Brandon J. Schmeichel, Jon K. Maner, and E. Ashby Plant. 2008. "Mortality Salience Increases Adherence to Salient Norms and Values." *Personality & Social Psychology Bulletin* 34 (7): 993–1003. https://doi.org/10.1177/01461 67208316791.

Gardell, Mattias. 2003. *Gods of the Blood: The Pagan Revival and White Separatism*. Durham, NC: Duke University Press.

Geertz, Clifford. 1973. *The Interpretation of Cultures*. New York: Basic Books.

Gilboy, James. 2020. "Proving Boomers Wrong Again, Millennials Are Getting Their Licenses in Record Numbers." *The Drive*. https://www.thedrive.com/news/31823/proving-boom ers-wrong-again-millennials-are-getting-their-licenses-in-record-numbers.

Ginzburg, Carlo. 2013 [1980]. *The Cheese and the Worms: The Cosmos of a Sixteenth-Century Miller*. Translated by John and Anne C. Tedeschi. Baltimore: Johns Hopkins University Press.

Girard, René. 1977. *Violence and the Sacred*. Baltimore: Johns Hopkins University Press.

Girard, René. 1986. *The Scapegoat*. Translated by Yvonne Freccero. Baltimore: Johns Hopkins University Press.

Girard, René. 1987. *Things Hidden Since the Foundation of the World*, with Jean-Michel Ourgoulian and Guy Lefort. Translated by Stephen Bann and Michael Metteer. Stanford: Stanford University Press.

Goldenberg, Jamie L., Tom Pyszczynski, Jeff Greenberg, and Sheldon Solomon. 2000. "Fleeing the Body: A Terror Management Perspective on the Problem of Human Corporeality." *Personality and Social Psychology Review* 4 (3): 200–218. https://doi.org/10.1207/S1532795 7PSPR0403_1.

Goldenberg, Jamie L., Tom Pyszczynski, Jeff Greenberg, Sheldon Solomon, Benjamin Kluck, and Robin Cornwell. 2001. "I Am Not an Animal: Mortality Salience, Disgust, and the Denial of Human Creatureliness." *Journal of Experimental Psychology: General* 130 (3): 427–435. https://doi.org/10.1037//0096-3445.130.3.427.

Goodrick-Clarke, Nicolas. 2002. *Black Sun: Aryan Cults, Esoteric Nazism, and the Politics of Identity*. New York: New York University Press.

Gray, Eden. 1960. *The Tarot Revealed*. Stroudsburg, PA: Signet (New American Library).

Green, Lesley. 2013. "The Day-World *Hawkri* and Its Topologies: On Palikur Alternatives to the Idea of Space." In *Contested Ecologies: Dialogues in the South on Nature and Knowledge*. Edited by Lesley Green, 69–89. Cape Town, South Africa: HSRC Press.

Greenberg, Jeff, Tom Pyszczynski, and Sheldon Solomon. 1986. "The Causes and Consequences of a Need for Self-esteem: A Terror Management Theory." In *Public Self and Private Self*. Edited by Roy F. Baumeister, 189–212. New York: Springer-Verlag.

Grimes, Ronald L. 1988. "Infelicitous Performances and Ritual Criticism." *Semeia* 41: 103–122.

Grimes, Ronald L. 1990. *Ritual Criticism: Case Studies in Its Practice, Essays on Its Theory* 1st edition. Columbia: University of South Carolina Press.

Grimes, Ronald L. 2000. *Deeply into the Bone: Re-inventing Rites of Passage*. Berkeley: University of California Press.

Grimes, Ronald L. 2002. "Performance Is Currency in the Deep World's Gift Economy: An Incantatory Riff for a Global Medicine Show." *Interdisciplinary Studies in Literature and Environment* 9 (1): 149–164. https://doi.org/10.1093/isle/9.1.149.

Grimes, Ronald L. 2014. *The Craft of Ritual Studies*. Oxford: Oxford University Press.

Grimfrost. 2020. "Open Letter to EU Businesses and Heathen Communities" Grimfrost Blog. https://grimfrost.com/blogs/blog/heathen-open-letter-to-businesses-and-heathen-comm unities.

Guédon, Marie-Françoise. 1988. "Du rêve à l'ethnographie: Explorations sur le monde personnel du chamanisme Nabesna." *Recherches Amérindiennes au Québec* 18 (2–3): 5–18.

Gundarsson, Kveldúlf. 2007. *Our Troth Volume Two: Living the Troth*. 2nd edition. Berkeley, CA: The Troth.

Gunnell, Terry. 2000. "The Season of the *Dísir*: The Winter Nights and the *Dísablót* in Early Medieval Scandinavian Belief." *Cosmos: The Journal of the Traditional Cosmology Society* 16 (2): 117–149.

Gunnell, Terry. 2007. "How Elvish Were the Álfar?" In *Constructing Nations, Reconstructing Myths: Essays in Honour of T. A. Shippey*. Edited by Andrew Wawn, Graham Johnson, and John Walter, 113–130. Turnhour, Belgium: Brepolis.

Guthrie, Stewart. 1980. "A Cognitive Theory of Religion." *Current Anthropology* 21 (2): 181–203. https://www.jstor.org/stable/2741711.

Guthrie, Stewart. 1993. *Faces in the Clouds: A New Theory of Religion*. New York: Oxford University Press.

Hail and Horn Gathering program. 2018. Raven's Knoll. (unpublished festival program).

Haley, Kevin J., and Daniel M. T. Fessler. 2005. "Nobody's Watching? Subtle Cues Affect Generosity in an Anonymous Economic Game." *Evolution and Human Behavior* 26 (3): 245–256. https://doi.org/10.1016/j.evolhumbehav.2005.01.002.

Hallowell, A. Irving. 1969. "Ojibwa Ontology Behaviour and World View." In *Primitive Views of the World*. Edited by Stanley Diamond, 49–82. New York: Columbia University Press.

Halstead, John, ed. 2016. *Godless Paganism: Voices of Non-theistic Pagans*. Online: Lulu.com.

Hamayon, Roberte. 2016. *Why We Play: An Anthropological Study*. Online: Hau Books.

Hamerton-Kelly, Robert G. 1987. *Violent Origins: Walter Burkert, René Girard and Jonathan Z. Smith on Ritual Killing and Cultural Formation*. Stanford, CA: Stanford University Press.

Harari, Yuval Noah. 2014. *Sapiens: A Brief History of Humankind*. Toronto: Signal (McClelland & Stewart).

Harmsworth, Joshua James. 2015. "Crafting the Web: Canadian Heathens and Their Quest for a 'Virtuous' Self." PhD diss., University of Edinburgh.

Harris, Adrian. 2014. "Embodied Eco-Paganism." In *The Handbook of Contemporary Animism*. Edited by Graham Harvey, 403–415. London: Routledge.

Harvey, Graham. 1997. *Contemporary Paganism: Listening People, Speaking Earth*. New York: New York University Press.

Harvey, Graham. 2006. *Animism: Respecting the Living World*. New York: Columbia University Press.

Harvey, Graham. 2013. *Food, Sex & Strangers: Understanding Religion As Everyday Life*. Durham, NC: Acumen.

Harvey, Graham, ed. 2014. *The Handbook of Contemporary Animism*. London: Routledge.

Harvey, Graham, ed. 2020. *Indigenizing Movements in Europe*. Sheffield: Equinox.

Heath, Cat. 2021. *Elves, Witches and Gods: Spinning Old Heathen Magic in the Modern Day*. Woodbury, MN: Llewellyn.

Heide, Eldar. 2006. "Spinning *Seiðr*." In *Old Norse Religion in Long-term Perspectives: Origins, Changes, and Interactions*. Edited by Anders Andrén, Kristina Jennbert, and Catharina Raudvere, 164–170. Lund, Sweden: Nordic Academic Press.

Henrich, Joseph, Steven J. Heine, and Ara Norenzayan. 2010. "The Weirdest People in the World?" *The Behavioral and Brain Sciences* 33 (2–3): 61–83. https://doi.org/10.1017/S0140525X0999152X.

Hirschberger, Gilad, Tsachi Ein-Dor, and Shaul Almakias. 2008. "The Self-Protective Altruist: Terror Management and the Ambivalent Nature of Prosocial Behavior." *Personality & Social Psychology Bulletin* 34 (5): 666–678. https://doi.org/10.1177/0146167207313933.

Holbraad, Martin, and Morten Axel Pedersen. 2017. *The Ontological Turn: An Anthropological Exposition*. Cambridge: Cambridge University Press.

Hornborg, Alf. 2006. "Animism, Fetishism, and Objectivism As Strategies for Knowing (or Not Knowing) the World." *Ethnos* 71 (1): 21–32. https://doi.org/10.1080/00141840600603129.

Hrafnhild, Nicanthiel. 2009. *Boar, Birch and Bog: Prayers to Nerthus*. Lulu: Gullinbursti Press.

Hubert, Henri, and Marcel Mauss. 1968. *Sacrifice: Its Nature and Function*, Translated by W. D. Halls. Chicago: University of Chicago Press.

Huizinga, Johan. 1955 [1950]. *Homo Ludens: A Study of the Play Element in Culture*. Boston: Beacon Press.

Hüsken, Ute, ed. 2007a. *When Rituals Go Wrong: Mistakes, Failure, and the Dynamics of Ritual.* Leiden: Brill.

Hüsken, Ute. 2007b. "Ritual Dynamics and Ritual Failure." In *When Rituals Go Wrong: Mistakes, Failure, and the Dynamics of Ritual.* Edited by Ute Hüsken, 337–366. Leiden: Brill.

Ibn Fadlan, Ahmad. 2017. *Mission to the Volga.* Translated by James E. Montgomery. New York: New York University Press.

Ingold, Tim. 2000. *The Perception of the Environment: Essays on Livelihood, Dwelling and Skill.* London: Routledge.

Ivakhiv, Adrian. 2005a. "Nature and Ethnicity in East European Paganism: An Environmental ethic of the Religious Right?" *The Pomegranate: The International Journal of Pagan Studies* 7 (2): 194–255. https://doi.org/10.1558/pome.2005.7.2.194.

Ivakhiv, Adrian. 2005b. "The Revival of Ukrainian Native Faith." In *Modern Paganism in World Cultures: Comparative Perspectives.* Edited by Michael F. Strmiska, 209–239. Santa Barbara, CA: ABC Clio.

Jackson, Anthony, ed. 1987. *Anthropology at Home.* New York: Tavistock Publications.

Janowitz, Naomi. 2011. "Inventing the Scapegoat: Theories of Sacrifice and Ritual." *Journal of Ritual Studies* 25 (1): 15–24.

Jonas, Eva, Jeff Schimel, Jeff Greenberg, and Tom Pyszczynski. 2002. "The Scrooge Effect: Evidence That Mortality Salience Increases Prosocial Attitudes and Behavior." *Personality & Social Psychology Bulletin* 28 (10): 1342–1353. https://doi.org/10.1177/014616702236834.

Kahneman, Daniel. 2011. *Thinking, Fast and Slow.* Vaughn, ON: Anchor Canada.

Kallgren, Carl A., Raymond R. Reno, and Robert B. Cialdini. 2000. "A Focus Theory of Normative Conduct: When Norms Do and Do Not Affect Behavior." *Personality & Social Psychology Bulletin* 26 (8): 1002–1012. https://doi.org/10.1177/01461672002610009.

Kaplan, Jeffrey. 1996. "The Reconstruction of the Ásatrú and Odinist Traditions." In *Magical Religion and Modern Witchcraft.* Edited by James R. Lewis, 193–236. Albany: State University of New York Press.

Kaplan, Jeffrey. 1997. *Radical Religions in America: Millenarian Movements from the Far Right to the Children of Noah.* Syracuse, NY: Syracuse University Press.

Kaplan, Jeffrey, and Tore Bjørgo, eds. 1998. *Nation and Race: The Developing Euro-American Racist Subculture.* Boston: Northeastern University Press.

Kaplan, Jeffrey, and Leonard Weinberg. 1998. *The Emergence of a Euro-American Radical Right.* New Brunswick, NJ: Rutgers University Press.

Karns, Christina. 2018. "When You're Grateful, Your Brain Becomes More Charitable." *The Conversation.* https://theconversation.com/when-youre-grateful-your-brain-becomes-more-charitable-105606.

Karns, Christina M., William E. Moore III, and Ulrich Mayr. 2017. "The Cultivation of Pure Altruism via Gratitude: A Functional MRI Study of Change with Gratitude Practice." *Frontiers in Human Neuroscience* 11: 599–599. https://doi.org/10.3389/fnhum.2017.00599.

Kauffman, Stuart A. 2008. *Reinventing the Sacred: A New View of Science, Reason, and Religion.* New York: Basic Books.

Kimmerer, Robin Wall. 2013. *Braiding Sweetgrass: Indigenous Wisdom, Scientific Knowledge, and the Teachings of Plants.* Minneapolis, MN: Milkweed Editions.

Kolbert, Elizabeth. 2015. *The Sixth Extinction: An Unnatural History.* London: Bloomsbury.

Koole, Sander L., and Agnes E. Van den Berg. 2005. "Lost in the Wilderness: Terror Management, Action Orientation, and Nature Evaluation." *Journal of Personality and Social Psychology* 88 (6): 1024–1028.

Kraft, Siv Ellen. 2018. "Protective Occupation, Emergent Networks, Rituals of Solidarity: Comparing Alta (Sápmi), Mauna Kea (Hawai`i), and Standing Rock (North Dakota)." In *The Bloomsbury Handbook of Religion and Nature: The Elements.* Edited by Laura Hobgood and Whitney Bauman, 185–198. London: Bloomsbury.

Kraft, Siv Ellen. 2019. "Protecting Mother Earth: Indigenous Religion(s) on Protest Scenes." At *Religion-Water-Climate: Changing Cultures and Landscapes*, a conference of the International Society for the Study of Religion, Nature, and Culture in partnership with the University College Cork, and the International Association for the History of Religion. Cork, Ireland. June 13–16.

Krzewińska, Maja, Anna Kjellström, Torsten Günther, Charlotte Hedenstierna-Jonson, Torun Zachrisson, Ayça Omrak, Reyhan Yaka, et al. 2018. "Genomic and Strontium Isotope Variation Reveal Immigration Patterns in a Viking Age Town." *Current Biology* 28 (17): 2730–2738.e10. https://doi.org/10.1016/j.cub.2018.06.053.

Kvavadze, Eliso, Ofer Bar-Yosef, Anna Belfer-Cohen, Elisabetta Boaretto, Nino Jakeli, Zinovi Matskevich, and Tengiz Meshveliani. 2009. "30,000-Year-Old Wild Flax Fibers." *Science (American Association for the Advancement of Science)* 325 (5946): 1359–1359. https://doi.org/10.1126/science.1175404.

Lacharity, Erik. 2018. *Holy Mother Redux* (unpublished pamphlet).

Lafayllve, Patricia M. 2018. *A Practical Heathen's Guide to Asatru.* Woodbury, MN: Llewellyn.

Lakoff, George. 2014. *The All New Don't Think of an Elephant! Know Your Values and Frame the Debate.* White River Junction, VT: Chelsea Green.

Lakoff, George, and Mark Johnson. 2003 [1980]. *Metaphors We Live By.* Chicago: Chicago University Press.

Larrington, Carolyne, Trans. 2014. *The Poetic Edda.* Oxford: Oxford University Press.

Latour, Bruno. 1993. *We Have Never Been Modern.* Trans. Catherine Porter. Cambridge, MA: Harvard University Press.

Leopold, Aldo. 1966 [1949]. *A Sand County Almanac and Sketches Here and There.* New York: Oxford University Press.

Letcher, Andy. 2000. "'Virtual Paganism' or Direct Action? The Implications of Road Protesting for British Eco-Paganism." *Diskus* 6. http://web.unimarburg.de/religionswissenschaft/journal/diskus.

Letcher, Andy. 2004. "Raising the Dragon: Folklore and the Development of Contemporary British Eco-Paganism." *The Pomegranate: The International Journal of Pagan Studies* 6 (2): 175–198. https://doi.org/10.1558/pome.v6i2.175.

Levinas, Emmanuel. 1969. *Totality and Infinity: An Essay on Exteriority.* Translated by Alphonso Lingis. Pittsburgh, PA: Duquesne University Press.

Levinas, Emmanuel. 1985. *Ethics and Infinity: Conversations with Philippe Nemo.* Pittsburgh, PA: Duquesne University Press.

Levinas, Emmanuel. 1989. "Martin Buber and the Theory of Knowledge." Translated by Seán Hand, *The Levinas Reader.* Edited by Seán Hand, 59–74. Oxford: Blackwell.

Levinas, Emmanuel. 1998. *Otherwise Than Being or Beyond Essence.* Translated by Alphonso Lingis. Pittsburgh, PA: Duquesne University Press.

Levinas, Emmanuel. 1990. *Difficult Freedom: Essays on Judaism.* Translated by Seán Hand. London: Athlone Press.

Lewis, James R. 2012. "The Pagan Explosion Revisited: A Statistical Postmortem on the Teen Witch Fad." *The Pomegranate: The International Journal of Pagan Studies* 14 (1): 128–139. https://doi.org/10.1558/pome.v14i1.128.

Llewelyn, John. 1991. *The Middle Voice of Ecological Conscience: A Chiasmic Reading of Responsibility in the Neighbourhood of Levinas, Heidegger and Others.* New York: St. Martin's Press.

Luhrmann, Tanya M. 1989. *Persuasions of the Witch's Craft: Ritual Magic in Contemporary England.* Cambridge: Harvard University Press.

MacLellan, Gordon. 2004. "Entertaining Faeries." In *The Paganism Reader.* Edited by Chas S. Clifton and Graham Harvey, 365–372. New York: Routledge.

Malinowski, Bronislaw. 2015 [1922]. *Argonauts of the Western Pacific: An Account of Native Enterprise and Adventure in the Archipelagoes of Melanesian New Guinea.* London: Forgotten Books.

Maniates, Michael F. 2001. "Individualization: Plant a Tree, Buy a Bike, Save the World?" *Global Environmental Politics* 1 (3): 31–52.

Margaryan, Ashot, Daniel J. Lawson, Martin Sikora, Fernando Racimo, Simon Rasmussen, Ida Moltke, Lara M. Cassidy, et al. 2020. "Population Genomics of the Viking World." *Nature (London)* 585 (7825): 390–396. https://doi.org/10.1038/s41586-020-2688-8.

Mauss, M. 1990 [1950]. *The Gift: The Form and Reason for Exchange in Archaic Societies.* Translated by W. D. Halls. New York: W. W. Norton.

McClymond, Katharine. 2004. "The Nature and Elements of Sacrificial Ritual." *Method & Theory in the Study of Religion,* 16 (4): 337–366. https://doi.org/10.1163/15700680 43079037.

McFarland Taylor, Sarah. 2019. *Ecopiety: Green Media and the Dilemma of Environmental Virtue.* New York: New York University Press.

McKay, Ryan, and Harvey Whitehouse. 2015. "Religion and Morality." *Psychological Bulletin* 141 (2): 447–473. https://doi.org/10.1037/a0038455.

McLean, Stuart. 2008. "Bodies from the Bog: Metamorphosis, Non-Human Agency and the Making of 'Collective' Memory.'" *Trames* (Tallinn) 12 (3): 299–308. doi:10.3176/tr.2008.3.05.

McNallen, Stephen. 1998. "Wotan vs. Tezcatlipoca: The Spiritual War for California and the Southwest." *Runestone: Celebrating the Indigenous Religion of European Americans.* http://runestone.org/wp-content/uploads/The-Runestone-Summer-1998.pdf.

McNeill, J. R., and William H. McNeill. 2003. *The Human Web: A Bird's Eye View of World History.* New York: W. W. Norton.

Mencej, Mirjam. 2011. "Connecting Threads" *Folklore* 48: 55–84. doi:10.7592/FEJF2011.48. mencej.

Moieni, Mona, Michael R. Irwin, Kate E. Byrne Haltom, Ivana Jevtic, Meghan L. Meyer, Elizabeth C. Breen, Steven W. Cole, and Naomi I. Eisenberger. 2019. "Exploring the Role of Gratitude and Support-Giving on Inflammatory Outcomes." *Emotion* 19 (6): 939–949. https://doi.org/10.1037/emo0000472.

Naveh, Danny, and Nurit Bird-David. 2014. "How Persons Become Things: Economic and Epistemological Changes among Nayaka Hunter-Gatherers." *Journal of the Royal Anthropological Institute* 20 (1): 74–92. https://doi.org/10.1111/1467-9655.12080.

Nelson, Richard K. 1983. *Make Prayers to the Raven: A Koyukon View of the Northern Forest.* Chicago: University of Chicago Press.

Norenzayan, Ara, Ian G. Hansen, and Jasmine Cady. 2008. "An Angry Volcano? Reminders of Death and Anthropomorphizing Nature." *Social Cognition* 26 (2): 190–197. https://doi.org/10.1521/soco.2008.26.2.190.

Norgaard, Kari Marie. 2011. *Living in Denial: Climate Change, Emotions, and Everyday Life.* Cambridge, MA: MIT Press.

Oboler, Regina Smith. 2004. "Nature Religion as a Cultural System? Sources of Environmentalist Action and Rhetoric in a Contemporary Pagan Community." *The Pomegranate: The International Journal of Pagan Studies* 6 (1): 86–106. https://doi.org/10.1558/pome.v6i1.86.

Offer, Avner. 1997. "Between the Gift and the Market: The Economy of Regard." *Economic History Review* 50 (3): 450–476. https://doi.org/10.1111/1468-0289.00064.

Olson, Carl. 2002. "Excess, Time, and the Pure Gift: Postmodern Transformations of Marcel Mauss' Theory." *Method & Theory in the Study of Religion* 14 (3–4): 350–374. https://doi.org/10.1163/157006802320909765.

Palmer, Craig T., Lyle B. Steadman, and Chris Cassidy. 2006. "Traditional Religious Ritual Sacrifice: Cultural Materialism, Costly Signaling, or Descendant-Leaving Strategy?" *Journal of Ritual Studies,* 20 (2): 33–42.

Patterson, Barry. 2004. "Finding Your Way in the Woods: The Art of Conversation with the *Genius Loci.*" In *The Paganism Reader.* Edited by Chas S. Clifton and Graham Harvey, 354–364. New York: Routledge.

Paxson, Diana. 2006. *Essential Ásatru: Walking the Path of Norse Paganism.* New York: Citadel Press.

Pearce, Maryanne, Erik Lacharity, Chantal Layoun, and Austin Lawrence, eds. 2020. *Bragafull*. Raven's Knoll.

Pike, Sarah M. 2001. *Earthly Bodies, Magical Selves: Contemporary Pagans and the Search for Community*. Berkeley: University of California Press.

Pike, Sarah M. 2004a. "Gleanings from the Field: Leftover Tales of Grief and Desire." In *Researching Paganisms*. Edited by Jenny Blain, Douglas Ezzy, and Graham Harvey, 97–112. Walnut Creek, CA: AltaMira.

Pike, Sarah M. 2004b. *New Age and Neopagan Religions in America*. New York: Columbia University Press.

Plumwood, Val. 1995. "Human Vulnerability and the Experience of Being Prey." *Quadrant*, 29 (3): 29–34.

Polanyi, Karl. 2001 [1944]. *The Great Transformation: The Political and Economic Origins of Our Time*. Boston: Beacon Press.

Polanyi, Michael. 2015 [1958]. *Personal Knowledge: Towards a Post-Critical Philosophy*. Chicago: University of Chicago Press.

Pollington, Stephen. 2010 [2003]. *The Meadhall: The Feasting Tradition in Anglo-Saxon England*. Little Downham, UK: Anglo-Saxon Books.

Price, Neil. 2019. *The Viking Way: Magic and Mind in Late Iron Age Scandinavia*, 2nd edition (revised and expanded). Oxford: Oxbow.

Price, Neil. 2020. *Children of Ash and Elm: A History of the Vikings*. New York: Basic Books.

Quilley, Stephen S. 2013. "De-Growth Is Not a Liberal Agenda: Relocalisation and the Limits to Low Energy Cosmopolitanism." *Environmental Values* 22 (2): 261–285. http://dx.doi.org.proxy.lib.uwaterloo.ca/10.3197/096327113X13581561725310.

Quinn, Daniel. 1995 [1992]. *Ishmael*. New York: Bantam.

Raffield, Ben, Neil Price, and Mark Collard. 2019. "Religious Belief and Cooperation: A View from Viking-Age Scandinavia." *Religion, Brain & Behavior* 9 (1): 2–22. https://doi.org/10.1080/2153599X.2017.1395764.

Ramos, Alcida Rita. 2012. "The Politics of Perspectivism." *Annual Review of Anthropology* 41 (1): 481–494. https://doi.org/10.1146/annurev-anthro-092611-145950.

Rappaport, Roy A. 1968. *Pigs for the Ancestors*. New Haven, CT: Yale University Press.

Rappaport, Roy A. 1979. *Ecology, Meaning and Religion*. Richmond CA: North Atlantic Books.

Rappaport, Roy A. 1999. *Ritual and Religion in the Making of Humanity*. Cambridge: Cambridge University Press.

Rasmussen, Rune Hjarnø. 2020. *The Nordic Animist Year*, revised edition. Estonia: Nordic Animism.

Rasmussen, Susan J. 2002. "Animal Sacrifice and the Problem of Translation: The Construction of Meaning in Tuareg Sacrifice." *Journal of Ritual Studies*, 16 (2): 141–164.

Reuter, Thomas. 2014. "Is Ancestor Veneration the Most Universal of All World Religions? A Critical of Modernist Cosmological Bias" *Wacana* 15 (2): 223–253. https://doi.org/10.17510/24076899-01502002.

Rezendes, Paul. 1998. *The Wild Within: Adventures in Nature and Animal Teachings*. New York: Tarcher/Putnam.

Rigdon, Mary, Keiko Ishii, Motoki Watabe, and Shinobu Kitayama. 2009. "Minimal Social Cues in the Dictator Game." *Journal of Economic Psychology* 30 (3): 358–367. https://doi.org/10.1016/j.joep.2009.02.002.

Roberts, Adrienne. 2019. "Driving? The Kids Are So Over It" *Wall Street Journal*. https://www.wsj.com/articles/driving-the-kids-are-so-over-it-11555732810.

Rood, Joshua. 2020. "Investigations into Asatru: A Critical Historiography" *Aura: Tidsskrift for Akademiske Sudier av Nyreliøsitet* 11 (1): 81–95. https://doi.org/10.31265/aura.359.

Rountree, Kathryn, ed. 2018 [2015]. *Contemporary Pagan and Native Faith Movements in Europe: Colonialist and Nationalist Impulses*. New York: Berghahn.

Sahlins, Marshall. 1972. *Stone Age Economics*. New York: Aldine de Gruyter.

Sahlins, Marshall. 2011a. "What Kinship Is (Part One)." *Journal of the Royal Anthropological Institute* 17: 2–19. https://doi.org/10.1111/j.1467-9655.2010.01666.x.

Sahlins, Marshall. 2011b. "What Kinship Is (Part Two)." *Journal of the Royal Anthropological Institute* 17: 227–242. https://doi.org/10.1111/j.1467-9655.2011.01677.x.

Schultz, P. Wesley, Jessica M. Nolan, Robert B. Cialdini, Noah J. Goldstein, and Vladas Griskevicius. 2007. "The Constructive, Destructive, and Reconstructive Power of Social Norms." *Psychological Science* 18 (5): 429–434. https://doi.org/10.1111/j.1467-9280.2007.01917.x.

Searle, John R. 1969. *Speech Acts: An Essay in the Philosophy of Language.* London: Cambridge University Press.

Seigfried, Karl. 2014. Worldwide Heathen Census 2013: Results and Analysis. Norse Mythology Blog, 6 January 2014. https://www.norsemyth.org/2014/01/worldwide-heathen-census-2013-results.html.

Seligman, Adam B., Robert P. Weller, Michael J. Puett, and Bennett Simon. 2008. *Ritual and Its Consequences: An Essay on the Limits of Sincerity.* New York: Oxford University Press.

Sheils, Dean. 1975. "Toward a Unified Theory of Ancestor Worship: A Cross-Cultural Study." *Social Forces* 54 (2): 427–440.

Shore, Lynn M., Amy E. Randel, Beth G. Chung, Michelle A. Dean, Karen Holcombe Ehrhart, and Gangaram Singh. 2011. "Inclusion and Diversity in Work Groups: A Review and Model for Future Research." *Journal of Management* 37 (4): 1262–1289. https://doi.org/10.1177/0149206310385943.

Sideris, Lisa H. 2017. *Consecrating Science: Wonder, Knowledge, and the Natural World.* Oakland: University of California Press.

Simek, Rudolph. 1993 [1984]. *Dictionary of Northern Mythology.* Translated by Angela Hall. Cambridge: D. S. Brewer.

Smith, Jonathan Z. 1987. *To Take Place: Toward Theory in Ritual.* Chicago: University of Chicago Press.

Smithers, G. V. 1959. "The Meaning of 'The Seafarer' and 'The Wanderer' (Continued)." *Medium Aevum* 28 (1): 1–22. https://doi.org/10.2307/43626769.

Snook, Jennifer. 2013. "The Construction of an Ethnic Folkway as Religio-ethnic Identity." *Nova Religio: The Journal of Alternative and Emergent Religions* 16 (3): 52–76. https://doi.org/10.1525/nr.2013.16.3.52.

Snook, Jennifer. 2015. *American Heathens: The Politics of Identity in a Pagans Religious Movement.* Philadelphia: Temple University Press.

Solomon, Sheldon, Jeff Greenberg, and Tom Pyszczynski. 2015. *The Worm at the Core: On the Role of Death in Life.* New York: Random House.

Strang, Victoria. 2004. *The Meaning of Water.* Oxford: Berg.

Strathern, Marilyn. 1988. *The Gender of the Gift: Problems with Women and Problems with Society in Melanesia.* Berkeley: University of California Press.

Strmiska, Michael. 2000. "Ásatrú in Iceland: The Rebirth of Nordic Paganism?" *Nova Religio: The Journal of Alternative and Emergent Religions* 4 (1): 106–132. https://doi.org/10.1525/nr.2000.4.1.106.

Strmiska, Michael. 2005a. "The Music of the Past in Modern Baltic Paganism." *Nova Religio: The Journal of Alternative and Emergent Religions* 8 (3): 39–58. https://doi.org/10.1525/nr.2005.8.3.39.

Strmiska, Michael., ed. 2005b. *Modern Paganism in World Cultures: Comparative Perspectives.* Santa Barbara, CA: ABC-CLIO.

Strmiska, Michael. 2007. "Putting the Blood Back into Blót: The Revival of Animal Sacrifice in Modern Nordic Paganism." *The Pomegranate: The International Journal of Pagan Studies* 9 (2): 154–189. https://doi.org/10.1558/pome.v9i2.154.

Strmiska, Michael. 2018. "Pagan Politics in the 21st Century: 'Peace and Love' or 'Blood and Soil'?" *Pomegranate* 20 (1): 5–44. https://doi.org/10.1558/pome.35632.

Strmiska, Michael. 2020. "Arguing with the Ancestors: Making the Case for a Paganism without Racism." In *Paganism and Its Discontents*. Edited by Holli S. Emore and Jonathan M. Leader, 1–21. Newcastle: Cambridge Scholars Press.

Sturluson, Snorri. 2005. *The Prose Edda*. Trans. Jesse Byock. London: Penguin Books.

Sturluson, Snorri. 2016. *Heimskringla*, volume 1, 2nd edition. Translated by Alison Finlay and Anthony Faulkes. Exeter: Viking Society for Northern Research, University College London.

Tacitus, Cornelius. 1970. *Agricola and the Germania*. Translated by Harold Mattingly. London: Penguin.

Taylor, Bron. 2001. "Earth and Nature-Based Spirituality (Part II): From Earth First! and Bioregionalism to Scientific Paganism and the New Age." *Religion* 31 (3): 225–245. https://doi.org/10.1006/reli.2000.0257.

Taylor, Bron. 2010. *Dark Green Religion: Nature Spirituality and the Planetary Future*. Berkeley: University of California Press.

Taylor, Bron. 2016. "The Greening of Religion Hypothesis (Part One): From Lynn White, Jr and Claims That Religions Can Promote Environmentally Destructive Attitudes and Behaviors to Assertions They Are Becoming Environmentally Friendly." *Journal for the Study of Religion, Nature, and Culture* 10 (3): 268–305. https://doi.org/10.1558/jsrnc.v10i3.29010.

Taylor, Bron, Gretel Van Wieren, and Bernard Zaleha. 2016. "The Greening of Religion Hypothesis (Part Two): Assessing the Data from Lynn White, Jr, to Pope Francis." *Journal for the Study of Religion, Nature, and Culture* 10 (3): 306–378. https://doi.org/10.1558/jsrnc.v10i3.29011.

Temper, Leah, and Joan Martinez-Alier. 2016. "Mapping Ecologies of Resistance." In *Grassroots Environmental Governance*. Edited by Leah S. Horowitz and Michael J. Watts, 45–70. London: Routledge. https://doi.org/10.4324/9781315649122-9.

Thaler, Richard H., and Cass R. Sunstein. 2009. *Nudge: Improving Decisions About Health, Wealth, and Happiness*, revised and expanded edition. New York: Penguin Books.

Thomas, Kirk S. 2015. *Sacred Gifts: Reciprocity and the Gods*. Tucson, AZ: ADF Publishing.

Thorsson, Örnólfur, ed. 1997. *The Sagas of Icelanders: A Selection*. New York: Penguin Books.

Tönnies, Ferdinand. 2001 [1887]. *Community and Civil Society*. Translated by Jose Harris and Margaret Hollis. Edited by Jose Harris. Cambridge: Cambridge University Press.

Traube, Elizabeth. 1979. "Incest and Mythology: Anthropological and Girardian Perspectives." *Berkshire Review* 14: 37–54.

Tsang, Jo-Ann, and Stephen R. Martin. 2019. "Four Experiments on the Relational Dynamics and Prosocial Consequences of Gratitude." *Journal of Positive Psychology* 14 (2): 188–205. https://doi.org/10.1080/17439760.2017.1388435.

Turner, Victor. 1969. *The Ritual Process: Structure and Anti-Structure*. New Brunswick, NJ: Aldine Transaction.

Valeri, Valerio. 1985. *Kingship and Sacrifice: Ritual and Society in Ancient Hawaii*. Chicago: University of Chicago Press.

Vandenbergh, Michael P. 2004. "From Smokestack to SUV: The Individual as Regulated Entity in the New Era of Environmental Law." *Vanderbilt Law Review* 57: 515–628.

Vandenbergh, Michael P. 2005. "Order without Social Norms: How Personal Norm Activation Can Protect the Environment." *Northwestern University Law Review* 99: 1101–1166.

van Elk, Michiel, Bastiaan T. Rutjens, Joop van der Pligt, and Frenk van Harreveld. 2016. "Priming of Supernatural Agent Concepts and Agency Detection." *Religion, Brain & Behavior* 6 (1): 4–33. https://doi.org/10.1080/2153599X.2014.933444.

Viveiros de Castro, Eduardo. 2015. *The Relative Native: Essays on Indigenous Conceptual Worlds*. Chicago: Hau Books.

von Schnurbein, Stefanie. 2016. *Norse Revival: Transformations of Germanic Neopaganism*. Leiden: Brill.

Wallis, Robert J. 2004. "Between the Worlds: Autoarchaeology and New-Shamans." In *Researching Paganisms*. Edited by Jenny Blain, Douglas Ezzy, and Graham Harvey, 191–215. Walnut Creek, CA: AltaMira.

Weaver, Harry. 2018. "Modern Pagan Ritual Sites: The Cultivation of Sacred Objects at Raven's Knoll." Master's thesis, York University, Toronto, Ontario.

Westley, Frances, Brenda Zimmerman, and Michael Patton. 2006. *Getting to Maybe: How the World Is Changed*. Toronto: Vintage Canada.

Wetherell, Margaret. 2012. *Affect and Emotion: A New Social Science Understanding*. London: Sage.

Wetherell, Margaret. 2015. "Trends in the Turn to Affect: A Social Psychological Critique." *Body & Society* 21 (2): 139–166. https://doi.org/10.1177/1357034X14539020.

Wild Hunt, The. 2020. "Pagan Community Notes: Apparel Company Files to Extend Trademark on the Term 'Heathen,' Controversy over Nashville Art College Merging with Christian University, and More!" *The Wild Hunt*. February 3, 2020. https://wildhunt.org/2020/02/pagan-community-notes-apparel-company-files-to-extend-trademark-on-the-term-heathen-controversy-over-nashville-art-college-merging-with-christian-university-and-more.html.

Williams, Chuck, Aaron Blaise, and Robert Walker. 2003. *Brother Bear* [Motion Picture]. Walt Disney Pictures.

Wilson, Shawn. 2008. *Research Is Ceremony: Indigenous Research Methods*. Halifax: Fernwood.

Young, David E., and Jean-Guy Goulet, eds. 1994. *Being Changed by Cross-Cultural Encounters: The Anthropology of Extraordinary Experience*. Toronto: University of Toronto Press.

Zola, Lia. 2011. "Ritual Continuity and 'Failed Rituals' in a Winter Masquerade in the Italian Alps." *Journal of Alpine Research* 99 (2). https://doi.org/10.4000/rga.1443.

Index